The
Secret World
of
Your Dreams

Other books by Julia and Derek Parker

The New Compleat Astrologer
The Immortals
How Do You Know Who You Are?
Do It Yourself Health
Dreaming
The Future Now
A World Atlas of the Supernatural
Life Signs

The Secret World of Your Dreams

A Complete, A-to-Z Dictionary of Dream Interpretations

JULIA and DEREK PARKER

A PERIGEE BOOK

for Pam and Chris Barlow

Perigee Books
are published by
The Putnam Publishing Group
200 Madison Avenue
New York, NY 10016

First American Edition 1991

Cover design © 1991 by Terrence Fehr

Library of Congress Cataloging-in-Publication Data

Parker, Julia.
The secret world of your dreams : a complete, A-to-Z dictionary
of dream interpretations / Julia and Derek Parker.
p. cm.
Includes bibliographical references.
ISBN 0-399-51700-6 (pbk.)
1. Dreams. I. Parker, Derek. II. Title.
BF1091.P266 1991   91-17602 CIP
154.6′3—dc20

Printed in the United States of America
3 4 5 6 7 8 9 10

Contents

Introduction

veryone has a secret world which no one else can enter, even if invited. It is the world of dreams – a world which keeps its secrets even from the dreamer.

Of course you can tell someone about your dreams. But however carefully you describe them, no one else can tell you what they mean, for they are in code – a code so difficult to break that a stranger could spend many years trying to unravel its mystery. Even a psychoanalyst can only suggest what your dreams *may* mean, and help you to work with them.

Your dream is scarcely ever what it seems: just as there are some areas of your personality which you are probably reluctant to reveal even to your nearest and dearest, so your dreams seem reluctant to speak to you directly, to reveal their meaning in a straightforward manner.

Suppose, for instance, someone is deceiving you; you may have some faint inkling that this is so, but you are reluctant to admit it to yourself. Then you have a dream that this person is helping you on with a pull-over. You probably dismiss this as one of those 'meaningless' dreams which seem to occur every other night. But what the dream will be telling you is that that person is 'pulling the wool over your eyes'.

It is at this point that many people, if you talk to them about dreams, will laugh and make an excuse to talk to someone else on the other side of the room. Yet there is conclusive evidence that dreams do work in this way – sometimes through puns, more often through even more subtle symbolism, to tell you the truth about yourself and the people about you. The deceiver may be a dear friend; you have put your suspicions about him or her behind you. But your real self knows better, and sends you a message through your dream to insist that you had better sit up and take notice.

It is only relatively recently that 'civilised' people have begun to realise how truthfully dreams speak to us ('primitive' people have always taken notice of their dreams, and used them – often regarding them as messages from a spirit world). For the past two thousand years or more, man's approach to dream interpretation has for the most part been fairly basic – and largely mistaken.

For centuries, for instance, writers have published 'dream books' in which you can look up something you have dreamed about, and which pretend to tell you what it 'means'. This is foolishness. At the end of a long life spent working on dreams, the great psychologist C. G. Jung wrote: 'No dream symbol can be separated from the individual who dreams it, and there is no definite or straightforward interpretation of any dream.' Only *you* dream your dream – and even you may not understand it, because dreams speak a language of their own – a language of symbols. Almost nothing in a dream is what it seems.

But there is a key which can help to break the code in which we dream. The most important symbols in our dreams have, mysteriously enough, roughly the same meaning for us all – for a middle-class white Englishman or an Indian street-sweeper, for a Texan oil baron or a Russian clerk. They inhabit a bottomless well of symbolic meaning which has existed as long as human life itself, and which holds the joys and fears, aspirations and frustrations of all mankind.

By using this timeless encyclopaedia of symbols and questioning yourself about them and their companions, you can begin to find your way into your dreams – which, once you have found the key to their code, once you have learned to translate them, can help you to understand yourself and your reactions to the world around you. Explaining these universal symbols, some of which form important elements of the great world myths and religions, we hope to show you how to unravel their personal meaning when they appear in your dream. We show how your dreams can introduce you to your *shadow* – the other you, in whom you can recognise the hidden, repressed and sometimes damaging aspects of your personality, but also the unrecognised creativity, the positive qualities you have perhaps never exploited.

But why should you bother to learn to interpret your dreams?

The answer is simple: because they can be of great practical help. They can advise, reassure, comfort and illuminate. There is nothing magical about this. Your dreams are not messages from strange gods: their language is the language of your most intimate self. The veneer of civilisation – of your upbringing, your education, your environment – is stripped away. In dreams we are not subject to the pressures that surround us in everyday life – we don't care what our wife will think, whether our children will respect us; we don't care how our boss will react, what the neighbours may say, whether we are behaving badly or selfishly; we don't put on our best clothes to dream; we don't bother with make-up. We are simply us: bare as on the day we were born, and as innocent.

Apart from anything else, we can feel an enormous sense of relief as a result of our dreams – and it seems most likely that we feel this even if we ignore them. Ignoring them perhaps diminishes their effect; but there is plenty of evidence to suggest that even just recording our dreams helps to bolster our self-confidence, build our personalities, helps us make the right decisions and encourages us to be ourselves.

Within the past few years there has been a greatly increased interest in dreams, with people meeting in groups or workshops to discuss them. These first began to appear in the mid-1960s, when the present interest in New Age matters began, and men and women in the Western world, who had a knowledge of the value of psychotherapy but did not wish to take professional advice, began to look about them for means of helping themselves come to terms with what seemed an increasingly threatening, technological world.

We think group dream analysis is a mistake. No doubt, if you are a beginner, discussion with people who have been interpreting their dreams for years can help to put you on the right track; but by their nature what dreams have to say to us is very private, and in our experience there are very few people who are prepared to be totally honest, in a group situation, about exploring their inner meaning. Talking to an individual, most usefully either a close friend or a total stranger, is another matter. So is working on your dreams with the help of a sensible book.

The present book is designed to help the absolute beginner. It is important to read the introductory chapters rather than to turn immediately to the dream dictionary. If you do that, you will be disappointed, for the suggestions we make and (most importantly) the questions we ask, can only be responded to if you know something about the way dreams work.

There are one or two more things to be said.

Don't be frightened by your dreams. Even nightmares can be dealt with and seen as friends, however frightening they are. Remember always that *you dream your dreams* – they are not sent by spirits to

9

torment you; those monsters are self-created: you made the Frankenstein, and he comes with a message from your innermost self.
Discover the message, and the monster is tamed.

Even more important, do not be frightened by the prospect of
discovering the *meaning* of your dreams. This is perhaps a little more
difficult. A few people will say, if one talks to them about analysis,
about discovering their real emotions and motives, 'Thank you very
much, but I'd rather not know.' You are not likely to be one of those
people: if you were, you would have stopped reading long before this!
Others fear that they will discover that they don't like themselves very
much. Well, there is a very good answer to that: change. One of the
most valuable things dreams show you is where your idealised picture
of yourself departs from reality. If self-improvement is really the name
of the game, there are no better weapons than dreams, the truth-
tellers.

One final warning: interpreting your own dreams is not easy, nor is
it something you should take too lightly. You have rejected the
traditional 'dream book', and chosen one which can show you how to
open the door into your dream world, or at least push it ajar. Don't
think it's going to be easy to get through the door into that fascinating,
strange, secret garden – but once you do, the air will help you to
breathe more freely, you will learn to move more surely and think
more clearly than ever before.

Derek and Julia Parker

Part One

· I ·
Talking
to
Yourself

Learn from your dreams what you lack.
W. H. Auden

The net of the sleeper catches fish.
Greek proverb

reams are so mysterious that it is hardly surprising that we treat them with extreme caution, or are even slightly afraid of them.

To start with, we cannot prevent ourselves from dreaming (we *all* dream, *every* night) and, on the whole, we cannot control our dreams: in them, we sometimes find ourselves behaving as we would never behave in our waking life, and feel frightened or revolted by our dream actions. Many people have, or believe they have, predictive dreams, and see sleep as a doorway into the fourth dimension, offering the possibility of time-travel, of seeing into the future. Sometimes we dream of our own deaths, or the deaths of loved ones, and may superstitiously think of this as an omen. The dead may themselves appear in our dreams, though often to reassure and bless us.

All in all, it is not surprising that men and women have always treated dreams with extreme caution, or that a great deal of silly superstition has grown up around them: that they 'go by contraries', for instance – 'dream of a death, you'll hear of a birth'; that if you tell a dream before breakfast you invite bad luck; or that 'A Friday night's dream on a Saturday told, Is sure to come true be it never so old.'

A lot of this folklore is extremely ancient. Apuleius, the Roman author, wrote about dreams going by contraries, almost two thousand years ago; the earliest known exhaustive book on the subject, Artemidorus' five-volume *The Interpretation of Dreams*, was written as early as the second century AD.

Perhaps man instinctively recognised, very early in history, what modern psychoanalysis has confirmed – that however they are produced, however we feel about them, dreams are an important part of our lives, and in some ways a key to our personality and behaviour. In a sense, we *are* our dreams.

Happily, however, only in a sense. If we dream of killing someone, that doesn't make us a murderer, or suggest that we are going to become one. It doesn't even necessarily mean that we would like to kill someone. It would be more likely to mean that we wanted to get rid of something that the victim represented, perhaps some trait of his or hers that we recognised in ourselves. But even that is a generalisation.

This, then, is the place for a confession which is also a warning. If you have picked up this book hoping that it will tell you what particular dreams mean, you are going to be disappointed. That is the confession. And any book which claims to be able to do that, is taking money under false pretences. That is the warning.

Sadly, there are still many such books about – usually reprints or imitations of 'dream books' which were popular in Victorian times, but had their roots in the superstitious beliefs of the ancients: that if you dream of a black cat, it 'means' good (or bad) luck; that if you dream of a sword it 'means' danger.

Life is not as easy as that; and dreams certainly aren't! Such books are like those astrological Sun-sign columns which promise that because you are 'a Scorpio' or 'a Capricorn' this or that is going to happen to you next week. Yes, a lot of people read them for fun, and enjoy doing so – and dreams, too, can be fun; they provide, after all, seven nights' free entertainment a week! But they are not (at least, not all) so simple.

If you think about it, the reason why dreams cannot be interpreted in a cut-and-dry way is very clear. If you dream of a cat, that dream will mean something very different to you from what my dream of a cat will mean to me. The reason is that your dreams are *your* dreams, and my dreams are *mine*. The cat which appears in your dream is, as it were, your own special 'essence of cat': it may perhaps be a cat you knew when you were a child, or a cat you have at present; its actions may relate to an experience you had with a cat when you were young, and will certainly have much to do with your attitude to cats – whether you like or hate them, whether you fear their claws or long to cuddle them. The cat in your dreams will behave in a way which only *you* can interpret, because only *you* know your deepest and innermost feelings about cats. The cat in my dream is the essence, so to speak, of all the cats *I* have known, so it will behave in a way which only *I* can interpret, because only I know my deepest and innermost feelings about cats.

There is one important qualification to make to this statement: and that is that in addition to our dream cat (or dog, or sword, or whatever) we all have within us a sort of instinctive conception or 'memory' of what humankind in general has, over many thousands of years, come to connect with the *idea* of 'cat' or 'dog' or 'sword'. This idea lives in what Jung called 'the collective unconscious'. The idea is a complex one, but the collective unconscious can be likened very roughly to a wide, deep well of universal memory containing what Jung called 'psychic structures common to all men'; or to put it another way, a great stream of images and symbols which drift in and out of our dreams, representing the deepest and most significant emotions humankind can experience.

More of this, later; for a knowledge of these universal symbols and what they mean offers one of the most helpful keys to interpreting our individual dreams, and it is a key we offer in the present book.

But for the moment, there is one particularly important fact to underline as strongly as possible:

YOU DREAM YOUR OWN DREAMS.

Yes, it does seem a truism, and to lay such emphasis on it seems ridiculous. But most people do not seem to believe it, which is why the silly idea persists that a black cat means good (or bad) luck whether it appears in your dream or in mine!

In dreams we are talking to ourselves. A few dream investigators have certainly questioned this, suggesting that dreams represent merely a way of clearing out of our minds the unwanted rubbish they accumulate during our lifetime: if every impression or memory remained consciously in our minds, it is alleged, they would be so numerous that they would get in the way of rational thought. So in sleep our minds run over the tape on which the images are recorded, and 'wipes' it.

This seems on the face of it a reasonable argument: but the difficulty is that once we have dreamed of an image or an incident, it *isn't* wiped from our mind; indeed, it is often reinforced. Similarly, psychoanalysis shows that it is likely that we never actually forget anything. Under hypnosis long-forgotten incidents from extreme childhood can surface.

So it is more probably that while some dreams are relatively 'meaningless' in that they are not very important, most have a significance for us, and are commenting or offering advice on situations which are perhaps unconsciously preoccupying our waking hours.

What dreams can do

'Offering advice?' Yes, absolutely. And that is probably the chief point of this book: that it is not only entertaining and interesting to find out what your dreams mean – it is *helpful*.

It is important to stress that we are talking on the most practical level. There is nothing mysterious about the way in which dreams can be useful – the mystery lies in learning how to recognise the way in which they can be useful, for there seems no limit to the ways in which we can use their advice.

On the most basic and obvious level, they can help us to understand ourselves. Most religions have at one time or another suggested that one day men and women will have to face their Creator in the knowledge that He will see them exactly as they are, all their pretences stripped away, with no possibility of hiding their faults or disguising their weaknesses. Not, perhaps, a very comfortable proposition, especially as it was usually supposed that the scene would be a very public one.

The idea was that we should be judged as we are, rather than as we present ourselves to the world. But another aspect of the notion was that perhaps for the first time we should see ourselves as we really are. An equally uncomfortable idea? Maybe, but a useful one. Most wise people have recognised that to know ourselves, warts and all, enables us to make wiser decisions, build better relationships, live lives which in the end are more fulfilled.

One of the most important things dreams do is show us, ourselves. Properly interpreting them, we can understand our motives in behaving, sometimes, deceitfully, in hiding our true selves behind a mask, in reacting over-violently to one idea or over-enthusiastically to another.

In ancient times, actors wore a mask known as the *persona*. Our *persona* (and Jung first used the word in this sense) is the self we present to the world: the picture of ourselves as we want to be seen. Our dreams rip the mask away. As the American writer Thoreau pointed out, 'In dreams we see ourselves naked and acting out our real characters, even more closely than we see others awake.'

This is good for us in several ways. For instance, the mask may not fit us very well. Many gays have found this, when they have felt it necessary to wear a mask of heterosexuality: they have felt insecure and unsure of themselves – for the mask has never really fitted them, and they have been fearful that it will slip.

One homosexual New York businessman, who had always concealed his real sexuality, dreamed that he was at a picnic with his boss and colleagues. His boss was about to sit down when he saw a large and ugly caterpillar. With an expression of disgust, he lifted his foot and was about to stamp on it when it broke apart and from it emerged a beautiful butterfly which flew up and perched on the boss' shoulder. There were expressions of admiration from everyone present.

The businessman's analyst pointed out that this was a clear indication that he felt, in his inner self, the desire to be honest and the conviction that his boss and colleagues would be sympathetic were he to do so. After some thought and considerable agony (because his waking self was still very unsure), he 'came out' and found not only that nobody minded in the least, but that his colleagues evidently admired his courage and now had additional trust in him.

This is only one of many examples of how a dream can help you make a decision – or even make a decision for you. The novelist D. H. Lawrence wrote to a friend:

I can never decide whether my dreams are the result of my thoughts, or my thoughts the result of my dreams. It is very queer. But my dreams make conclusions for me. They decide things finally. I dream a decision. Sleep seems to hammer out for me the logical conclusions of my vague days, and offer me them as dreams . . .

Dreams and creativity

Dreams are part of the process of thinking: the part that has been called 'lateral thinking'. We have all been told that it is valuable to learn to look at problems from an unconventional viewpoint: when we see them from a different angle, a solution often suggests itself. There is plenty of evidence of this: writers and composers have had works inspired in them by their dreams. One of the most famous was the violinist and composer Tartini who, in old age, told the astronomer Lalande that he once had a dream in which he sold his soul to the Devil, who took his violin from him and played:

. . . with consummate skill a sonata of such exquisite beauty as surpassed the boldest flights of my imagination. I felt enraptured, transported, enchanted; my breath was taken away, and I awoke. Seizing my violin I tried to retain the sounds

I had heard – but in vain. The piece I then composed, the 'Devil's Sonata', was the best I ever wrote, but how far below the one I had heard in my dream!'

Just as famous is the incident in which the poet Coleridge fell asleep while reading, and dreamed his poem *Kubla Khan*; but other writers have profited too. Robert Louis Stevenson had been thinking for some time of writing a story on the theme of *Dr Jekyll and Mr Hyde*:

For two days I went about wracking my brains for a plot of any sort; and on the second night I dreamed the scene at the window, and a scene afterward split in two, in which Hyde, pursued for some crime, took the powder and underwent the change in the presence of his pursuers . . .

The novelist Sylvia Townsend Warner woke one morning from a dream in which she had seen a man standing, wringing his hands, on the beach of a South Sea island, tears streaming down his face. She knew that he was a missionary, that he had made a single convert, and now found that the convert was a false one. She sat down immediately and shortly finished her best novel, *Mr Fortune's Maggot*, in which the island of her dreams became Fanua, and the figure that of the Rev. Timothy Fortune.

The German chemist F. A. Kekule dreamt the solution to the problem of the ring structure of benzene:

The atoms were juggling before my eyes . . . my mind's eye, sharpened by repeated sights of a similar kind, could now distinguish larger structures of different forms and in long chains, many of them close together; everything was moving in a snake-like and twisting manner. Suddenly, what was this? One of the snakes got hold of its own tail and the whole structure was mockingly twisting in front of my eyes. As if struck by lightning, I awoke. . . . Let us learn to dream, and then we may perhaps find the truth.

But, dreams sometimes pull one's leg unremittingly. William Morris wanted to dream a poem, and at last did so: but waking, he remembered only the first line – 'The moonlight slept on a treacle sea.'

Dreams and religion

Until the conviction grew that since they were often sexual in nature, dreams must be sent by the Devil, the early Christians believed that they were messages from God, often injunctions that man should look to the state of his soul. Many theologians have subsequently believed this, or at least have been convinced that they were means of revealing His will. Sir Thomas Browne, in 1650, suggested that:

. . . if there be guardian spirits, they may not be unactively about us in sleep, but may sometimes order our dreams, and many strange hints, instigations, or discoveries which are so amazing unto us, may arise from such foundations.

Such a view is less prevalent today, and though many people have had their feelings about religion clarified by dreams, they can work two ways. In 1958, a clergyman, the Rev. John Bradley, resigned from the Church of England, and later admitted that for some time he had been concealing even from himself the doubts he had had about his faith – until in a dream he had attended a sermon preached by St Peter, in which the saint had argued that honesty was so basic to life that it must be embraced whatever the discomfort, even at the risk of offending God. Mr Bradley concluded that he must place honesty before any social discomfort, and left his living. It might be argued that his conscious – and subconscious – had made itself heard above the subdued argument of his theoretical convictions.

Your view of the connection between dreams and faith must depend on your own attitude to religion. If dreams are indeed truth-tellers – if their chief activity is to tell us about ourselves – then any religion founded on truth can only, surely, approve and take notice of them? It is also the case that they can often be most helpful at times of distress: many people have been 'visited' in their dreams by loved ones who have died, and have been reassured and comforted.

Predictive dreams

We have always treated predictive dreams with great caution. There are some published examples which are, to say the least, extremely persuasive, and if many of them can be rationally explained, there are others which cannot. It would obviously be silly to look for predictions in every dream we have. Many people, on the night before a long flight, dream of an aircraft crashing. It is impossible to know for how many this has been a fatal prediction, but the number seems unlikely to be large.

Treat such dreams with caution and good sense. If you dream that your plane is crashing, there is no good reason to cancel your flight: the dream will simply be a reflection of your tension and a (perhaps unconscious) fear of flying. If you dream that that plane is piloted by a red-haired man with only one arm, and you are welcomed on board next day by a red-haired pilot with an empty sleeve, you might do well to be worried!

Practicality should always be underlined when we think of dream interpretation. It is not a modern, untried theory – it has been used in many cultures throughout world history (the Aboriginal and Amer-Indian cultures are particularly rich) – though it is only in the present century that a general concensus has been reached about the way in which we should look at our dreams and discover how they can help us.

Do dreams exist?

Though most of us 'know' that we dream, we would be hard put to it to *prove* that we do so. Speculation about the 'reality' of dreams is in a sense academic – it need not concern us any more than the philosophical argument about whether a cow continues to exist when we have stopped gazing at it. It may be difficult to *prove* that it does; but we all suspect that it may. Similarly, most people would accept that dreams exist: they are often too vivid, sometimes too uncomfortable, to be denied. On the other hand because they are so ephemeral and often vanish into thin air at the moment the dreamer wakens, a small number of people say that they 'never dream'. It is always worth asking them how, in that case, they know what a dream is? After a moment's thought, they will usually admit that they 'used to dream' once upon a time, when they were children – but no, these days, they never do.

They are mistaken. In fact, you may be able to prove it: watch someone go to sleep, and continue to watch them. After a while, you will notice that their eyes seem to be moving beneath their eyelids: wake them at that moment, and almost certainly they will remember what they have been dreaming about.

Nevertheless, while the majority of people simply find it difficult to remember their dreams, there is a minority which finds it impossible. The problem seems to be that in the nature of things we sleep when we are tired, perhaps exhausted, and there is a direct connection between good memory and a state of wakeful alertness: good memory control and accuracy fail in proportion to how tired one is. So when we awake from a sound sleep into which we have fallen when really tired, we are less likely to remember a dream than if we slept more lightly (there may be a connection with the fact that nightmares often take place during fitful, 'bad' sleep). We may perhaps be conscious that we have 'had a dream' without being able to recall it.

In extreme cases, it is almost impossible to convince non-dreamers that they do in fact dream. Trying to tackle the task of convincing someone who 'never dreams' that they do so, scientists have resorted to hypnosis, under which non-dreamers have given vivid details of dreams they have experienced. Yet when they came out of hypnosis, they have denied dreaming, and when recordings were played of their descriptions of their dreams, they simply failed to recognise them.

But these are extreme cases: most people who claim they 'never dream' can teach themselves to recall their dreams.

What *is* a dream?
Most people will have had the experience of dreaming that someone is ringing the door-bell, and waking to find that it is true. Can we call that experience a dream? Surely not. Similarly, most people at one time or another will have fallen into a 'day-dream' in which they will have been thinking so concentratedly about a situation that they have in a way entered it, and have 'awakened' with a jolt, just in time to escape being run down by a car! But day-dreams are not dreams in the sense in which most people understand them.

What most of us mean when we speak of a dream is something 'unreal' – an experience which we have while we are asleep, which *while it is taking place* seems entirely real, but which when we are awake is seen to have been – what? The word 'unreal' doesn't really apply, because in our dreams some sort of reality exists: we are recognisably ourselves, we recognise other people, things, situations. Fantasies? But we are usually in control of our fantasies. Hallucinations? Illusions?

There is a sense in which our dreams are very real indeed; but for the time being let us accept the proposition that a dream presents a kind of reality 'different' from that which we recognise when we are awake. People who are mentally ill have hallucinations which are very much like waking dreams, only they believe them to be true; they are not 'day-dreams' like those which rational people occasionally enjoy but, like dreams, seem much more real.

When waking from a particularly vivid dream, we may be convinced for a split second that it was 'real', but then we reject the idea a moment later, because the events of our dreams are usually noticeably different from the events of our waking lives. It is as though the instant we fall asleep someone lets in a clutch, and the cogwheels of our mind begin to spin out of control. What happens in our dreams doesn't seem to be anything rational, and is certainly nothing which we can control. In waking life, we are to a great extent our own master or mistress, particularly where our emotions are concerned. But not in the dream world.

Yet this doesn't mean that we are conscious of living in a fantastic and unreal world when we are asleep: dreams are very real indeed, while they last. In fact, psychology claims that they are in a sense more real than real – that in our dreams our pretensions and poses are stripped away, and we can, if we want to, see ourselves not as we or other people see us, but as we really are.

· II ·
Dreams
as
Therapy

*Dreams are faithful interpreters of our inclinations; but
there is art required to sort and understand them.*
M. de Montaigne

Judge of your natural character by what you do in dreams.
R. W. Emerson

hile for centuries it was generally felt that dreams
were important – whether as messages from the gods
or one's ancestors, as a means of predicting the future
or merely of exploring some strange world parallel to
our own – since about the beginning of the twentieth century they
have provided the raw material for psychoanalysis.

This new view was largely the result of the work of two psychologists – Sigmund Freud (1856–1939, the founder of psychoanalysis)
and his sometime colleague C. G. Jung (1875–1961), who concentrated on analysing his patients' conflicts, and found dreams invaluable as an index to them.

Apart from the enormous volume of work published by these two
men and their colleagues and disciples (who included Alfred Adler,
A. A. Brill, S. Ferenczi, Ernest Jones, J. Sadger and others), a great
library of books has grown up which comment on, expand and
theorise about their work. Here, we can give only the briefest idea of
their respective approaches to dream analysis.

The unconscious: Freud

It was Sigmund Freud whose name will always be associated with the
modern theories of dream interpretation – with the conviction that we
dream because our unconscious wants to tell us something, usually

about the way we really, secretly, want to live, as opposed to the way we are living at the moment.

It is worth trying to define what psychologists – and Jung in particular – mean by 'the unconscious'. It is at once a very simple and a very complicated concept. At its most basic, our 'unconscious' holds motives and desires of which we are unaware, but which are nevertheless very important to us. Jung, as usual, put it most succinctly and forcefully:

Everything of which I know, but of which I am not at the moment thinking; everything of which I was once conscious but have now forgotten; everything perceived by my senses, but not noted by my conscious mind; everything which, involuntarily and without paying attention to it, I feel, think, remember, want, and do; all the future things which are taking shape in me and will sometime come to consciousness; all this is the content of the unconscious.

In other words, we may think we know ourselves, and to some extent, we do; we know that we are reckless or like playing safe, that we are generous with money, shy in personal relationships, and so on. But, as Freud suggested, we do not know about other elements of our personal identity, buried in our 'unconscious'. When working with patients, Freud discovered – to his surprise and growing excitement – that elements of their unconscious were betrayed by their dreams. When they told him their dreams, he recognised that the fantasies which their minds constructed during sleep were to a very large extent based on motives, desires, energies to which they would not lay claim when awake – indeed, some of which they would fervently deny!

Of course, the basic idea was not as simple as that. Freud learned that, for instance, in dreams things were often 'condensed' (as he put it) – to some extent a shorthand was being used. There was another difficulty – dreams were highly symbolic, a not always recognisable symbol being used to express an idea, person or thing. He called this idea 'displacement'.

When told that an event in a dream probably stands for something else, dreamers almost always ask '*Why?*' If dreams want to tell us something, why can't they be clear about it? Why disguise the message? Why put it into a code which is difficult, sometimes almost impossible, to break?

Freud's answer was that dreams are in code for the same reason that underground workers in occupied Europe put messages in code during the Second World War; to get them past the censor.

In our ordinary, waking lives, we are under great pressure to conform – sometimes to the society around us, but sometimes simply to our own idea of ourselves. We may set out to work against the system, to be different from the crowd; but we are still often concerned to behave as we feel we *should*, according to our own lights – while buried deep within us is the desire to shock ourselves by some deviant behaviour; inside almost everyone there seems to be a revolutionary of some kind. In order to make life tolerable, so that we can observe some kind of discipline, we are our own censors: the person who protests violently against society may, deep inside, be a conformist longing to live within the confines of the society he claims to despise. A dream which expressed this too obviously would be extremely distressing and perhaps damaging – Freud thought it might even be 'too shocking to be understood'.

His pronouncements on dreams were shocking in themselves, for he became sure that not only were dreams a means of fulfilling repressed sexual desires, but that the *latent* content of dreams (the hidden meaning, as opposed to the *manifest* or immediately recognised content) was not only always sexual, but often incestuous. He also insisted that even infants experienced such dreams, and that 'infantile sexuality' was very real, and often very important.

Freud was very ingenious at interpreting dreams to fit his theory of our natural predisposition to incestuous feelings. A man dreaming of travelling in a train which entered a tunnel would be accused of really dreaming of sexual intercourse with his mother. It is difficult, in the 1990s, to realise just how shocking these ideas were – until one discovers in conversation that many people still find them shocking today.

Most psychologists now discount Freud's insistence that all dreams are always sexual. However, it is generally agreed that dreams transmit their meanings in code – the revolutionary may dream that he or she is carefully mending a piece of broken china, or meticulously building a scattered deck of cards into a house.

The method Freud used in order to show a patient the true meaning of his dreams was largely that of *free association*. Having persuaded the dreamer to remember the chief elements of a dream, he would invite her to say what each element first suggested to her, and then tried to help her to understand the connection. Naturally, considering the direction which Freud expected the interpretation to take, his patients were often severely inhibited – and when this happened, Freud accused them of resisting a real interpretation, and interpreted their dream for them.

Sometimes the symbolism he suggested was fairly easy to grasp –
sometimes more private, and therefore more difficult. In 1915, Freud
gave some examples in one of his *Introductory Lectures on Psychoanalysis*:

*People have dreams of climbing down the front of a house, with feelings
sometimes of pleasure and sometimes of dread. When the walls are quite smooth,
the house means a man; when there are ledges and balconies which can be caught
hold of, a woman. Parents appear in dreams as* emperor *and* empress, king
and queen *or other exalted personages; in this respect the dream attitude is highly
dutiful. Children and brothers and sisters are less tenderly treated, being symbolised by* little animals *or* vermin. *Birth is almost invariably represented by
some reference to* water: *either we are falling into water or clambering out of it,
saving someone from it or being saved by them, i.e., the relation between mother
and child is symbolised. For dying we have setting out upon a* journey *or
travelling by train, while the state of death is indicated by various obscure, and,
as it were, timid allusions;* clothes *and* uniforms *stand for nakedness. You see
that here the dividing line between the symbolic and the allusive kinds of
representation tends to disappear.*

*In comparison with the poverty of this enumeration, it cannot fail to strike us
that objects and matters belonging to another range of ideas are represented by a
remarkably rich symbolism. I am speaking of what pertains to the sexual life – the
genitals, sexual processes and intercourse. An overwhelming majority of symbols
in dreams are sexual symbols.*

Freud's basic idea – that dreams often betray unconscious emotions
or desires – was very quickly grasped, but that most dreams are of a
sexual nature was immediately disputed. It may be that this belief
was a product of the age: of all topics, sex was the one about which it
was most difficult if not impossible to speak, even to a doctor, and
Freud may for that reason have inferred that it was the topic which
the dreamer's 'censor' was most concerned to disguise. But this led
him into an overemphasis on sexuality: all along pointed objects
symbolised a penis, all hollow objects a vagina. He took the theory to
extremes which at times even became absurd. At one time he insisted,
for instance, that a man's tie was *always* a sexual symbol!

Of course, since sex is of enormous importance in most people's
lives, he was very often right; sometimes the symbols in dreams are
inescapably sexual, and extremely revealing about the sexual nature
of the dreamer. One case so typical that it is almost too obvious is that
of the Victorian writer and art critic John Ruskin. Ruskin was

severely inhibited – so much so that his marriage was never consummated. What could be more obviously symbolic than the snake in the following dream, set down in his diary for March 9, 1868?

Dreamed of walk with Joan and Connie, in which I took all the shortcuts over the fields, and sent them round by the road, and then came back with them jumping up and down banks of earth, which I saw at last were washed away below by a stream. Then of showing Joan a beautiful snake, which I told her was an innocent one; it had a slender neck and a green ring round it, and I made her feel its scales. Then she made me feel it, and it became a fat thing like a leech, and adhered to my hand, so that I could hardly pull it off – and so I woke.

The whole story of Ruskin's sexuality seems to be there: the insecurity of his standing with women, the penis-symbol declining to respond to a woman's touch while responding to his own. But it is difficult to imagine Ruskin setting the dream down so frankly, even in his diary, had he realised its implications; and it is not surprising that only a few decades later most people were disgusted to think that their dreams could have such, to them, revolting implications.

Carl Gustav Jung

However, a grasp of Freud's general theory set his colleagues off on their own exploration of dreams, and dreams speedily became *the* essential element of psychoanalysis. Jung, who shared with Freud the highest plateau of early twentieth-century psychology, went down a slightly different path. He took a more general view of his patients' dreams than Freud, believing that the overall content was of more importance than any single ingredient: Freud might concentrate on the tie, while Jung would look at who was wearing it, why, and what part it played in the 'plot' of the dream. He refused to be led off in the direction of 'free association' ('What does the *tie* mean to you?'), and would rather lead the dreamer on a walk around his dream, considering the general landscape, the weather, the circumstances ('What does the *dream* mean to you?'). While Freud's view was that dreams *concealed* the dreamer's most secret joys and fears, Jung felt that they *revealed* them. 'I was never able to agree with Freud,' he wrote, 'that the dream is a façade behind which its meaning lies hidden – a meaning already known but maliciously, so to speak, withheld from consciousness. To me dreams are a part of nature, which harbours no intention to deceive but expresses something as best it can, just as a plant grows or an animal seeks its food as best it can.'

Agreeing with Freud that dreams were 'the royal road to the unconscious', Jung's main premise was that they enabled us to see things from a different point of view, and in a different perspective. They could not only suggest ways of solving practical and personal problems, but they could help us to develop our personalities – indeed, they were 'our most effective aid in building up the personality'.

Must we dream?

Is it *necessary* to dream?

It is an unanswerable question. But we can guess at the answer, and Freud's general theory suggests perhaps the most reasonable response. If there is some hidden cavern within us which can conveniently be called 'the unconscious', where all sorts of hidden desires and emotions lie, and if this were to be so severely restricted that no hint of them could escape, a pressure might build up which would lead to an explosion. But if those desires and emotions are allowed to escape through dreams – even if we do not remember our dreams or recognise their symbolism when we wake – the pressure is relieved, the tension fails to build up; we can only be happier and healthier.

But if this is the case, you might argue, then why should we bother to interpret our dreams? Millions of people live entirely happy and fulfilled lives without pausing for a moment to consider their dreams and what they may mean. On the other hand, the twentieth century has been the great age of self-discovery, and a great many people have the desire to discover more about themselves and their motivations – some by entering psychoanalysis, some by consulting astrologers and, increasingly, many by recording and attempting to interpret their own dreams.

Some people are afraid of self-knowledge; they have no desire to discover the reasons why they act as they do, why they may dislike some people on sight, yet trust and love others; they make decisions on the basis of emotion and instinct, without recognising their real motives; their personal lives are led entirely without reference to the background against which their emotional responses were formed.

If they are happy and fulfilled, there is no reason to persuade them to probe the inner meaning of their lives. On the other hand dreams offer many clues to our motives and emotions which it is wasteful not to examine, especially when we have problems.

In this book we take neither a strictly Freudian nor Jungian view of dreams: in a popular book written by two people without training in psychiatry it would be impertinent to do anything else. But take into account the benefits each suggested could come from a study of one's dreams: Freud felt that our repressed feelings can be revealed to us, and therefore controlled; Jung that we can recognise aspects of ourselves which otherwise we would fail to recognise – which comes to the same thing. Freud felt that in our dreams we do things we wish to do in waking life, but repress (wish-fulfillment); Jung believed that dreams range over the whole of our experience – that is, they deal with all aspects of our lives, feelings and emotions, recognised as well as unrecognised.

We do however reject Freud's view that almost all the elements of dreams consist of sexual symbols, and find Jung's view of them much more sympathetic: that is that they are, certainly, highly personal, but that they also relate to the collective unconscious, that deep within us we carry the same motivations as every other human being, reflected in broadly the same images, many of them enshrined in myths, legends and superstitions which we 'know' even if we have never learned about them – for they come down to us not only in Homer but in fairy stories, not only in philosophy but in instinctive hopes and fears.

Our sympathy with Jung is not only instinctive, but stems from the fact that he positively encouraged dreamers to treat themselves: dreams, he believed, were a natural part of our lives, and were *meant to be understood*, though he himself did not attempt to devise a way in which ordinary people could learn to understand them.

Should we work on our own dreams?

There is obviously a limit to the amount of work which we can do on our dreams. Some analysts have suggested that in analysing our own dreams we are consciously resisting psychoanalytical treatment, and that we should only enquire into the meaning of our dreams while in analysis. It is difficult not to reply with Mandy Rice-Davis' famous words, 'They would, wouldn't they?' The psychoanalysts who suggest this are protecting the closed shop which in the past was the domain of fortune-tellers and witch-doctors, who were on the whole as interested in manipulating their patients as in curing them.

Even Freud himself thought that there was something to be learned by people from studying their own dream; after all, his early work consisted to a large extent of self-analysis. Jung believed that an intelligent layman was probably capable of a fairly accurate 'reading' of his own dreams, though a thorough grounding in mythology, folklore and the psychology of primitive people was perhaps essential to really deep understanding.

It is certainly true that if our dreams are dealing with an emotion or an area of life which we have repressed since childhood, and which is very deeply mysterious or worrying to us, we may not be able to approach it through the kind of self-analysis which they can provide us with. Our inhibitions may simply be too strong to allow it. But most of us can get a great deal of help, encouragement and reassurance from a study of our dreams, provided we relax sufficiently, forget ourselves as others see us, or even as we would wish to see ourselves, and let the symbolic language of our sleeping selves to speak to us.

The Secret Code

We may expect to find in dreams everything that has ever been of significance in the life of humanity.
C. G. Jung

Symbolism

he language of dreams is based on symbolism and we must now look at the language of symbols and see how far it is possible for people with no training in psychology to learn it.

A rough and ready description of a symbol is that it is an object, or perhaps an action, which stands for something else; in psychology, it represents another object or action which is not directly connected with it. It is rather like a code.

One way of looking at symbolism and seeing how it works is to look at the Christian religion, which is particularly rich in it. One of the most powerful symbols in world history is the fish which, from the very earliest years of Christianity, has been the symbol of Christ. This arose not because Christ or his actions were in any particular way fish-like, but because of the capital letters of five Greek words

Ἰησοῦσ Χρισνόσ, Θεοῦ Υιάσ Σωτήρ

Jesus Christ, Son of god, Saviour – which made up the word,

ιχθύσ

a fish.

The symbolism which made a ship the representation of the Christian church was arrived at in a different way. A ship carries people safely over the ocean, and the Church set out to carry people safely over the sea of life. Christianity also made use of the animal kingdom to represent Christ and the Church's qualities. He was called both Lamb and Lion, while the peacock stood for immortality, the phoenix for resurrection, the dragon or serpent for Satan and the stag for a soul thirsting for baptism.

It is easy enough to see how most of these symbols were arrived at: the lamb is meek, the lion brave (or he has that reputation); the phoenix was believed to renew itself, the dragon and serpent were fierce, consuming men by fire or destroying them by poison.

Freud, of course, saw the snake as a symbol of the penis, whereas the early Christians thought of its qualities, its 'personality', and likened them to those of the devil.

The theory behind dream analysis is that the things about which we dream, the actions in which we dream we are involved, the thoughts we dream, represent other things, other actions, other thoughts. This is fairly easy to accept. What is more difficult to believe is that symbolic meanings of certain things or actions are the same for all mankind. (Here, as everywhere else in this book unless we specifically say otherwise, when we speak of one sex we include the other.)

Common dreams

We all at one time or another dream of falling, of being pursued or attacked, of repeatedly trying to finish a particular task, of the work in which we are engaged during our waking hours and of sex, in one form or another. How do we know this? Well, there is plenty of anecdotal evidence. Talk of most people, mention those five categories, and you will find that on the whole they agree with you. But there is some statistical evidence, too. In his book, *The Dragons of Eden* (1977), Carl Sagan reports an experiment in which he recorded the dreams of a number of college students, and they reported that their dreams included those five elements. As a matter of fact, we have listed them in order of their frequency.

Obviously, if we dream of our work we all have slightly different dreams, but as Anthony Stevens points out in his *Archetype* (1982) the four other categories of dreams are probably common to all humanity. He suggests that our dreams of falling are:

. . . not surprising in a creature which, in the earlier stages of its evolution, spent its life in trees; nightmares of being attacked and pursued are only to be expected in a species whose primordial conflicts have involved hunting, fighting and striving for dominance; repeated attempts to perform tasks would reflect our never-ending

preoccupation with the need to master environmental vicissitudes, physical skills, social customs, etc., while the fifth category [sex] scarcely requires comment.

Now it may not seem very helpful that if we dream we are repeatedly trying to screw a top on to a bottle, the dream is reminding us that in waking life we are trying to 'master a physical skill'. But such a dream would be extremely unlikely to have such an obvious meaning: dreams are devious – they scarcely ever say what they mean in such simple terms. Such a dream would be more likely to mean that we were 'bottling something up', keeping it to ourselves, to prevent the knowledge being spilled. In other words, in such a dream the bottle and its top would perhaps be symbols of some knowledge (we 'contain' knowledge as a bottle contains liquid) which we do not want to let out (the bottle-top being a symbol of our attempts to retain it). Our continual attempts to screw the top on the bottle would then represent some difficulty which we were experiencing in doing so – perhaps because we are a natural gossip, or because we feel other people should know what we know.

Even such a simple explanation is not obvious until it is pointed out to us; once we have been told or have realised the explanation it seems so obvious that we instantly accept it: and this is one of the few bonuses where dream analysis is concerned – it is often true that once we hit on the meaning of a dream symbol, we realise instinctively that it is the right one. But this is very rarely as easy as in the example we have given. Dreams take their symbolic objects and actions from every area of our lives and experience – perhaps from an incident in our childhood, perhaps from a scene we saw on television half an hour before going to sleep, perhaps from a book or a newspaper report we saw last week. Sometimes the reference is to an incident or fact we have forgotten or not thought about for years – and if so, the difficulty of recapturing it and applying it to our dream is very great indeed. Sometimes our dreams choose a symbol which can have several meanings (in psychiatric language, it is said then to be *overdetermined*), which is another problem.

The difficulty of interpreting our dream symbols can scarcely be overstated. To do so, we must grasp at every possible clue, including some which we might at first thought discard: and these include traditional associations of which we may not consciously be aware. We are not merely twentieth-century men and women, after all – we are part of a great stream of life which has been flowing over the surface of the earth for millennia, and our collective unconscious retains meaningful symbols which may seem unimportant to us.

If we doubt this, we have only to think about the appeal of art: of why we should be moved by certain rhythms, certain chords in music; by primitive drawings which were done by men so different from us as to seem like spaceman from a distant galaxy. We are responding to sights and sounds which have grown into the very stuff of which our bodies and minds is created. Similarly, we may never have heard of some of the myths and legends from which potent symbols have been drawn, yet they will appear in our dreams, with meanings at which we could not guess, and which we can only approach by careful reading and thought.

This is why Jung claimed that a sound knowledge of world mythology was essential to anyone working seriously on dream analysis. It may be that relatively few people would be prepared to study that immense subject with sufficient thoroughness to be able to 'read off' each symbol as it occurred in their dreams. Our dream dictionary contains references to the major myths and legends from which some of the more common symbols are drawn. Please do not neglect these, or think they are unimportant. If you consider them carefully, you will be astonished at how often they have a keen and incisive comment to make on your personality or your life.

Archetypes

The greatest difficulty, until we have grasped, understood and accepted it, is that many of the symbols in our dreams seem not to be personal – that is, they don't seem on the face of it to have much to do with us as individuals, or our own particular problems. Yet they do.

How? The answer is fairly obvious, if we think of the human mind as having evolved, over many thousands of years, like the body. Evolution has made our bodies what they are, has developed fins into hands, turned gills into ears, taught us to walk on two legs rather than four, diminished what were once tails into rudimentary fragments of bone at the base of our spines.

Our minds have evolved, like our bodies. Embedded in them, like our rudimentary tails, are inherited images of love or fear, hatred or mistrust. In other words, the human mind has a history, just like the human body. Freud called the historical traces of ancient emotions and attitudes which hide within the mind of modern man, *archaic remnants*; Jung referred to them as *archetypes*.

These are not the same as instincts. Our instinctive reactions to certain situations, even certain people, are very often immediate. We will say to ourselves, 'I don't like that man or woman', though we may not have any special reason for not liking them –

> *I do not like thee, Dr Fell –*
> *The reason why, I cannot tell;*
> *But this I know, and know full well –*
> *I do not like thee, Dr Fell.*

But sometimes someone's charm or looks will swamp such an instinct: and it is then that our dreams will prompt us, not necessarily by showing us Dr Fell himself in some satanic context, but by giving us a sideways glimpse of him, or of some symbol representing him, which will make it quite clear, if we have learned to read our dreams correctly, that something in us mistrusts him. So, our instinctive mistrust of someone is just that – instinctive; our *unconscious* mistrust will be shown by a symbol, an *archetype*.

We shouldn't believe that these archetypes are individual to us: we aren't the only human beings to have rudimentary tails at the base of our spines! When we have a dream which has a strong, perhaps frightening image in it, we should remember that while it may refer to a particular situation in which we are involved, the image itself will probably be a universal one. Jung recalls (in *Man and his Symbols*) a professor who had had a very disturbing vision in a dream, and came to see him in a serious panic. Jung listened to him, then showed him a 400-year-old book in which there was a woodcut showing that very vision. The professor was comforted: it was not that he had once seen that woodcut and forgotten it – it was that the artist who had drawn it had had the same vision as himself; it was an *archetype*.

Certain dream images, archetypes, seem to be inevitably attached to certain states of mind: they may be coloured by some personal references, but their general tone will be the same for us all, wherever we live, whatever our social position, whatever our language or level of intelligence. Children do not learn these archetypes as they learn a language or learn to walk; they are inherited just as certain instincts are inherited, such as a fear of fire or of the dark. We do an awful lot of things instinctively, without understanding why, and all the evidence is that many of our instinctive gestures or reactions date from a past so remote that we cannot trace their beginning – they may have developed before man was capable of reasoning.

Some people deeply mistrust this kind of talk. They like to think that they are completely rational, that they behave according to the laws of reason; they find it distasteful to think that their actions may be the result of a million years of conditioning rather than forty years of education and experience in the modern world. Interestingly, such people are generally among those who have claim that they 'never dream'. They find it safest to repress their dreams, and they certainly deeply mistrust them.

This is not an uncommon attitude, even among the more enlightened of us. There is something 'magical' about dreams which at worst can instil a sort of superstition. It is a deep-seated instinct as most common superstitions are.

But when we overcome our mistrust, we find our dreams can give us valuable support through the symbols, the ancient archetypes they offer. These cling tenaciously to the primeval forces which once drove us, and represent them to us in forms which are certainly difficult to perceive and understand, but which are enormously valuable. If we can grasp and comprehend them, we can gain enormous strength because they are concerned with all the major themes of life: love, hate, war, birth, death.

Many dream symbols seem to be directed at helping us to achieve a psychological balance. We need balance and discipline in our pyschological lives just as we do in our physical lives. As diet and exercise help us to keep our bodies healthy and 'well-balanced', so our dreams (Jung believed) help us to keep our psychological balance – when we lean too far in one direction, they will prompt us to remember that for every argument there is a counter-argument, that every emotion has its opposite.

Dreams and our relationships

A large number of dreams have to do with our relationships – not only sexual, but social. This is not surprising, for most of us spend a great deal of our time dealing with other human beings in one way or another, but at the same time we defend ourselves against them. The most devoted lovers need to keep a corner of themselves private; and because they often feel that this is an unworthy desire – that they should be prepared to open themselves completely to their partner – some tension arises. In dreams, the inhibition vanishes; dreams are nothing if not personal, and seem very much concerned with reconciling our individuality with the necessity that we must live, sometimes on very close terms, with others. So a lot of our dreams send us messages about our successes and failures in this area of our lives.

If we are to benefit from our dreams, we must learn to trust them, to accept the way in which they criticise us. This is not easy. If our friends criticise us, we can always pretend that they are wrong. Our dreams are never wrong! It is no use saying, 'Ah, but I'm not *like* that.' You are – because the criticism expressed by your dreams doesn't come from someone else; it comes from you; and not from the outward, posturing you who may happily pretend that your faults don't exist, but from the inner you who recognises the faults which you most hate to acknowledge.

The shadow
Jung had a term for the unacknowledged area of one's personality which is often shown in dreams: he called it 'the shadow'. It is a wonderfully vivid term, because not only does it represent the side of oneself which one prefers to keep in the dark, but the particular fault under discussion is often personified. Someone may appear in our dream who we think of as incorrigibly mean, and he or she will actually represent some mean area of our own personality.

The *shadow*, at best, perfectly balances the *persona*. When the two get severely out of balance, or one almost vanishes, we have either someone who is all 'self', who is so concerned about appearances and other people's good opinion that he never acts in any other way than to placate others, or someone who is all 'shadow' and cares so little for society that at worst he can become a criminal, entirely serving his own selfish motives.

We sometimes come across our shadow in waking life. How often we have said, when two people seem to dislike each other, 'Ah, they're too alike.' Each recognises in the other those defects which they possess but refuse to acknowledge – each sees his shadow in the other; the shadow always represents those qualities which we dislike most in other people, and which we ourselves possess but deny. By forcing us to recognise our defects, our dreams provide a valuable service – they are that 'best friend' who will point out our faults without fear or favour, and on whose honesty we can absolutely rely. Such honesty might provoke a quarrel with a human friend, but there is no point in flying into a rage with our dreams, especially when we know, consciously or unconsciously, that they're right!

Anima and animus
Apart from the shadow, another human figure may appear in our dreams, not representing our shadow but personifying other problems. In a man's dreams this figure will often be female (Jung called

this the *anima*); in a woman's, it will often be male (the *animus*). The anima represents the female aspects of the male personality, the animus the male aspects of the woman (we are all male *and* female).

The anima's effect is generally negative, but it will act in different ways according (Jung believed) to the relationship between the man and his mother. If it was a bad relationship, the anima will have a depressing effect; if a good one, it will at worst tend to make the subject somewhat effeminate, impractical, over-sensitive, too dependent on women.

The anima, like the shadow, is often recognisably a particular person, or perhaps a type of person. Some psychologists claim that when a man suddenly and fiercely falls in love with a woman it is because he recognises her as his anima – she is, literally, the woman of his dreams. At best, the anima helps a man to discover the most suitable partner. It can however be a thing rather than a person – very often a car (men usually refer to their cars as female ['She's running beautifully!] or sometimes a ship [also invariably 'female']). Psychologists suggest that the anima figure in men's dreams often takes the form of an erotic fantasy, which can become more pervasive when the dreamer lacks a satisfactory sexual relationship in waking life; the anima may then encourage him to search out pornography as a substitute.

The animus – the male figure in the female dream – can, like the anima, be a figure of good or of ill; and just as the character of the anima is related to the man's relationship with his mother, so the animus is affected by the woman's relationship with her father. He is frequently a hard and cruel man, often representing death. Sometimes however he can be a handsome, 'perfect' man, representing some impossible ideal, contrasted in the sleeper's mind with the real man who is on her mind, and whose faults she is busily cataloguing. Popular heroes and heroines, such as film or pop stars, often appear in dreams and represent anima and animus, suggesting that we will never find perfection in another human being, and might as well stop looking for it – which could be either a dangerous or a very valuable opinion to offer. Just like the anima, the animus has both a negative and positive side.

It is very important to realise that neither the shadow nor the anima/animus are fantasies; recognising them is not merely a game. In dream analysis it is very important indeed. What anima and animus do, when working at their most powerful, is prompt us to question ourselves about our objectives and convictions, to clear our

minds of pretence and open them to the suggestions of our unconscious; to allow ourselves to speak to us – to become whole.

They can also, incidentally, be important, crucial, in partnership.
Couples in a heterosexual partnership must, if it is to succeed, recognise the degree to which they embody the qualities of each other's
anima or animus. When we fall in love at first sight it is because we
think we see, across that crowded room, our anima or animus – a
living dream. Living with that dream, we have to learn that he or she
is not going to be the complete embodiment of everything we ever
dreamed of in man or woman, our own anima or animus. We have to
recognise that our partner is not the partner of our dreams; he or she is
real, in his or her own right, with his or her own needs. We must learn
to forgive when it turns out that the qualities we expected are missing.
We must allow our partner his or her own dreams.

· IV ·
Working with Your Dreams

We often forget our dreams so speedily: if we cannot catch them as they are passing out at the door, we never set eyes on them again.
William Hazlitt

emembering your dreams is not difficult. The first step is to begin to record them. Only a word or two, jotted down as you awake, will help you to recall a whole dream later, and as you grow more practised, you will not find it difficult to recall your dreams in considerable detail.

You will not be able to remember them all. Unless you wake in the middle of a dream, or just as it finishes, you are very unlikely to remember it at all. This means that even the most practised of us will only be able to record perhaps one-fifth of our nightly dreams, or even fewer. There is no way of knowing whether the ones we are able to examine in detail are our most important dreams, but on the other hand the evidence seems to suggest that really important dreams do manage to break through to consciousness sooner or later, and that we know which *are* the important ones. Sometimes we remember very vividly in old age a dream we had when we were quite young; this seems to be a sure indication that it is important.

Recurring dreams are significant too. Sometimes these take the form of nightmares, and are very frightening; we may need help to interpret these dreams and abolish them. On the other hand, recurring dreams can be delightful and reassuring. The French novelist, Julien Green, set down one in his journal:

Maybe I shouldn't breathe a word about the most beautiful, the most mysterious dream I ever had. I dream it once or twice a year. Suddenly, I see myself on a road that skirts the top of a cliff and I know that the dream is beginning and with it, a feeling of happiness such that human speech cannot give the faintest idea of it. Farther on, there will be a big iron gate, so difficult to turn on its hinges, then the long avenue of trees, then once again the cliff and I pause to look at the sea, but instead of water I see an immense forest that stretches to the horizon and covers the whole countryside, and at that moment I feel as happy as someone who has passed beyond death.

More about recurring dreams later: but first, what about those people who believe that they never dream?

Tonight I will dream

If you want to remember your dreams then say firmly to yourself when you go to bed: 'Tonight I will dream; and in the morning I will remember one of my dreams.' The chances are very strong that you will wake tomorrow morning and remember a dream. If this fails, and you have a partner or friend who is prepared to help, ask them to sit with you while you sleep, and to wake you when they see your eyes moving beneath your eyebrows. You will then be in REM sleep, and will almost certainly be able to remember your dream when you are shaken awake. (Rapid eye movement is very obvious: but to show your partner the sign, simply close your eyelids and move your eyes about below them.)

If you begin to remember your dreams, but only a very few of them, there is a technique which you can try in order to encourage yourself to remember more. It was devised by the psychotherapist Dr Frederick A. Perls, and though it sounds a very strange and quirky idea, it almost always works. It can also be used as a way to decipher particularly difficult dreams, as we will explain later.

Take two chairs and place them opposite each other. Sit in one, and think of your dreams as sitting in the other. Now, simply question them – and do so aloud. You will feel distinctly self-conscious the first time you do this; but persevere! Ask them why they aren't remaining in your memory when you wake up.

Now move into the other chair, and answer yourself, in the very first words that occur to you. You will find that more often than not, you will give yourself the right reason. It may be that your dreams say, 'Life's busy enough as it is; we don't want to give you more to worry about'; or, 'We're pretty dull, really; we don't think you'll be interested in us'; or, 'We don't think you'll be able to understand us.'

You will find that the answers are almost always excuses, to which you will have a very good answer. Simply tell your dreams you have plenty of time for them, or that you *will* find them interesting (it's why you're trying to remember them). You will probably find that the log-jam will clear.

Recording your dreams

Now, about recording your dreams.

The first thing is to try to record *all* the dreams you remember. You may find this more than a little trying. When you first start, you may wake up three or four times a night with a dream asking to be noted down. Note it down! You will find that in time experience will tell you which dreams are important enough to need as many notes as you can make, and which you can more or less 'let go'. But in the beginning, it is important to get into the habit of making notes on them all.

Keep a notebook – better still, loose-leaf paper which can be bound – and pencil at your bedside, and, if you want to avoid waking your partner, a torch. If you sleep alone, then a tape-recorder is ideal. It's important to make your notes as soon as possible after you awake, but don't sit up in bed, put on your spectacles, open the note-book, fumble for the pencil . . . lie still for a moment or two, letting the dream lie still in your mind, as it were. Then jot down the most important symbol or incident in the dream. If it has already begun to slip away, as they often do, don't panic and try desperately to remember; the harder you try, the faster the dream will run. Again, lie still and let your mind play around the idea of the dream until it comes up with something.

When you are fully awake, make sure your dream is dated, and set aside a few minutes at least to begin the process of examining it. You may not have much time, unless you are prepared to set your alarm to wake you half an hour earlier than you need in order to get the day under way. But at least read your rough notes and add anything that occurs to you – you will find you can often elaborate your notes considerably after a gap of only ten minutes or so. Note the *mood* of the dream (happy, sad, nostalgic?). How do you feel about the dream *now*? (Reassured, frightened, worried, pleased?) Try to remember whether anything you had on you mind as you fell asleep could have prompted the dream, and make a note of that.

Later, when you have leisure, transcribe the dream properly. You may find it useful to use the same format for each dream. On page 44 is a form you could use or adapt. You may only be able to fill in the lower parts of the form at first.

43

Jung asserted that there were three stages in approaching a dream. First, look for obvious ways in which the dream is commenting on your present situation, your life as you are living it at the moment. Then look at the 'cultural context' of the dream – the way in which it relates to your own time – in your case, the way of the world and of your own country in the 1990s, and what society would make of your dream, not only its actual content, but its mood and atmosphere. Thirdly, Jung emphasises the probable archetypal meaning – your dream seen in the context of the whole life of mankind, the instincts and emotions we all share as a natural heritage of the millennia during which mankind has developed.

DREAM RECORD

Date   Approx. time

1 DREAM   Using your notes, write the dream in the form of a 'story' (however weird or fantastic).

2 MOOD   How did you feel during the dream? How do you feel *now*? Do you think the dream was (a) warning you about something, (b) reassuring you, (c) giving advice – etc.

3 SYMBOLISM   What was the main symbol of the dream, and who or what did it represent?

4 CONTEXT   What or who may have prompted the dream?

Of course you will not be able to make sense of your dream as a trained Jungian analyst might. So don't be worried if the very basis of dream interpretation seems to elude you at first, if you can't even get your dream into logical sequence, so that when you have finished recording it, it still seems like a jumble of incidents or symbols rather than a story or narrative. This may well quite often be the case. We all know how rarely dreams are 'sensible'. The main thing is that you should get down everything you remember about the dream, and your immediate reactions to it – both while you were dreaming and now that you are awake. Thinking about your emotional response will quite often bring back symbols or incidents which you thought you had forgotten, and it is very important to get as much of the dream down as you can (without inventing anything!). When you start interpreting, you will have to think of absolutely everything about the dream as a clue to what it wanted to tell you; you can't count on anything in a dream, however insignificant, being unimportant.

Interpretation

Having got as much of the dream down on paper as you can, try to remember whether something might have happened on the previous day to trigger the dream. This is quite often the case; even if a dream obviously relates to, say, a problem which you have been concerned with for months, some incident or thought may well have suggested the particular dream you are considering and often the 'trigger' will seem to have nothing to do with the problem itself.

People are very often ready to say, 'Ah, yes, I dreamed of my house catching fire because late last night I watched that TV documentary on the Fire Brigade.' The TV documentary may well have been the trigger, but the dream may have been connected with something going on in your life about which you feel very strongly – fire is a potent symbol, for instance, of sexual passion. The 'trigger' will often be a firm clue, indeed, to the context of the dream, but don't automatically dismiss a dream founded on something you saw on TV or read in a book. Rather ask yourself why your dreams chose those subjects, out of the thousands of symbols harvested into your subconscious during the day.

You will sometimes be at a loss to connect your dream with anything. When this is the case, you can use Dr Perls' technique again. This time, sitting on the chair, confront your dreams and say, firmly: 'I didn't understand that dream. What were you really trying to tell me? What did such-and-such a symbol represent? Who was the man in the mask? Who was the woman driving the fast car?'

What you are doing is not questioning an empty chair, or even your dream as such; you are questioning your unconscious. If you do the exercise seriously, you will receive serious answers.

If you are still at a loss, there is another avenue open to you. Remember that, to a certain extent, while you do not control your dreams as such, you can certainly make suggestions to them. So before you go to sleep, simply tell your dreams: 'I didn't understand the dream I had last night, though I think it is probably important. Please send me another with the same message.' You will be surprised how often this works.

We said just now that your do not control your dreams: but some people are able to do just that. Very occasionally, most of us have a dream during which we are conscious that we are dreaming. This can be a very enjoyable experience; sometimes it leads to 'out-of-body' experiences during which we see ourselves lying in bed, and may travel to other rooms, other places. With practice, some people are able to have lucid dreams almost at will: involved in a dream of adventure, they can throw themselves off a precipice, knowing that they are dreaming and will therefore be able to fly – or they can direct the course of the dream. Some psychologists consider (and we tend to agree) that lucid dreams do not fulfil the purpose for which dreams seem to exist. If we direct the course of our dreams, they cannot be the channels for what our unconscious wants to tell us but become the tools of our conscious minds, just as our imagination is, when we are awake.

Looking at your dream record, when it is as complete as you can make it, and trying to make sense of it, you can approach it in various ways, some of them less obvious than others. One of the clues which can be very obvious when you have spotted it, but seems so strange on the face of it that many people resist it, is the pun. Dreams are, for some reason, very interested in puns – even when the dreamer, while awake, may find it quite difficult to make a good one! Why dreams should work in this way is beyond explanation, yet they do.

Such dreams will depend to a large extent on your vocabulary: if you dream of a clock, there may be the suggestion that you want to rebuke or fight someone – but only if you know the slang expression, *to clock someone*! But in this sphere too there are universal ideas which have been around for so long that they mean something to everyone: a dream of a mouse sitting or lying quietly before you may very well mean that you should keep quiet about something: 'as quiet as a mouse' is a phrase everyone knows.

Not only verbal, but visual and even aural puns can occur in dreams. Once again, the clue to spotting the pun and interpreting the dream will be obvious once you have seen it. It will be something which is preoccupying you, or some incident that has occurred to you the day before you dreamed that particular dream.

Another thing to watch out for in your dreams is *yourself*: and we do not mean that you're very likely to see yourself in your dream – at least, not in the sense that you see yourself walking around, as though you were looking in a mirror. But you may be in the dream, all the same, disguised as someone or something else! If a telephone is ringing in your dream, *you* may be that telephone: your unconscious may be desperately trying to send you a message. If someone is uprooting a plant or a flower, especially one which you are very fond of, someone may be trying in some way to uproot or displace *you*.

We have already suggested that you should think carefully about the *atmosphere* of your dream: this is because the same dream may have one of several meanings, and the way you feel about it may be the only available clue to interpreting it. Suppose, for instance, that you dream that you are flying – a fairly common dream. If you feel happy, released, free, the dream is obviously a very positive one – a dream of some kind of release, of soaring towards your objectives, of achieving them; you have lift-off!

On the other hand if the dream has a depressing feeling about it, if you feel frightened, if you are flying low among trees or through clouds, clearly the dream is less positive: you may be flying from something, trying to get away, indulging in some kind of unwise escapism.

One of the major problems in dream interpretation – probably the main problem – is to decide which of several possible meanings one symbol or symbolic action has. A rough and ready rule, but one which seems to work more often than not, is to consider first whether the thing or person at the centre of your dream is *real* to you in waking life. If you dream of a house, and it is a familiar house, then the dream is probably connected in some way with that house. If you dream of an unfamiliar house, it is probably symbolic: it may represent some new area of experience which you are about to explore, for instance; a new job, even a new person.

So a dream which involves someone or something which is a part of your everyday life should be read, first of all, quite literally. It may well be one of those dreams which can be extremely useful, perhaps as a warning. If you dream that your dog's lead breaks, then check the lead before you take him for his next walk: you may unconsciously have noticed that it has a weak spot in it, and your dream is reminding you about it. Similarly, if you dream your car goes off the road at a particular corner, take care when you next approach it: your dream may be nudging your elbow and suggesting that you usually take it just that little bit too fast.

47

If your dream really doesn't seem to contain anyone or anything which you recognise as part of your life at present, then comes the time to think about what it represents: consider whether it may be a pun; whether you may figure in it, disguised as a car or a mountain or a sheep (feeling sheepish about something you've recently done?).

You are in for a tough time when you settle down to interpret your own dreams. We hope that the suggestions we make in the remainder of this book will help, but remember that it is quite possible that none of them may make any kind of sense to you. We all lead very different lives, we undergo different emotional experiences, do different jobs, have different feelings; even identical twins who seem as like as two peas in a pod and who share remarkable instinctive reactions (as so many twins do) are sufficiently different for the same dream to mean different things to each of them. So for us or anyone else to pretend that they can interpret your dreams for you is nonsense. It may even be true that you will find the task of discovering what your dreams mean to you simply too taxing – or maybe too unsettling.

In the latter case remember that, as far as we can see, the whole purpose of dreams is to help you, to tell the truth about yourself; and that this is bound to be unsettling! Dreams don't simply reinforce your prejudices; they explore the reasons for them, suggest that you may be wrong, point out where your arguments are weak, illuminate other people's points of view. Dreams don't comfort you by telling you that everything in the garden is lovely: they are very good indeed at pointing out where weeds are strangling healthy plants, where a little organic fertiliser would do the world of good.

A part of their remarkable power is that you know when you have interpreted them correctly: just as, when you work with Shiatsu, or acupressure, a quite unmistakable twinge makes it clear when you have your finger on precisely the right spot, so you know when you have interpreted your dream aright: *of course*, you say to yourself, *of course* that's what it means. You will feel satisfied, relaxed and often deeply affected by what you have discovered about yourself, what you, who know yourself better than anyone else, have told yourself about yourself!

· V ·
Ten Questions about Dreams

Can nightmares be dangerous?

Nightmares will only damage you if you allow them to. Of course a repetitive nightmare which wakes you night after night in a cold sweat of terror is worrying, and if it persists over a long period there is no doubt that it can have an effect on your confidence and self-assurance. The answer is not to give in to it; go to bed, not fearful of the dream that is waiting for you, but ready to face up to it, to ask what it is trying to say to you, and to answer its statement.

Nightmares are not the product of overeating, overdrinking, or any other physical activity. They are the result of some waking anxiety which is so acute that it bursts into your dreams. Childhood, in particular, is full of such anxieties, often attached to the process of getting used to the world and facing problems which may seem stupidly minute to those who have forgotten what it was like to be five years old. If your child wakes screaming in the night, it will usually be the result of a 'bad dream' which has been forgotten by the time you reach the bedside. There is nothing you can do other than comfort the child, reassure her, tell her that 'it won't happen again' – which will probably be true, for she is very unlikely to have another nightmare the same night. If nightmares occur night after night, the problem is more serious, and you must look for the waking problem which is prompting them. Your child may feel insecure at school or at home; may be being bullied by a fellow-pupil or even a teacher; or may be distressed at your response to something she has done or not done.

Most importantly, consider your relationship with your partner. Children are remarkably susceptible to atmosphere, and often (especially if they do not have enough vocabulary, or feel they cannot discuss things with you) pick up tension or stress. Loneliness or jealousy can also be turned inwards and emerge in frightening nightmares.

Recurring nightmares in adults also deserve careful study (cf also, the *recurring dream*, p. 51). Jungians would suggest that nightmares

49

are the work of your *shadow* (see p. 37); instincts which for some reason you don't feel you can show to the world during your waking life break into your dream world and show their anger at being repressed. Ann Faraday, in her book *The Dream Game*, aptly quotes the fairy story of Beauty and the Beast: once the beast has been recognised and accepted, loved for what he is, he turns into a handsome prince.

You may have as much, or more, difficulty in recognising the true meaning of a nightmare as recognising the motive behind any other kind of dream. Follow the same process, remembering, if the nightmare recurs, to note even the slightest change which may take place in it (see, again, *recurring dreams*). Once you have recognised the area of your life – whether it's an aspect of your personality or your actions – which the nightmares are attacking, you may find that that alone dismisses them; you will also find it very worthwhile to think seriously about it and whether it needs modification (which is extremely likely).

Do I/should I dream in colour?

Some people simply do not know whether they dream in colour or not, and there is no evidence that it matters. Some authorities have suggested that extrovert, imaginative people are more likely to dream in colour than introvert, practical people, but there is not a great deal of evidence to support this view, though it would be very unlikely if an artist, for example, dreamed in monotone.

Needless to say, a colour which you particularly remember from a dream, or which appears again and again in a series of dreams, will be as important as any other symbol, and you should think carefully about its possible significance. Green, for instance, may represent a regenerative, creative force, though there is a traditional association with jealousy and envy, too; red may stand for danger; yellow is the colour of cowardice, but also the colour of the sun; people who are depressed are said to be 'blue'. Consider all the options (and see *COLOURS*).

Does it really matter if I forget my dreams?

Of course not. Millions of people probably never give their dreams a thought, either forgetting them or simply not trying to remember them, and live entirely happy and fulfilled lives. But there is no doubt at all that dreams can be helpful, possibly even to those who don't remember them. The Freudian view is that they act as a safety valve, releasing tensions which we may not even know exist.

I have one dream which is repeated again and again. What does this mean?

Repeated or *recurring dreams* are fairly common, and it can safely be said that they are important to whoever dreams them, carrying a message which will be very well worth recovering. If your recurring dream is one which you have had since you were very young, which occurs again and again, it very probably refers to an aspect of your personality which has been a problem to you for your whole lifetime, though not one which has necessarily caused you waking problems. When you have recognised the issue which the dream is confronting, and trying to force you to confront, it will disappear.

Remember, however, that a recurring dream may also have a relevance to some current problem or preoccupation. Consider, for instance, a recurring dream in which a dog appears in a frightening context. It may be based on a subconscious fear of dogs; maybe one frightened you when you were in your cradle, an incident which you have completely forgotten. If you dream of being chased by a dog, the dream may well have its basis in such an incident, but it may recur when you are consciously or unconsciously feeling insecure and vulnerable, under circumstances as different as being offered a position of authority at work, for which you feel unready, or trying to decide whether to make an approach to a woman you fancy, but fearing rejection. Or it may be triggered by something as simple as seeing an advertisement for this year's Crufts Dog Show!

In trying to work out the relevance of a recurring dream it is specially important to note any changes in the dream itself, even the slightest modification in the events that usually occur in it. This will give you valuable clues as to the dream's real meaning.

Can dreams foretell the future?

Many people would immediately answer 'yes', and it's true that most of us will at some stage in our life stop in our tracks as we recognise a situation or a place about which we remember dreaming.

Sometimes the answer is simple and straightforward. Many people claim to have dreamed of President Kennedy's assassination. This seems, on the face of it, remarkable. But consider: everyone in the world dreams five or six dreams a night. President Kennedy was a world-famous man. Many people must have dreamed about him on almost every night of his presidency, and presidents are vulnerable to assassination.

On the other hand there have been records of predictive dreams which have convinced extremely intelligent and thoughtful people that they are a means of breaking the bonds of time and looking into the future. The most famous book on the subject is J. W. Dunne's *An Experiment with Time* (Faber & Faber, 1927), and no one interested in this aspect of dreams should fail to read it. Meanwhile, scores of accounts of apparently predictive dreams have been published, many of them very persuasive, but equally many of them entirely anecdotal and with no means of checking their accuracy or otherwise. One of the more acceptable is related by Jung himself in his autobiography, *Memories, Dreams, Reflections* (Collins, 1963):

I dreamed that my wife's bed was a deep pit with stone walls. It was a grave, and somehow had a suggestion of classical antiquity about it. Then I heard a deep sigh, as if someone were giving up the ghost. A figure that resembled my wife sat up in the pit and floated upwards. It wore a white gown into which curious black symbols were woven. I awoke, roused my wife, and checked the time. It was three o'clock in the morning. The dream was so curious that I thought at once it might signify a death. At seven o'clock came the news that a cousin of my wife's had died at three o'clock in the morning.

That is fairly inexplicable, though Jung does not tell us whether his wife's cousin had been seriously ill and likely to die, which might have prompted the dream. As with so many other psychic and inexplicable experiences, the safest thing is to go by one's own experience: and while you should not be frightened by a dream which seems to predict some awful disaster, it is well worth treating such a dream in precisely the same way as any other, making a note of the date and time in particular – it will certainly be trying to tell you something, and maybe its message will be of considerable practical value.

Should dreams of death frighten me?

They often will, of course; on the other hand, people who one has loved and lost often appear in dreams to comfort and reassure.

In general, remember that dreams are never what they seem. So if you dream of the death of a person, or of your own death, that certainly doesn't mean that anyone is going to die: it may well mean that someone will die *to you* – that your feeling for them has died; or that someone's feeling for you has died. A dream of someone who has been dead for some time will probably refer to some incident or emotion connected with that person.

Such dreams can be warning dreams, of course; you may unconsciously have thought 'Doesn't X look ill?' when you met her; your dream may be drawing attention to the fact. Whether you warn the person concerned is another matter; it would certainly be unwise to tell them you think they're going to die, but you might suggest a check-up by their doctor.

Don't think that because you dream of the death of someone close to you, you're wishing them dead. But it might be well worth while thinking about your relationship with them; it may need renewing. There may be the suggestion that a distance is growing between you.

Finally, dreams of death often seem, ironically, connected with birth and renewal. This is perhaps more common with someone who lives within the western Christian tradition, where death has been seen as renewing rather than destructive; but dreams of birth can often signal the beginning of a new project or period of life, often after the end, or death, of a previous one. Thus, death can mean change. The dream may be suggesting that you are ready to make important changes in your life, in your opinions or behaviour. These may be represented by the person who died in your dream (see *shadow*, p. 37). Dreams of birth often refer in the same way to change or the need for change.

What is happening when I realise, in the middle of a dream, that I am dreaming?

You are experiencing what is known as a *lucid dream*. Some people cultivate this trick to the extent that they can take part in their dreams almost as an actor takes part in a play – except that they can depart from the script and direct the play in any way they want it to go. Though relatively little research has been done on the subject, it is at least possible (see p. 46) that a lucid dream cannot perform the function of a 'free' dream: if you are consciously directing it, it cannot spring freely from your subconscious.

It does not matter if you have this kind of dream occasionally – in fact, most people do so (usually when they first fall asleep) and they are usually more 'realistic' than ordinary dreams, not as fantastic or outrageous. Certainly it can be useful in dealing with a nightmare if you are able to realise, while you are dreaming, that the fantastic and frightening circumstances are 'only dreams'.

Can a dream lead to sleepwalking?

Sleepwalking is not specially uncommon in children, and can be the result of emotional disturbance; occasionally it seems that a nightmare can be a trigger. It is rare for a child to hurt herself when sleepwalking: she will stumble about, occasionally knocking into the furniture, and perhaps talking to herself; eventually she will return to bed of her own accord. You can try very gently to waken her – it is not dangerous to do so, as has sometimes been claimed. But all things being equal it is probably best to leave her alone.

Sleepwalking in adults is more unusual, but when it happens (never during REM sleep, and usually during the first two hours) it can be spectacular. One American woman put on a dressing-gown, got into her car and drove for over twenty miles on a freeway before waking to find herself at the wheel. Sleepwalking can run in families, and to that extent there may be some physical trigger; but it can be the result of some psychological or emotional disturbance which dream analysis may help to resolve.

Is it important if I talk in my sleep?

It is not of very great significance – unless, of course, you say something which it would really have been better to keep to yourself! There seems no rule about talking in your sleep: some people do it, some don't; sometimes they talking during an REM period, sometimes at other times. Talk during REM sleep seems to be related to dreams which are going on at the same time; talking at other times may be nonsense, or relate to physical facts – the bedroom being cold, a noise going on, or whatever.

Can dreams answer my questions?

The way in which dreams can solve problems is one of the most interesting things about them. Artists and scientists alike have found that their dreams can provide the answers to problems, or at the very least put them on the right track (for in this as in everything else, dreams like to work in an opaque way). Whatever your problem, it is worth laying it before your dreams just before you go to sleep, and inviting them to comment. The result may not, probably will not, be what you expect; but time and time again dreams will suggest a course of action, or a new way of looking at the problem, which will be rewarding.

Part Two

The Dream Dictionary

We can only make suggestions about the possible meaning of the symbols in your dream. Remember that the context and mood of the dream are very important, and think about the possible symbolic meaning, even if this seems unlikely; there is very often an association. We suggest here some questions you might ask yourself, but as you continue to work on your dream, many more will suggest themselves.

Individual ANIMALS and BIRDS are to be found under those general headings.

Where possible, as in the first section of the book, we have used asexual pronouns; when this has seemed clumsy, we have used he, but of course the reference is almost always to either sex.

Abyss A dream of an abyss can certainly be rather frightening. If you found it distressing, try to approach your interpretation as rationally as possible. Is there an area of your life, a problem perhaps, which seems unfathomable? – too deep to be plumbed? Your state of mind in the dream will be very important: i.e. were you frightened, resigned or determined to get out of or avoid the abyss?

Acorn In mythology a symbol of life, of immortality – and of fecundity. Surely your dreams are giving you considerable encouragement, and making a statement about the development of potential! Remember that the oak into which the acorn grows is solid, strong and very long-lasting: that 'great oaks from little acorns grow'. Have you the germ of an idea which needs nurturing?

Actor   See **Stage**.

Altar   Almost every world religion has used an altar of some kind, so it is a profoundly religious symbol which can represent a divine presence or a sacrifice, or perhaps a thanksgiving. Its shape, resembling a tomb, can have intimations of immortality, and it often represents the immortal part of man. In Christian mythology – which will be important to most Westerners, whether or not they subscribe to the religion – it represents both the tomb and the resurrection, death transformed into life, so it can be a very positive symbol. It may suggest renewal in a personal sense; a new line of approach or thought. It may suggest that you should take a less worldly view of any problems. But ask yourself, too, whether the altar in your dream was merely a pun; are you about to change (alter) your mind? Or have you just done so? Or is there some situation which is changing, or needs your intervention to change it?

ANIMALS   Animals in general are symbols of the power of the life-force, but also (because they must reproduce in order to survive) of our sexual and emotional urges. An animal which you feel you must kill, in a dream, usually represents an animal instinct which must be subdued. Friendship with animals represents our wish to return to the simplicity of the Golden Age, before we murdered them for food and killed each other for gain. An animal which is helping or in some way advising you represents an aspect of your own nature which is urging you to take a particular line of thought or action. If you dream of yourself as an animal, or if you are imitating an animal, perhaps by wearing a mask or a skin, you are instinctively wanting to use those natural instincts which we humans all too often repress.

   Mythological pairs of animals (the lion and the unicorn, the bull and the bear) represent opposite emotions or powers – positive and negative, male and female, ying and yang. Consider these possibilities. But think too of your waking reaction to the kind of animal in your dream. Do you love or hate, admire or envy it? Are you frightened by it, or have you recently behaved in a manner you

associate with it, i.e. been 'catty', been involved in 'monkey business' and so on? The allusion may not always be in the form of a
pun: you may have been as proud or as brave as a lion, as feline as a
cat, as stubborn as a mule. Don't forget to try to put yourself in the
animal's place when interpreting your symbol – this is most
important.

Antelope Elegant, strong, horned animals, with herding
instincts, capable of moving at considerable speed. In several world
mythologies associated with divinity, and always with fierceness
and a sense of danger. Does the animal symbolise your approach to
someone or something? Perhaps you are ready to move on in some
way – but remember that herding instinct, which might work
against you in waking life.

Ape Apes have always been associated with mischievousness,
malice, cunning – sometimes with conceit; the Christians saw an
ape in chains as a symbol of sin overcome. Most of us have various
feelings about apes: they're lovable, amusing and clever; but often
their behaviour strikes a chord which identifies us with them in less
desirable ways. Have you been 'aping' someone lately? If so was
this a positive or negative thing to do? Did you admire or loathe
your dream ape?

Ass In Christian mythology the ass represents humility, patience
and peace, but elsewhere it often stands for stupidity, obstinacy
and lewdness; as a beast of burden, it can represent poverty, or
sometimes a faithful but stubborn friend or servant. The phrase
'silly ass' springs to mind, but remember too the gentle donkey, and
the fact that your dream ass may well have been a pun. Have you
made an ass of yourself or are you about to do so? Are you being too
patient – or stubborn – in dealing with some problem or situation in
you waking life?

Badger A persistent and hard-working animal that is sometimes
hunted or baited, and now receives a lot of support from conser-
vationists. It is not surprising that 'badgering' has become
common parlance. Your dream badger is probably summing up
your present situation. Are you badgering someone, or even some
problem? If so, are you making progress? Was your dream badger
making progress or did you feel sorry for him? Are you feeling that

you're making little or no impression? Could this be a warning that you are nagging someone too much?

Bat The bat has often been a frightening symbol, perhaps because the early Christians regarded it (a cross between bird and rat) as 'the bird of the devil' – a representation of Satan who was often shown wearing bat's wings. The context will as always be important: is there a warning of some kind? Bats are clever at flying in the dark: should you rely on your instinctive judgement in confusing circumstances? But remember 'blind as a bat'. Or are you 'bats' about someone?

Bear The fact that bears hibernate made them a strong symbol of the resurrection and rebirth – emerging each spring 'a new animal'. But its alleged natural cruelty made it a Christian symbol of evil and greed. Although they are dangerous animals we usually love bears, perhaps because of their cuddly appearance and what seems a natural sense of humour. Your dream bear may represent someone who has some of its qualities. Is there a connection with your childhood 'teddy bear'? Have you recently bared your soul to someone, or should you do so? Have you far too many heavy burdens to bear?

Boar In Christian mythology the boar represented cruelty, brutality, anger and the sins of the flesh. The animal is strong, persistent, stubborn, usually fat, delicious when cooked. This could well be a warning symbol of the first order. Have you behaved chauvinistically? Are you being treated chauvinistically by your partner? Should you try to become less boring?

Buffalo For the AmerIndians the buffalo is the symbol of supernatural strength, power and fortitude, and the popularity of the Western film may well have attached this feeling to our image of them. We tend to think of buffaloes in herds, so your dream buffalo may represent a herd instinct relating to your present situation. Is public opinion persuading you to make a decision or take a certain line of action? Do you really want to go along with it?

Bull In most mythologies the bull represents more or less rampant masculinity, male strength; often it stands for royalty, kingship. To dream of riding a bull is probably still a very positive symbol. Sometimes, however, it represented brute, unthinking force. Bulls are slow to anger but once aroused are difficult to control. It may well be that you are extremely angry and about to have a blazing row with someone. Your dream bull may be prompting you to clear the air. There could also be a warning that you're behaving in a rather 'bullish' (or over-optimistic) manner, or are you ready to take the bull by the horns in some way? There may be sexual overtones, so consider this area of your life too. Could your dream bull be questioning your sense of security or your expression of emotion? Is your Sun-sign Taurus, or have you a Taurean within your circle? This may be significant.

Camel A dignified, indifferent animal, traditionally associated with royalty, obedience and stamina, and with the Magi. It kneels to receive those who ride it, and so represents humility. Were you the camel? If so, what is your burden; who is 'riding' you? Remember the last straw that broke the camel's back: is there a clue there? Are you standing on your dignity and maybe not asking for help when you inwardly know you really need it?

Cat Cats have always been associated with night and mystery, hence their association with witches. Black cats in ancient times were always symbols of evil and death (Satan was often disguised as a cat); only in modern times have they been believed to bring good luck. Consider your own personal attitude to cats and how you react to them. If you decide *you* were the cat, is your attitude to someone stealthy or even underhand? Are you simply as contented as a domestic cat? Were you purring or snarling? But always try the puns: have you been 'catty' to someone (or vice versa)?

Centaur The mythical horse with the torso and head of a man has always represented the balance between our physical (lower) and spiritual (upper) natures, and sometimes the conflict between them. Is there such a conflict in your personality or behaviour? Christians saw this creature as symbolising the simple battle between good and evil, though the Greeks revered it as a symbol of wisdom. The context of the dream should suggest the creature's meaning to you. Remember the centaur represents the Zodiac sign Sagitarius, the Archer: the centaur is often shooting off arrows, which symbolise power. Where are they aimed? But might he represent a Sagittarian friend? If you are a Sagittarian, this is obviously an important dream for you.

Chameleon The amazing ability of this creature to change its colour according to its surroundings makes it a fascinating dream symbol. Christian myth equated it with Satan, able to adopt various guises in order to deceive mankind. Could it refer, in your dream, to any deceit on your part? Are you presenting a false self to the world, or even to yourself? Should you change in some way – habits, opinions, image?

Cow In every religion the cow has signified the mother, the maternal instinct. In Egypt she was Hathor, the Great Mother; in Hindu religion, as a sacred animal, fertility and plenty; in Scandinavia the first cow licked the ice to produce the first man. Is this a dream associated with your mother? A woman dreaming of a cow in calf should consider her own maternal instinct (or might she be pregnant, perhaps without knowing it?). If the dream cow was giving milk, this might relate to the milk of human kindness, or again to the dreamer's maternal or even paternal instinct. Is the dream saying anything relating to your attitude towards your children or your desire, or otherwise, to have them? If you are a nursing mother there may be a reference to your milk, or your breasts. Is this a warning dream? Remember such phrases as 'holy cow', 'silly moo', 'stupid cow': any could be relevant. Have you behaved stupidly recently? Or was the dream warning you of possible future actions which you might later regret?

Crocodile Being swallowed by a crocodile has illustrated the descent into hell, and the creature has almost always represented brute force, evil, treachery and hypocrisy ('crocodile tears'). Living both on land and water, it has been thought to represent the dual nature of mankind: good and evil. Think of all these possibilties. There may be significance in its behaviour: lashing its tail (have you lashed out at someone recently?) or just lying in wait, only its eyes above water. Your dream may well relate powerfully to some deep inner emotion, especially if *water* was also emphasised. Or have you merely snapped up a bargain recently?

Deer Deer have always been a pleasant and inoffensive symbol, associated with benevolent magic, meekness and gentleness. Have you, or should you have, some of these qualities? But again, remember the possible pun – have you or someone else simply been a 'dear'?

Dog   The most domesticated of all animals has from prehistory played an important part in the life of mankind. In general mythology it is associated with fidelity, watchfulness, nobility; it has guarded the gates to the Underworld and has attended the dead, has been the messenger of man as well as his friend (though sometimes associated, like the cat, with witches, male and female). The Christians have seen the dog as the protector of the shepherd's flock, therefore sometimes as symbolising priesthood. Jewish tradition saw the dog as impure and evil or even demonic. Your own feelings towards dogs should however be the starting-point for interpretation: does the dog represent yourself or someone else? Then think of common phrases: the dirty dog, the black dog (depression) or man's best friend. Are you being 'dog in the manger' in some respect? Have you behaved badly? (Greek mythology saw dogs as impudent flatterers.) Were you 'dog tired' when you went to bed? Would you like to own a dog (wish-fulfilment?) Is your bark worse than your bite? Have you been bitching it up? Are you in conflict with some 'bitch'?

Donkey   See **Ass**.

Dragon   See main entry, page 104.

Elephant   Elephants have been long associated with strength, faithfulness, wisdom, good memory and in general, with good fortune. The Hindu elephant-god, Ganessa or Ganesh, is the god of prosperity, prudence, longevity and intelligence. Christian myth represented the elephant as Christ treading down evil. Most recently it has become an endangered species, and even more sympathetic. All these possibilities merit consideration, as does its possible representation of marriage and long partnerships (it is the most domestic and family-orientated of animals; 'aunts' helping to look after 'nieces' and 'nephews'), so there could be a strong association with your family. But also: are you clinging on to some memory which would be best forgotten (an elephant never forgets)? Are you overweight? Do you need to make your life a little more exotic – for instance was your dream elephant suggesting a need for exciting travel, to India or Africa perhaps? Does your dream symbol have any relevance to your present financial situation?

Fox   The fox has usually been regarded as crafty and cunning, but is now, because of a general reaction against hunting, a more sympathetic symbol (your own attitude to hunting may be crucial, especially if there was a dream hunt in process). Christianity has seen the fox as the attacker of domestic animals, and therefore as evil attacking good. Are you being sly or cunning at present? Was your dream fox suggesting that you should 'go to ground' to avoid the enemy? What happened to the dream fox is obviously important. See also **Pursuit**?

Frog   For no very good reason the frog was often an erotic symbol (hence, kissed, he became the most handsome of princes!). The Christians (therefore?) saw him as evil. Had the dream a bearing on your self-esteem? Are you a handsome prince/princess, waiting to break out of a less appealing disguise? Are you 'puffed up' with pride? Could the frog be someone whose inner self is more appealing than their image? The frog is also a symbol of transformation and change.

Goat   Almost every civilisation has associated the goat with virility and sexual power, though some have thought him unduly lewd (early Christians used him to represent lust, and therefore the damned). To the Greeks and Romans he symbolised creative energy, to the Hindus creative heat. The goat has sometimes represented the female urge towards motherhood. Think about this. But the goat is also a dextrous climber, a leaper from crag to crag; so there may be a reference to ambition. Or, if he was tethered to a post, restriction. Which kind of goat are you, ambitious or resigned? Is your sex-life spectacularly active or complicated at present? Was your dream suggesting you've been a silly goat? Remember the goat is the symbol of the Zodiac sign Capricorn which might be a reference to yourself, or a friend.

Hare   The early Christians, the Greeks and the Romans used the hare as a representation of lust, but it also stood for mildness and resignation. Most other mythologies have connected it with the moon, sometimes with the dawn and springtime and therefore with hope. Modern Westerners probably think of the Mad Hare. All these allusions could be meaningful. Then there is the famous Aesop fable of the hare and the tortoise, with its moral of more haste and less speed. Is your dream hare suggesting that you are taking short cuts, or 'haring around' too much at present? Is the month March? Was your dream suggesting something about your hair?

Hedgehog   The hedgehog has a very special form of self-protection; apart from its spines, its tendency to curl up in a ball has served it well during its evolution, until the terrors of heavy road traffic. Are you trying to get away from some harsh 'prickly' words or behaviour which has upset you, or which you regret inflicting on another person? Are you pretending to be what you're not? Are your defences strong enough? (Spines are no protection against a heavy lorry.)

Hippopotamus   Vast, contented, sleepy, living a life of ease. The delightful Egyptian goddess Tauret, goddess of childbirth, was a hippo – perhaps helping her worshippers to feel relaxed about their coming confinement. There is also an emotional emphasis, since hippos spend so much of their time in *water* – peaceful, placid, if somewhat muddy water. Was your dream hippo encouraging you to take things more easily and to relax, even cool it a bit? Was he summing up your present situation – i.e., content and secure? Are you overweight, even if pregnant?

Horse   The horse is a most important symbol because of its long and close association with man. Its symbolism is complex just because of this long history: it has signified both life and death but also wisdom, nobility, speed (including the speed of thought), and animal instincts (in particular, those psychic powers man has neglected). The Buddhists have seen the horse as symbolic of the hidden nature of things, the Chinese of fertility and power, the Christians of courage, the Hindus of the body (while the rider is the spirit). But obviously you must consider how the horse appears in your dream – as a favourite pony, the Derby winner or a police horse. Were you riding him and in control, or being taken for a ride? Are you in control of your life? Is your outlook positive? Should you be making some kind of move? Is speed of the essence in your present situation? Are you riding roughshod over other people, or they over you? Is there an element of wish-fulfilment in your dream horse? Or, quite simply, was your horse symbol making a comment on your vocal chords?

Hyena A howling scavenger, unpopular but cunning. Your dream hyena could be suggesting that you should pit your wits against society or your present situation – that you can improve your lot if you approach problems more shrewdly. It may be a question of you against 'the rest' – whoever 'they' may be. Should you make more of a fuss about your current problems? Think of the hyena's howling – are you trying to attract attention in some way?

Leopard In Christian mythology yet another symbol of sin and of the Devil's treachery (perhaps because, while looking so beautiful, it is so deadly). Other civilisations have seen cruelty and aggression but also bravery in the animal. The fact that leopards are known for not changing their spots could be relevant, but the agility of these animals should also be considered – are you trying to outrun someone, or to outdo them in some way? Do you need to take quick action or is there something or someone you need to chase up? See also **Cat**.

Lion The king of the jungle, brave, sexually potent, proud, seemingly arrogant, has always been a major symbol for man. The Christians have seen it as representing both good and evil – the power and majesty of Christ were represented by the lion, but it was from the evil of the lion's mouth that He rescued man. The Devil was seen as 'a raging lion'. Supposed to sleep with its eyes open, the lion symbolised watchfulness; its cubs were supposed to be born dead, and the mother to breathe life into them, hence the beast symbolised the resurrection. He is the symbol of many saints, including St Mark. The Chinese saw him as a symbol of bravery, the Egyptians as the great protector, the Hebrews as cruel, the Romans and Iranians as royal. The lion and lamb together represented the peace and happiness of paradise or the Golden Age. The lion was often connected with the sun. Maybe your dream lion was reassuring you that you are 'Monarch of all you survey'. But you should consider whether you might be throwing your weight about or simply being too bossy towards other people. Do you feel specially secure? Is all well with you and your life, or are you, lion-like, licking your wounds? Do you know a Sun-sign Leo whose actions or characteristics might have prompted your dream?

Lizard The lizard, supposed to have no tongue, was often the symbol of silence: the Greeks and Egyptians thought it was divinely wise and a symbol of good luck. For the Christians it was evil, but the Romans thought it symbolised death and resurrection. These small creatures are liked for their love of the sun, lazing on walls after their hibernation. So are you taking things easy at the moment? – or do you need, and deserve, to do so? Are you, like the lizard in spring, feeling content, warm and blissful – in relation to your sex-life in particular? Lizards move quickly if threatened, sometimes rather nervously so. Are you threatened? Are you scuttling away from some problem or difficulty?

Monkey See also **Ape**. Representing impudence, mischief and comedy the monkey has usually been (for its artful cleverness) the symbol of trickery. One of the Chinese signs of the Zodiac is the monkey, and the characteristics the sign bestows are those we commonly associate with this creature; western astrologers often find similarities between monkey characteristics and those of Gemini. Remember the three Mystic Monkeys enjoining us to 'see no evil, hear no evil, speak no evil.' Has this a significance for you at present? Ask yourself whether you were your dream monkey. Have you been involved in any 'monkey business' lately? Does the phrase 'he/she is a little monkey' make special sense for you at present?

Mouse Often feared, often liked (perhaps usually because of charming childhood stories); quite rightly considered dirty and shy. Maybe your dream mouse is suggesting that you are vulnerable in some way, or that you are rather too timid. Are you a mouse in a trap? Do you think your image is a bit 'mousey'? Was your dream suggesting that you should attempt to be more forthcoming or liven up your image in some way? Are you being chased or chasing something you cannot get? If so refer to **Pursuit**, possibly **Cat**.

Ox See **Bull**.

Pig See **Swine**.

Rabbit For some reason the moon has often been associated with a white rabbit, but most commonly the rabbit has been, for obvious reasons, a symbol of fecundity and lust, not dissimilar to the *hare*, but without the 'mad' connotation. Your dream rabbit could well be a pun on 'rare bit', or suggesting that you might have been 'rabbiting on' in some way; if so consciously try to stop nagging. But are you feeling hunted or 'got at'? Are you considering starting or increasing your family? Could your dream be expressing your unconscious readiness to have another child?

Ram Above all indicative of virility and creative power; in the Zodiac, Aries the ram is the first sign, the renewed power of spring. The Christians saw the ram as symbolic of Christ, but in almost every other mythology the beast has been seen chiefly in sexual terms, so for men a dream including this animal is most likely to be a reference to their sexuality. But the ram also, not least in astrological terms, puts himself first, wants to win. Is your dream ram encouraging you to be more assertive and self-confident? Have you been trying hard to 'ram home' some opinion or point of an argument?

Rat Nobody loves rats, and the rat in your dream may well refer to someone for whom, in waking life, you have little affection – who is, in fact, 'a dirty rat'. Unless you have ratted on someone. Or are you showing rat-like cunning? Or being 'ratty'? Rats were associated with the plague, and therefore with death.

Sheep 'All we like sheep have gone astray.' Sheep are often considered stupid creatures only capable of blindly following a leader (hence, perhaps, the reference to Christ as the Shepherd). Are you being too easily led at present? Do you feel vulnerable when having to stand up for your rights or do something alone? Are you apprehensive about being 'different' or attracting too much attention? Was your dream sheep suggesting that you have a sheep-like mentality – so should you try to develop your own opinions and aim for original ideas?

Snake See **Serpent** in main index.

Squirrel The squirrel is often a symbol of acquisitiveness because of its sensible habit of putting food aside for times of want. The dream could obviously be a reference to your own sense of security or lack of it. Are you hoarding unnecessarily, being too 'careful' about money or affection (the two are often linked)? Think further; perhaps you are not hoarding possessions or even money, but old injuries, bad memories, negative feelings? Should you let go of the past and begin to plan more for the future? Even save for the future to make it more secure?

Stag   Because of its antlers the stag was often connected with the Tree of Life, and therefore was a symbol of creation and renewal. Though strong and a stout fighter against evil (trampling the serpent underfoot) the stag is also a symbol of peace and piety, so, a rather mixed symbol. We tend to think of the stag as a powerful creature, who even if hunted often survives, so the dream may comment on a present fight against something – or on your own position in a struggle of some kind. Are you seeking a way out of some really tricky situation? Have you been invited to a 'stag night', or are you considering some last fling before commitment? What could the horns symbolise?

Swine   See also **Boar**. Though a fertility symbol, the pig is also equated with greed and gluttony, and often regarded as unclean. The only god who had any time for him was Zeus, to whom he was sacred. Pigs are often considered 'lucky', and are sometimes a symbol of prosperity – perhaps because, like the elephant, they are fat! The pig is also a Chinese astrological sign. Have you a particularly low opinion of someone's behaviour? Have you behaved like a swine to anyone? Was your dream suggesting that you're chauvinistic? Do you feel 'unclean', psychologically?

Tiger   The tiger is, symbolically, similar to the lion – regarded also as a king of beasts, and to the Chinese the Lord of Land Animals. It is larger, fiercer, more dangerous than the leopard. Your dream tiger may represent someone exotic, sexy and dangerous. Is this how you would like to see yourself – or be seen by others? Do you think that you need more excitement in your life? Was your dream tiger about to eat you up? Are you being engulfed by some stormy, passionate, dangerous love affair which is getting out of hand? In which case, was your dream a warning?

Toad   'The loathsome toad, ugly and venomous' has an undeserved reputation for evil and if you were strongly conscious of its identity, that idea is reinforced (unless you are specially fond of toads in waking life). It may represent something in your current waking life which, perhaps unconsciously, is disturbing you – an action you have been forced to take, of which your inner self thoroughly disapproves, or of which society disapproves. What did you do to the toad? Did it hop away and hide? If so, were you intent on exposing it? Or was it, rather ingratiatingly, apologising for its ugliness?

Tortoise   One of the four Chinese sacred animals, representing winter. The Christians saw this animal, enclosed in its shell, as symbolic of a married woman living safely and modestly in her husband's house. In Hindu legend the tortoise supported on her back the elephant which held up the world: she is almost always feminine. Slow, steady, careful and very self-contained, she may represent meticulous, slow progress. But think of that hard, impenetrable shell – your dream tortoise may be suggesting that you should look after yourself. Or is someone trying to 'get through' to you and you aren't taking any notice. Should you? On the other hand, should you be taking things more steadily and carefully? Are you putting up some pretence of strength whereas in reality you're feeling terribly vulnerable? In that case, should you unburden your problem to a sympathetic friend? Are you thinking about moving house – or clearing out, lock, stock and barrel?

Turtle   See **Tortoise**. But this animal represents longevity, and in China is the god of examinations! The turtle spends a lot of time in the *water*; there could well be a direct connection between your dream turtle and your emotions, especially if your turtle was swimming or in a pool.

Unicorn   This mythical beast represents virginity, purity, chastity, femininity. It is the emblem of the Virgin Mary. Its horn was always said to be an antidote to poison, and to the early Christian therefore it symbolised the power to destroy sin. Ground unicorn's horn is an irresistible aphrodisiac, though the horn seems, perhaps surprisingly, infrequently to be a sexual symbol (however, do not reject this possibility out of hand). In English myth the unicorn often partnered the Lion – a very masculine principal. She was often shown encircled by a protective fence or wall – another allusion to purity and other-worldliness. The wall, was, however, always low enough to be jumped, if necessary or desirable! The unicorn's legends are numerous. If you are a woman your dream unicorn may be saying something about your need for protection; if young there may be a reference to your virginity. A man's dream unicorn could suggest a certain vulnerability concerning the feminine side of his personality, or represent some woman who seems unattainable. Are you apprehensive about certain areas of your love life? Do you feel in need of protection, or want to protect someone you love? Are you coping with a somewhat complex or confusing emotional conflict? Was your dream unicorn representing someone you desire but to whom you cannot or should not declare your feelings? Is this symbol a statement concerning your own or someone else's innocence?

Wolf   Similar to the *hyena*, and generally fierce and 'evil'. The wolf was reputedly unable to turn its head, and early Christians therefore believed it to represent proud, unyielding people. In Western Europe, the story of Little Red Riding Hood may be significant. In Roman mythology a wolf suckled Romulus and Remus, and indicated valour and protection, showing the best sides of the wolf's nature. Can you identify with any of the wolf's characteristics at present? Are your present actions somewhat wolf-like? Have you been giving – or getting – 'wolf whistles' recently?

Ankh   See **Cross**.

Ant   The ant has been seen in almost every civilisation as suggestive of endless busy-ness, non-stop work – also of order; it is very much part of a feudal system, and one that works well. So the symbol is most likely to refer to your work, whether at home or outside it. Is your dream suggesting that you are working hard for no real advantage? Is the system taking advantage of you? But perhaps your dream ant is really an aunt?

Anvil   In many mythologies, the world was forged on an anvil: and the hammer and anvil represented male and female. Are you hammering out some specific problem, or re-shaping your life in some way? – or perhaps you should do so. The symbol might also be suggesting that you are in need of change. There is a direct connection here with *horses* and *iron*, both extremely masculine symbols relating to assertiveness and potency (remember the tradition of eloping couples getting married at the smithy at Gretna Green). So your dream anvil might be a statement about your relationship, or a proposed one. Should you become more assertive? Should you make some important decision that will have a direct effect on your partner? Should you quite simply be bolder, make your voice and opinions more heard?

Apple   In many civilisations the apple has been a magical fruit: in Greek myth it symbolised love and desire – it was sacred to Venus, awarded to her by Paris after a contest to find the most beautiful woman. No good came of this. The Christians (of course) saw the apple as representing lust, and therefore evil, and depicted it as the source of sex – the fruit of knowledge offered by Eve to Adam, and enthusiastically accepted. It is not insignificant that the contemporary 'big apple' is the city with its teeming life. The first taste of the apple can never be forgotten, innocence never regained. For all these reasons the apple is a very potent symbol. Was your dream apple suggesting a taste of the 'big apple' – in whatever form? If so, was what you tasted sweet and delicious, or bitter? If sweet, consider the possibility of wish-fulfilment; if bitter, was this a warning about a 'bitter' experience? Are you being faced with several alternatives, all of which seem equally attractive?

Apron   Here is a symbol of hard work, of getting down to some task (especially if you were actually donning the apron, or wearing it). Here too is a potent symbol of protection, and of being 'tied to mother's apron strings'. There is also symbolic secrecy if one considers the ritual aprons worn by Freemasons and other secret societies. Are you cherishing some secret? Are you about to start some challenging, or hard but boring, task? Was your dream suggesting that you are still tied to your mother's apron strings, or that you are keeping your child too tied to yours? Do you need to protect yourself in some way?

Arch   Mythologically representing the arch of the sky, but in Indian myths the *yoni* or female genitals. In both senses protective, and in architecture suggestive of strength, support. Your dream arch may be symbolically expressing the range of your experience of life, from innocence to maturity. Or perhaps you are being protected from difficulties or the heavy burden of life – don't forget we sometimes shelter 'underneath the arches'. Does your dream arch say something about material security, or the security that comes from religious faith? Having had your dream do you now feel inspired in some way to carry on, because you feel more secure? Are you merely being arch?

Ark   In the Christian world the symbol is inevitably one of rescue and protection (interestingly this is also the case in Hindu, Egyptian and Semitic myth) – so, protection against the storm, the gathering together of the family, a feeling of togetherness against all ills. Today the ark may also symbolise the green movement and conservation. Any of these issues may have been on your mind, but in addition it would seem that your dream ark was a positive symbol reassuring you of security, of the closeness of loved ones and your ability to do a great deal for them. Have you been thinking about home improvements or extensions to make space for an increasing family? Do you feel like Mr or Mrs Noah? Were conservation issues on your mind? If the flood came into your dream see also **Water**.

Arrow   A symbol of penetration, and therefore potently sexual, though anger and antagonism may also be indicated, and indeed martyrdom. So who were you shooting at – or whether you were the target – is obviously most important. Was there a statement about your potency (i.e., how far did the arrow travel, and how successfully)? Do you need to father a child? Did your arrow suggest that you need challenge, need to break away and aim for some specific objective? Have you hit a particular bull's eye? The arrow is the symbol of Sagittarius: is there a reference to someone you know?

Ashes   These would seem to represent an ending of some kind, or at least a reference to the fact that nothing lasts for ever. If you were raking through ashes, perhaps you are trying to cling on to something which is over. If you were scattering ashes or burying them do not be frightened into thinking that you or some loved one will die – the dream is probably suggesting that you are ready to make changes, to rid yourself of some trait you've been aware of in another person (the person of whose ashes you were disposing?). Was your dream suggesting that you are trying to keep something alive? Were you burned by hot ashes? Did the dust from the ashes cloud your vision?

Axe   In world mythology (except the Christian) the symbol of power, often of a powerful man, sometimes of divinity. Modern men dreaming of an axe could well have fears of castration or impotence. A more common suggestion might be that you fear 'the chop' – redundancy from your job. If you feel insecure in your work your dream axe is probably very aptly summing up your present apprehension.

Ball Sometimes the symbol of either *sun* or *moon*, but also a *mandala*, symbolising psychological wholeness and strength. Your dream was probably a very reassuring symbol, suggesting that you are in a strong position – perhaps that the ball is in your court. Maybe it indicates that you have come to terms with your personality and are a 'whole' person. But as always the context will be vital: were you a goalkeeper failing to hold the net? – your dream ball in that case could be encouraging you to think about your problems so that you can counter weaknesses in your personality by further developing your positive traits. If you are a man, there is always the pun: should your genitals be medically checked? Or haven't you the balls to face something important? If you are a woman, have you symbolically or realistically been prevented from 'going to the ball'? Are you involved in a particular 'ball game'?

Bamboo The symbol suggests flexibility and versatility. In the East, because bamboo is always green, it symbolises youth. Would you like your life to be a little more varied, interesting or exotic? Or are you being 'bamboozled' into taking a line of action that you're not too keen on?

Banner The symbol of victory, of 'flying the flag', of standing for something, putting yourself on the line. So have you had a great victory recently? Or do you want or need to proclaim something to the world? Is your sense of pride in your beliefs – political, religious or whatever – involved? If you are rather a shy person, somewhat lacking in self-confidence, your dream banner may well have been a positive symbol, suggesting that you are now ready to show off a little, to be rather more extrovert and show others what you are capable of. Should you be flying the flag? Have you something to shout about? Were you saluting the flag – if so what does your dream flag/banner represent to you?

Basket   As a container, the basket generally symbolises fruitfulness in one way or another. The symbol could well suggest that you are gaining experience. It may represent your personality as a whole. What was in the basket is particularly significant – if it was empty you should consider whether your life is 'empty' in some way. Are you 'putting all your eggs in one basket'? Was your dream basket a heavy burden? Do you feel under pressure – have you a great many problems at present? Did you spill something from your basket? – if so, what did it represent?

Beard   A symbol of virility, sometimes wisdom. A young male dreaming of a beard is probably wishing he had one, or desires to be grown-up. To dream you have a beard when you have not may suggest you have something to hide, or are adopting some disguise. A woman dreaming she has a beard could well be receiving a warning from her unconscious that she is behaving too assertively, and should consider whether to redress the balance and allow the more feminine side of her nature more fulfilling expression. The father figure – even the grandfather figure – may be emerging in the dream, and that relationship should be questioned. How did the beard feel? Was it soft and welcoming or harsh and bristly? Women: does the dream beard say anything about your sexual attitude to men? Men: did you feel your dream beard was very much part of you or did you grow it 'for show' or to give the impression that you have changed or appear to others to have changed? Were you scared of having to shave it off? If so, does this dream represent castration fear for you? See **Old Man**?

Bed   Beds are associated with rest, so this could simply be a reflection of your need to take things more easily, or it could refer to laziness! But there is also the sexual dimension (wish-fulfilment?) – and perhaps a reference to the daily task of making the bed: is there a situation which you need to neaten up? Or having made your bed, must you lie in it? And could that lie be an untruth?

Bee   The bee (like the *ant*) symbolises order, industry and duty. Bees were also often connected in myth with the afterworld (remnants of the belief can be seen in the custom of 'telling the bees' if someone has died). Bees also represent well-run communities and community spirit; even communism (in its finest theoretical sense). The bee as a pollinator of flowers may also be significant (if you are a man, are you ready to start a family? – if a woman, are you pregnant?). Perhaps you should examine your attitude to the community or (consult the context), your attitude to women. If in your dream you were stung by a bee, was the dream telling you to keep off – not to meddle with affairs which do not concern you? Was your dream punning – do you want to 'be' somebody? See also **Hive** and **Honey**?

Bell   The bell was supposed to swing between good and evil; its sound has been associated both with joy and celebration and with death. It can be a warning. So was your bell ringing clearly, merrily, or tolling – was it clear or muffled? Are you at a starting-point in your life? Did your dream bell echo your present state of mind – gloomy, happy or whatever? But if you awoke with a start at your alarm bell or hearing the phone ringing, you can probably disregard your dream.

Bicycle   The interpretation of the dream will depend on your associations with bicycling: whether it was something you merely did as a child and remember with pleasure, or something you do today, perhaps with apprehension, on busy roads – or associate with the unpleasant prospect of going to work. Look at your dream in that light: wish-fulfilment, or an allusion to some particular part of your life? If you are worried, in your dream, about the state of your brakes, or the safety of the bicycle, do not dismiss this: you may unconsciously have noticed a fault to which your dream is drawing attention. Lastly, there is the vulgar reference to a woman with free morals as a bicycle. A comment on your own morals – not necessarily sexual?

BIRDS   Birds, with their ability for free flight, have always represented spirituality, ascent, aspiration, thought and imagination. They were often messengers plying between man and the gods; Christianity saw them as representative of souls in paradise, the Egyptians as the spirit released after death (the *ka*). So dreams of flight (and see **Flying**) are often an indication that we are attempting to distance ourselves from our problems and the concerns of everyday life. Flocks of birds may well symbolise a need to be one of a group we admire and identify with. Remember too that birds have a very powerful and wide range of vision. The air is their element, air representing free thought, ideas and self-expression. The type of bird occurring in our dreams will be vital to your interpretation.

Albatross   The association with misfortune made by some sailors is no stronger than the association with long, powerful flight: the ability to endure a long journey. So relate the dream to an arduous task ahead of you, or perhaps an intellectual journey. Or are you there confronting some tenacious problem? Must you come to terms with some emotional upset or difficulty? (Consider this approach especially if the *sea* came into your dream.)

Bat   See under **Animals**.

Blackbird   A Christian symbol of temptation (associated with its handsome black appearance and sweet song). Could it refer to some black friend, or an admired black singer?

Cock   Above all, in every mythology, the cock has represented alertness, vigilance; in Christian myth watching out for evil, warning against it. The cockerel is a symbol sacred to Mercury, the messenger god (remember Pathé News, with its opening credit of the crowing cock?). So is this a warning dream? Or have you something to crow about? If so why don't you do just that? Is your dream cock encouraging you to show off a bit, to be proud of your achievements? Of course there is always the pun, and a possible sexual connotation. (Even if this is a word you would never use in conversation, remember your dreams are no respecters of convention!)

Dove   A symbol of the spirit, and not only in Christian myth, though it is in that context that it has most potency, representing the Holy Spirit. But doves have also always been associated with faithful love – and with peace and the renewal of hope (it was a dove which brought an olive branch back to Noah after the flood). Are you at peace with your particular world? Is your dream dove representing a fulfilling love-relationship or a symbol of future happiness? Did the dove represent your partner? Was it associated with some gesture of hope?

Duck   Associated with floating lightly on the surface of the *water*, ducks have often been seen as symbols of superficiality. There could be a reference to your emotional life; are you taking it too lightly? But remember the water which runs off a duck's back. A possible reference to some difficulty which you are ignoring, or should ignore?

Eagle   A potent symbol through the centuries, sometimes of victory, sometimes of release; with its reputation for being able to stare straight at the sun, a symbol of great daring and achievement (representative of Christ gazing on the Heavenly Father, Christians believed). So there may be a focus on your inspirational and spiritual life. But remember that the eagle is a ruthless bird of prey; there could be a warning here. There is also a connection between the symbol of the eagle and the eighth sign of the Zodiac, Scorpio, which bestows on its subjects great energy, sense of purpose and powerful emotions. Do you have these qualities, or are they representative of someone close to you? If you are an American citizen was the dream eagle your national emblem – was this a patriotic dream?

Goose   Associated with watchfulness (sometimes used as guardian birds, instead of dogs) but also with creativity (sometimes even laying golden eggs!), though rather easily led. Have you been a 'silly goose' lately? Is your dream warning you not to kill the goose who lays your particular golden egg?

Hawk   Very similar to the *eagle*, but smaller and consequently concerned with smaller prey. Was your dream hawk representing someone 'hawkish', or with a 'hawkish' attitude?

Hen   A charming mother symbol, but hens worry and are constantly clucking their concern for their young. Are you being a clucking hen with your children? Are you disproportionately worried over small problems and allowing them to dominate your life? A black hen is a symbol of evil.

Heron   Representative of quiet vigilance, these birds are extremely shy. Symbolically, a combination of two elements, *air* and *water*. It may be that logic and feeling are well integrated for you at present, but the fact that the heron is a fishing bird could suggest that you are delving into your emotions or fishing for new emotional experiences. Are you particularly aware of your feelings and responses to them at present? Are you being objective and more aware than usual of your actions? Maybe you are out to catch someone – a new lover? Are you trying to overcome shyness or any tendency to hide your true feelings?

Kingfisher   This beautiful, colourful, rather rare bird, has in the past been symbolic of dignity – but also of speed. If you decide that you were the kingfisher, you should consider whether you are fishing for compliments. There could be some connection with pride, perhaps in your image; also consider carefully any connection with water. Do you think your dream kingfisher was a combination of two dream symbols – e.g., 'king' and 'fisher'? (in which case there could just be some Christian symbolism).

Ostrich   The fastest bird on earth, but one that cannot fly. Whether the ostrich was running away from or towards you will be significant, also whether it was pursuing you, or you it. Crosscheck any other relevant symbolism. But there could be a warning here: are you, ostrich-like, burying your head in the sand – not facing up to some decision or problem? Think what the ground was like in your dream – are you concerned with money problems or your materialistic security at present? Were the bird's splendid feathers featured in your dream? In ancient myth they symbolised justice. But are you tending to show off or trying to attract flattery? The large ostrich egg was often preserved in churches and mosques as a symbol of creation and resurrection.

Owl   The owl has been the symbol both of wisdom and of death. The Chinese saw it as evil, as did the early Christians – the bird's call was the Song of Death. But to the Greeks the owl was sacred to Athene as a creature of great wisdom. Do you think your dream owl was suggesting that you need to study your way of life or re-think your attitude to important issues? Did the owl represent some wiser, maybe older person – a teacher or someone whose opinions you respect? Did your dream owl hoot, and if so, was this a warning to be cautious or circumspect?

Parrot   Colourful, noisy, but delightful creatures, above all connected with mindless repetition and talk. Did your dream parrot stand for someone you know, who is extremely talkative but has few opinions of their own? Or could that be you? Was your dream parrot suggesting that you should think and speak for yourself and not simply go along with others' opinions? If your parrot was caged, does this sum up your present situation – is your speech restricted by your nature or by circumstances?

Peacock Always associated with love and immortality; the tail was seen as representing the sky and its stars, and there was therefore an association (especially among Christians) with immortality. The Chinese saw it as symbolising dignity, rank and pride. Its exotic appearance could well be making a comment on your life-style – that you'd like it to be more colourful or romantic. You should also consider whether your sense of pride is in question in some way. Have you been showing off too much – or not enough? Does your dream peacock represent some vain male known to you? Was there a peahen in your dream? – a much less flamboyant bird, and just a little dull. If so, do you think that she was you?

Pelican This strange-looking bird is uncommon in northern Europe. For Christians it represented sacrifice, for it was thought to feed its young with its own blood. With its large beak for carrying food, it still suggests concern for its young. Did your dream pelican represent your family situation – that you are having to work very hard to supply their everyday needs? Are your efforts being appreciated?

Phoenix Cremating itself, the phoenix was said to be born again, after three days, from its own ashes – so it was *the* symbol, in ancient myth, of immortality. It is also a symbol of the sun. Whether or not you knew its story, your dream could well relate to rebirth of some kind, suggesting that you are changing your opinions, making a new start of some sort. Are you in a hopeful state of mind? If not, your outlook may be gloomier than it should be. If your dream phoenix was on fire, do you feel very passionately about someone or something?

Raven Like the parrot, the raven talks – but has generally been seen as more intelligent, or at least slyer. Associated with prophesy, but thought by many civilisations to be in touch with the gods of the dead. Its colour is no doubt responsible to some extent for the gloom associated with the bird – Christians contrasted it with the white dove, and artists often showed it perched on a branch of the tree from which Eve picked the apple of knowledge. Noah was disappointed when his raven failed to return. Your dream may refer to the long-term future. Do you see this as bleak? The context will be important: which area of your life was being shadowed by this rather negative symbol? Or could there be a reference to someone with raven hair?

Stork   The association of the stork with childbirth is too well-known to need emphasis. It has been known for women to dream they are pregnant and only later discover that it is true. A dream could make this point, or simply be the product of wish-fulfilment. It is worth remembering that the stork represented to the early Christians the promise of coming spring, so in every way a positive and hopeful symbol.

Swan   All ease, grace and beauty – a bird much associated with poets and poetry (traditionally, it sings as it dies). But think too of the swan's strong webbed feet and just how hard they work to propel themselves so placidly through peaceful but fast-flowing water. Flying swans symbolise power, and because Zeus changed himself into a swan to father Leda's children there are also fertility connections here. Can you identify with any of these characteristics? Perhaps you work really hard, and as a result all is peace and harmony? In which case the dream may be a reassurance.

Woodpecker   A shy bird said to have magic powers, and in some mythologies sacred to the gods, though the Christians saw it as the conveyer of heresy. We usually see it as hard-working – an achiever. Its tapping suggests a search, or hard work in pursuit of something – in your case, a new principle, or perhaps knowledge? But is the sound an aural pun, related to typing or tap-dancing?

Blindness   This can be a frightening dream symbol, especially if you dream that you are blind. The association seems inevitably to be with your blindness in relation to some issue or situation. Look at other aspects of the dream for a clue; and take the dream as a warning. If someone else is the blind person, consider what he or she represents: love, for instance? *Your* love, perhaps – for do not forget that anyone or anything in your dream may represent you, yourself.

Blood   If you found your dream distressing, try to be rational about its interpretation. If you were bleeding, is someone in waking life bleeding you in some way, perhaps financially? Were you injured – cut or stabbed maybe? If so, are you giving your 'life blood' to your family or your loved ones? If the bleeding came from an area of your body which seems sound, this could be some kind of health warning, and it might be worth getting a medical check-up. (Women often dream of bleeding – and on waking find they have started their period.) Blood represents strength, life itself (hence blood sacrifice, in many religious rites – and the wine in the Christian communion service). But might there be a hint that you should become a blood donor?

Bonds   To find yourself bound – by cords, handcuffs, chains or whatever – is certainly a symbol of restriction; what is important is to decide the reason. Were you being restrained (perhaps for your own good) from doing something, or confined because of some misdeed? Were you struggling, or relatively content? If the latter, there may be a hint that you should restrain yourself. If you were struggling to free yourself, then in waking life there is no doubt some restriction from which you need to be free. As with all 'warning' dreams, look for other symbols to point you to the area of your life with which the dream is dealing. Could your dream bonds relate to your marriage or permanent relationship? – has this imposed too much restriction on your life? There is also the possi-bility that the dream is a reference to the kind of bondage which for some people accompanies sexual gratification: if so, do not be shocked, but consider the matter rationally – the instinct is neither uncommon nor shaming. Should you ask your dreams for further assistance (see p. 45–6). Was your dream symbol a pun – saying something about investment?

Bones   Your dream bones may be telling you something about the past – perhaps the very distant past if they were being dug up from an archaelogical site or a graveyard. Are you getting down to the 'bare bones' of some problem, project or research? Do you want to be very thin, skeleton-like? Or *are* you too thin? Were your dream bones a skeleton in some cupboard? If so, is your secret really necessary? If your dream bones were linked to *death* see p. 52. This is an interesting as opposed to frightening symbol. A famous dream in which Jung discovered a skull in a deep cellar under his house convinced him that he should become a psychologist, plumbing the depths of man's mind.

Bonfire See **Fire**.

Book A symbol of knowledge, though sometimes of life itself, the universe. Was the book open or closed? What sort of book was it? It seems likely to refer to something or someone who is an open or closed book to you: and your attitude to the book will no doubt relate to your waking attitude to them. The title of the book, or its appearance, should offer a clue. There could, on another level, be a reference to your own search for knowledge, either general or particular; even your search for 'the meaning of life' – and again, the book itself may offer a suggestion. Closing or destroying a book obviously has other implications.

Bow A bow that accompanies an arrow, or a true lover's knot? The bow can represent both masculinity and femininity: the crescent has always been a female symbol, but the strength of the bow (propelling the arrow) masculine. There may be a comment on your current relationship: think of the dream's context. Whether the bow was simply hanging, useless, at your side, or being positively used will certainly be important. And, of course, if it was used. See **Arrow**.

Bread In almost every civilisation, the symbol of life, the symbolism spanning thousands of years. There may be a reference to your work as provider for a family, if that is what you are – or to your money. If you were begging for bread, the dream suggests a cry for help: what kind of help? No doubt you will know. Are you being starved of something other than bread – is it love? Is this a pun or someone who you think of as 'well-bred'?

Breasts For a male dreamer, perhaps a simple sexual dream. However, the breast is a universal and powerful symbol of motherhood, and for a man may represent a need for maternal, non-sexual affection and care. For a woman there is the strong probability that it has something to do with her attitude to motherhood, perhaps a desire for that role. Some women are concerned about the size of their breasts; this is another possible interpretation. Women should regularly check their breasts for any malformations, and any dream which seems to suggest concern should prompt you to make a close inspection as an obvious and wise precaution. Remember that the breast is a source of nourishment, and that in dreams food is often a symbol for money; strange though it may seem, yours may have been a comment on your economic situation!

Breath Were you out of breath? If so you may have fallen asleep under the bedclothes and simply needed to take in more oxygen! But perhaps in your dream you were taking in breaths of fresh air, or were in need of some. In that case ask yourself whether you need to let some fresh air into your life.

Bridge World myth has seen the bridge as a means of communication between heaven and hell, and as the bridge of death between this world and the next. Your dream may not refer to this, but it will almost certainly be referring to two 'worlds' of some kind, and to your ambition to cross from one to the other. A bridge always spans something – a river, a railway, sometimes the *water* between two islands. It would seem that you could be in a state of transition or important change. The context of the dream should suggest the area of your life on which it is making some comment. And its advice? Think of the bridge – was it strong and steady, or was it worn, or swaying in the wind? The quality of your waking sense of security will have prompted this. Should you act with greater caution, or move quickly, before the bridge gives way?

Butterfly A very pretty but frail creature, and one with a short life. The Victorians referred to a girl as a butterfly if she was fickle, indecisive, failed to know her own mind, but fatally attractive to men. If you were the butterfly, perhaps you are looking or feeling especially attractive at present, but if you are flitting about, you could be enjoying life a little too much at the expense of your long-term well-being (and that of other people). Should you take life a little more seriously? The butterfly can also symbolise a free spirit, one who has achieved well-deserved freedom. Does this apply to you? If you are a butterfly emerging from a chrysalis, or struggling to do so, the inference is obvious. It is also a symbol of transformation and change. And remember, the butterfly is also a religious symbol of the soul.

Candle   Its light was always a symbol of knowledge. In Jewish mythology, the seven-branched candlestick (according to Josephus) represented the Sun, Moon and planets and also the seven days of the week. To modern Westerners, candle light seems more personal than 'artificial' electric light, so the symbol too is likely to be personal. On what area of your life do you need to shed light? The context of the dream should give you the clue. If the candle was blown out, are you trying to evade an issue? Or hide something? For a male dreamer a candle could be a sexual symbol: was it refusing to burn, guttering, melting too quickly? Remember 'the game's not worth the candle'. What game?

Cane   Freudians would suggest that a cane is probably always a phallic symbol; either agreeing with or setting aside this possibility, consider who was caning whom. In waking life, have you recently deserved punishment, or do you wish to punish someone else – or threaten to do so? The sexual allusion may be sadistic or masochistic. If you think this is the case, do not let it worry you; for the most part this is an entirely innocent tendency, though if it is compulsive, ways should be found of satisfying it in order that it should not be dangerously repressed.

Car   For a man, a dream car seems usually to be a reference to the phallus; psychology has always made the assumption, and it is very likely to be the case in your dream, if you are a man. So dreams of a breakdown, a repair, of speeding or being in need of fuel, will very possibly have sexual connotations. Think of the context of the dream, who else was in it, and so on. A woman dreaming of a car may unconsciously be making the same allusion: the identity of the driver will obviously be important. The car could however have something to do with her assertiveness or lack of it.

Cards   The fifty-two cards may represent the weeks of the year (the red cards the warm seasons, the black the cold); but individual cards can have a personal significance – who is the King, the

Queen, the Knave in your life? If you are dealing the cards, are you busily regulating other people's lives (meddling, perhaps?) What does the game represent? Are you winning or losing? The suits – hearts, clubs, diamonds, spades – may have some significance, perhaps as puns. Hearts traditionally represent emotion and love, diamonds youth and finance, clubs adulthood and enterprise, spades old age, obstacles and enemies. Or was your dream of the Tarot cards, which have other meanings, too elaborate to detail here? The significance of this dream may need considerable teasing out.

Cauldron See **Saucepan**.

Cave On the whole, a dream of a cave is likely to be somewhat daunting. In most world myths a cave symbolises a place of initiation, the underworld, the place of the dead – though also a shelter (the womb of the earth). The Hindus saw caves as 'places of the heart', and it is certainly likely to represent something profound about yourself or your situation. If you were taking refuge, from what? If you were exploring, maybe this represents your need to explore your own psyche, either by private meditation or in analysis. A cave is always feminine, so perhaps there is a reference to someone (your mother?) whose personality in some way offers reassurance or shelter. If the cave holds a *monster*, what does it represent? Was the cave totally dark, or was there a light towards which you were making progress? – this may represent your ultimate aim. If you are carrying a light, what waking situation should you illuminate? Are you sure the cave was not a *tunnel*?

Chains See **Bonds**.

Chair A means of support, generally firm and preferably comfortable, though very occasionally there can be instability and a collapse. Does any of this ring a bell when you refer to your waking life? Were you sitting confidently in the chair or was it wobbling dangerously? Does the dream relate to a situation in waking life in which your confidence in someone or something is misplaced?

Cherry The obvious, immediate association is with loss of virginity, but don't neglect the ancient association. Since the cherry flowers before its leaves are out, it was always taken to represent humanity in its most basic state, naked and alone. This could then be a dream about loneliness or destitution.

Chess The most intelligent and civilised of games often symbolises life itself, the battle between good and evil, male and female, the two sides of any argument. Because the intellect is involved, as well as slyness, plotting and deviousness, your dream could be a comment on your attitude to any present conflict in your life. The identity of the pieces may be important (who is represented by the White Queen, the Black King, or whatever?). A cry of 'mate!' may be significant if you are thinking of consolidating a relationship. If you are a chess-player, the significance of the dream may be much more difficult to discern: try to find the parallels between the game itself, the way it is going, and any waking circumstances.

Chimney The image of a falling factory chimney is often used in a jokey way in films to represent the collapse of the penis – it is such a common phallic symbol that it is almost unreasonable to suppose that your dream chimney was anything else! If you are a woman, is the dream a comment on your partner's sexuality – does it reflect your opinion of or reservations about him?

Chisel As a chisel is a sharp, cutting tool the symbol may well refer to something you are either trying to carve out for yourself in your life, or something that you are trying to hack away at, rid yourself of. Did you cut or injure yourself with your dream chisel? Has someone hurtfully rebuked you recently? All sharp instruments were believed by Freud to be sexual symbols; don't reject the possibility out of hand.

Christmas Tree See also **Tree** – but especially if it is nowhere near Christmas your symbol is probably saying something very specific and special to you, more than likely relating to your family and your relationship with its members. If your dream occurs around Christmas time it could be that responsibilities connected with the season are pressing in on you. Were there lights on the tree? – if so, are you about to 'light up' in some way? Are you high-spirited and feeling positive? – or depressed? Were you planting your tree and trying to make it stand upright? If so this could be a comment on your sex-life; and bear in mind that the tree is wooden, and that this symbol sometimes emerges when we are concerned about our security or our concern for the preservation of the species.

Cinema Much will depend on the film you were seeing (and see **Picture**, **Photograph**). Was the film distorted in some way? The sound or vision quality bad? What does that suggest? Waiting for the film to start? – maybe, then, you are not sufficiently involved in life, for a film is a vivid depiction of reality. An old, black-and-white film may suggest your life needs colour and lacks immediacy.

Circle A circle is one of the most universal of all symbols, representing wholeness, eternity. Your dream circle may well be making a statement about your psychological condition. If the circle was perfect it is likely that you are content and at one with yourself – you have achieved psychological wholeness. If you were inside the circle and felt apprehensive or trapped, are you trapped in some aspect of your life? – unable to get away from problems, claustrophobic living conditions or a sterile relationship? Perhaps you were drawing or looking at circles, in which case your unconscious may be telling you that you are striving for psychological wholeness. Was the circle accurate or wobbly? – in other words, are you in control or do you still have many lessons to learn about life? A circle with a dot in the middle, incidentally, represents perfection, and is the astrological symbol for the Sun. Are you going around in circles getting nowhere? See **Mandala**.

Cloak A protective symbol but also indicative of a need to hide from something or someone – or to hide something. But kings, and beauty queens, wear cloaks, so sometimes a symbol of majesty or success – in this case perhaps representing self-congratulation. It may be, however, that you are trying to protect yourself against someone or something, trying to be less conspicuous. Did you feel more secure in your dream cloak? Was the cloak itself pleasant, warm, well-made? – or old and full of holes? Your attitude and feelings in your dream will be very important. Was there an element of the 'cloak and dagger' in it?

Clouds Angels are often represented standing on clouds, so they can be a symbol of spiritual conviction. More than likely your dream clouds were summing up your life at present. Were the clouds rolling by, letting the sun through, or were they clouding the

Sun? Are storm-clouds gathering in your waking life? Has your life taken a turn for the better? – or perhaps this is about to happen. Your dream may either be warning you or giving you encouragement.

Club A phallic symbol? Quite possibly, but not inevitably, because a club can be a general symbol of strength. If you were hitting someone or something with a club it is likely that in waking life you are extremely angry and may even be nursing ideas of violence. But perhaps you were being clubbed. If so, are you living under great stress and pressure? Your dream could well be warning you. Perhaps you saw some poor animal being clubbed to death, a baby seal, maybe. Who is attacking you so violently? Or who are you attacking? Or are you being urged to support animal rights?

But perhaps your dream club was a meeting of like-minded people or friends, in which case how significant were the other people, or the club room itself? See **Crowds** or **Cards**? One final thought: you wouldn't by any chance have put someone 'in the club' – or be pregnant yourself?

COLOURS People seem quite concerned as to whether they dream in colour or not. As we have pointed out (see p. 50) this is not a matter of great importance, but if you have a dream which seems positively soaked in a particular colour, is it obviously reasonable to think about the significance of this. Consider first whether the colour has a particular personal importance: is it associated with a person or place you know, a woman, perhaps, who often wears it? But then think of the traditional symbolic meaning of the colours: this has a long history, and we can only summarise –

Black Black is traditionally the colour of *death* and of evil – it seems uncommon to dream of black except as a memory of or reference to death or funerals. It has often been associated with witchcraft, so it will be worth considering whether, even unconsciously, you are thinking of putting the evil eye on someone! Dreams in which black features strongly often reflect the black mood of a dreamer who is depressed or pessimistic.

White The opposite of black: the symbol of purity, hope, innocence. It may be inviting to you to shed light on something, or to strive to see some situation (or person) more clearly; it might be a comment on someone dressed in white (in your dream). It may be worth remembering that in the Middle and Far East white is the colour of mourning.

Red   A vibrantly energetic and vigorous colour, which has always, but especially in modern times, signalled danger. But it has been the symbol of many things – of royalty, battle, sexuality, vengeance. Think of it first, however, in the sense of warning – especially if it is associated with a traffic light, a red flag or some other obvious warning symbol. Look as ever to the general context to take you further. It is on the whole a masculine colour (as opposed to blue, which is feminine).

Orange   Like red, orange has been a symbol of royalty; a warm, generous colour, it is above all encouraging and reassuring. It is also the colour of health, especially the glands.

Yellow   Light yellow is usually on the side (as it were) of red and white – it represents warmth of understanding and general goodness. The darker the yellow, the more prevalent the sense of unease, for it then tends to stress the shadier side of the colour, standing for jealousy, treachery and perhaps cowardice.

Green   Traditionally the colour of jealousy, and this is perhaps most likely to be the connotation. It has also stood for bad luck (perhaps because it was the colour traditionally worn by the Little People, fairies, pixies). Remember that green is made by mixing blue and yellow: could that be significant? Or there may be a reference to the increasing importance of 'green' matters – the preservation of the environment. Green is the colour of life, growth and healing.

Blue   The colour of cold intellect, fidelity; unemotional, it encourages all the processes of thought, and suggests depth (perhaps because it is, or should be, the colour of the deep ocean). It is on the whole a feminine colour (as opposed to red, which is masculine).

Purple   *The* colour of royalty: so suggestive of self-congratulation. It is also associated with spirituality, and with immaturity.

Compass   Are you at a crossroads in your life, or about to make some change of direction? Was the pointer showing you the way? If any of the compass points emerged very distinctly, what do these directions actually mean to you?

Compasses A pair of compasses usually symbolise order, justice: they enable man to draw the perfect circle, and are much associated with quasi-religious orders such as freemasonry. You were probably about to draw a **Circle** in your dream, so see that entry; but should you have been stabbed by the point, which stands at the centre of the circle, there might have been a statement about the very centre or core of some problem or aspect of your life. See **Prick**, **Needle**?

Conjurer See **Trick/Trickster**.

Cooking In dreams, food and drink are very often allusions to the emotions; if you were cooking in your dream, the recipe and how you were preparing it may be relevant to your present emotional state. If you were adding sugar, for instance, this could be an indication that you are not finding life sweet at present, that maybe you in some way lack affection; adding salt or pepper, on the other hand, may suggest that life lacks savour, or needs 'pepping up'. Try to relate other elements of the dream to your emotions: were you over- or under-cooking something? Look at the ingredients and refer to the entries which describe them. Of course if you are the family cook there may be an element of wish-fulfilment, or are you 'cooking something up' in the sense of plotting or scheming, in your waking life? What did your family or guests think of the food? – and were you yourself pleased or disappointed by the result?

Cord In ancient mythology a silver cord held the spirit and body together; Zeus literally had the world on a string. The symbolism clearly related to the umbilical cord, but it may be more simple than that. Are you becoming attached – too attached – to something or someone? Should you cut some cord in your life – in order to break free? What was the cord attached to? Was it a telephone cord? – if so, do you want to cut yourself off from someone? Are you, in other words, telling them to shut up? If you were paying out a cord as you walked along, your dream could represent your need for independence, though with security – in which case, again, what was the far end of the cord tied to or in contact with? Were you making something with cord, knitting or sewing? What are you making of your life at present; is it, or your dream cord, 'all knotted up'?

Corn   A potent ancient symbol of life, fertility and promise. A lot will depend upon the state of the corn. If it was waving, golden, strong and ready to be harvested, the symbol is obviously a very positive one – you may well be about to reap the benefit of your labours. If it was 'sowing time' in your dream you may well be quite literally sowing for the future – again a positive symbol (don't forget the fertility angle; have you an eye on parenthood?). If the corn was withered or beaten down by wind and weather you may well be experiencing a period during which your efforts seem not to be worthwhile, and your state of mind is somewhat negative. Was your dream corn simply a pun on something 'corny'? The Corn Goddess, incidentally, is associated with the astrological sign of Virgo. (A simple point: we hope your corns aren't troubling you.)

Crab   The creature hoards, is snappy, has a hard shell and a very soft interior. Is this reminiscent of your recent behaviour? Are you about to snap someone's head off, or has someone done this to you? The crab can also be a positive and protective symbol, however. Compare your dream crab to the characteristics of the Zodiac sign, Cancer: are you a Cancerian, or do you know anyone of this sign who could have been represented in your dream? If you were cooking a live crab and perhaps trying to hold it down in the water, are you repressing some inner injury or anger?

Crescent   A new *Moon* which has usually been taken to symbolise motherhood, and was the symbol of all Moon goddesses. Hence the custom of wishing on the New Moon, the wish coming true as the moon waxed. So are you very much wishing for something or someone? If there were negative elements in the dream, are you failing to face up to reality? In any case it would seem that you are in a hopeful state of mind at present – but wishing for the Moon?

If your dream crescent was a terrace of houses or buildings, these symbolise a change of direction within your personality; are you developing or changing your outlook, or becoming more aware of certain aspects of your personality?

Cross   Of course the cross is a very potent Christian symbol but in fact crosses have, from the very distant past, been highly symbolic in all known civilisations, representing not only universal values but mankind at the highest point of aspiration. For the Egyptians the *ankh* combined the male and female symbols and therefore represented life itself, and the coming together of heaven and earth. For the Chinese it was the symbol of the earth and everything upon it. The Africans used it as a symbol of protection in childbirth; for the Buddhists it stands at the centre of the Wheel of the Law; the Hindus see the upright as representing celestial being, while the crossbar stands for humanity in its baser condition. The Mexicans showed man crucified upon a cross, but their god himself was often also fixed to it. The Romans used it as a symbol of doom. The Christian meaning needs no comment.

In view of all this, any dream with a cross as its central symbol is likely to be an important one. It may well be a symbol of hope and inspiration, so that even if you are experiencing a difficult period in your life your unconscious is helping you to realise that all is not lost. It may represent the cross which you have to bear at present in waking life. But do not neglect the obvious punning attribution; are you very cross about something, or behaving like a 'little cross patch'?

Crossroads   As a symbol, a crossroads represents choice; but there is also an ancient magical connotation; witches were buried at crossroads, evildoers hanged there. Were you approaching the crossroads? If you had actually reached it, did you know which way to turn, or were you going straight on, ignoring the intersecting roads? Were you in your *car*? – if so were you in control of it? Were there traffic signals? Were they at stop, go or caution?

Crowd   Crowds often represent problems surrounding us. If you are in a crowd of people known to you, the characteristics of those with whom you can identify can represent aspects of your own personality, desirable or otherwise. Were you trying hard to get away from the crowd? Were you waiting to see someone or something spectacular? If so, perhaps you are living in hope of something you desire. Were the circumstances suggesting that you should break away, become more of an individual, less one of the common crowd?

Crown   The obvious symbol of majesty, of being the best: a supreme winner. But also a bitter symbol – remember the crown of thorns, and the unease of the head that wears the crown. So here is a symbol of responsibility as well as glory. Could your dream crown have related to promotion to a top job? If you were reassured by your dream, it could have been suggesting that you carry responsibility well. Remember that crowns are usually extremely valuable and should be treated with respect, as should the wearer. But perhaps you wish you were a *King* or *Queen* of some kind? Are you drifting towards some fairyland and getting out of touch with reality?

Crystal Crystal anciently symbolised purity (because it was clear, and hid nothing of itself). The crystal ball was supposed to tell all, so there is a reference, too, to honesty (unless the crystal was seen in an unreliable end-of-the-pier context). Maybe your dream crystal was quite simply saying that you can now see your problems more clearly. But if you were consulting a crystal-gazer, remember that you might well have been the gazer herself. Did you take notice of what she had to say? If you are feeling rather depressed there's a distinct possibility that your dream was somewhat negative – but think again: was it reassuring or warning? Particularly in the United States, crystals are used in alternative medicine as a means of healing or simply providing good health; so could your dream be referring to this area of your life?

Cup A feminine symbol, which often represented something passive, something from which you could draw sustenance. In Western Christian culture there is considerable mystical significance, such as the search for the illusive Holy Grail. Sometimes cups overflow, and there is an outpouring. Was your dream cup making a statement about your emotional life? Are you giving too much of yourself to your partner – or withholding emotion? Was your cup a chalice, and were you taking communion? Perhaps the dream was centring on your attitude towards spiritual matters?

Dance The dance has always represented energy, both physical and emotional. The Lord of the Dance is not only a Christian reference – dancing has been at the centre of most world religious ceremonies. There is less ponderous symbolism too, however: were you keeping both feet on the ground, or really 'taking off'? Consider very carefully who or what you were dancing with and what that dream partner represents to you. Are you leading someone a dance, or they you? Was this wish-fulfilment? – perhaps you long to be a ballerina?

Darkness Presumably a rather frightening symbol (see **Blindness**) which may suggest that you cannot see your way round present difficulties – unless there was light at the end of the *tunnel*, when your dream could be saying that there is darkness before the dawn. If you are feeling depressed, the dream is focusing on your specific problems: it will definitely be worth your while to ask your dreams for more help.

Dawn Presumably you are getting your problems into a coherent perspective and beginning to see your way ahead. Perhaps something has 'dawned' on you – an answer to some tricky intellectual problem? Are you starting a new phase in your life?

Death Dreams of death are rather more common than you may realise. Very often the dreamer is seeing someone put in a coffin, or himself being buried. Sometimes we dream we are actually dead, or for some unknown reason feigning death. Do *not* be frightened or apprehensive. Such dreams do not mean that you or others in your dream are going to die. Often such symbols simply suggest that we are ready for change, for new phases in our lives, that we have changed our opinions, or that we are ridding ourselves of certain character traits. These often surface in our dreams as people known to us who have these characteristics. Have you had any other similar dreams recently? Looking back over recent months, do you think you have changed in some respects?

Diamond See **Jewels**.

Dice Dice have been seen as representing fate: they fall as they will, or as they must. But there is also the association with gambling. Are you taking a chance? Was it worthwhile in your dream? Will it be worthwhile in real life? Did you throw a double six? Were any of the number combinations significant as puns, do you think? Were you confident that you could influence the fall of the dice, command fate? If any particular number was emphasised, look it up under **Numbers**.

Door   A door can bar you from something, be an entrance or an exit: try to make the connection with your waking life. Were you trying to unlock a door or close it? Were you hanging or repairing the door? The symbol is probably saying something important about various spheres of your life or, more personally, specific aspects of your personality. Are you, for instance, shutting yourself off from emotional or sexual expression? Are doors being opened for you spiritually or careerwise? Are you closing some phase of your life? To what, if anything, are you saying 'I don't want to know'? or, 'Yes I want to experience that – I am ready to do so?' Even if you don't think so, your unconscious may. See **Lock**?

Dragon   A very ancient and complex symbol which was originally positive, often representing kingship; but later, especially in the East, destructive and antagonistic to man – and woman. It has much the same significance as the *serpent*, now representing something against which we are expected to fight, so it can stand for anything in your character which you want to eradicate, anyone or anything you want out of your life. Since the dragon had a liking for virgins, he has (though invariably masculine) extremely close connections with old, fierce women – the mother-in-law in particular. Was your dragon some oversexed beast known to you, or was it, quite differently, a dragon of an old woman – an authority figure of some kind – a headmistress, a strict nursing sister or matron? Have you been a dragon lately?

Drinking   It may be that your spirit or body needs refreshment, that you will benefit from some kind of spiritual sustenance. If you dreamed you were drunk, are you trying to escape from some dreary aspect of reality? Had you had too much to drink before going to bed? Were you very thirsty, or did you need to go to the bathroom as soon as you awoke? Was your dream warning you of the negative effects of too much drinking?

Drowning   See **Water**, if relevant. Your dream may well be suggesting that you are reacting over-emotionally at present. Perhaps problems are getting the better of you, and you feel as if you are drowning in them. Was there any connection between drowning and sinking financially? Are you trying to 'keep afloat?'

Drum Once believed to be the sound in which all speech originated, the drum was also often used in religious ceremonies, so it is associated with messages, truth-telling. It is also noisy, and makes an immediate impression. Do you want to be noticed? What is making you bang your drum? Are you drumming something out of your life?

Drunk See **Drinking**.

Dwarf Dwarfs are small and not usually very handsome earth creatures, sometimes miners. Do you feel plain and rather small at present? Did your dream dwarf represent a problem or someone who you should cut down to size? Garden dwarfs or gnomes are usually figures of fun. Does the bobble hat fit?

Ear Oddly enough, some religions associated birth with the human ear, perhaps because it resembles the whorls of a shell, which is a birth-symbol. But such a dream is more likely to be warning you that you have an ear ailment so it might be worth getting a hearing check. Are you listening to advice? Or what other people are saying? Are you turning a dear ear to what is going on, or agreeing too readily with other people – a pun on 'Hear! Hear!'?

Earth Mother Earth, the symbol of creativity. The dreams could be reflecting your need for material security. Was the ground sound beneath your feet? Were you on shifting soil? Was the ground giving way, or were you involved in an earthquake? Perhaps you were gardening. Are you planning for the future? Was your dream suggesting that you should be more creative, or warning you of financial risks? See **Grave**, **Death**?

Eating Were you hungry and enjoying your food, or being gluttonous? Your dream could be making a statement about emotional or sexual hunger, or hunger for greater experience of life. That is a decision you must make. But you should also ask yourself whether you are being greedy? Whether you should lose or gain weight? Whether you are emotionally or sexually deprived? Whether you were, in your dream, tasting the sweetness of success and fulfilment? Also, most importantly, what or who were you eating and what does that represent? – be honest!

Egg A very potent and ancient symbol: from the World Egg (or in Hindu, Chinese and Greek mythology, the Cosmic Egg) came all existence, so it can represent the womb. Buddhists see the eggshell as symbolising the falsehood through which we must break to attain the truth. So the dream symbol is likely to be a very positive, hopeful one. Perhaps you have a private desire to conceive, or to begin some creative project? Were you trying to crack open your egg? If so, do you think that you are seeking some knowledge, or the solution to a baffling problem? Do you want to 'egg someone on' in some way?

Eye The human eye has always been a potent symbol, the all-seeing eye representing the power of God – or a god – to see through human nature right to the core of man's motives and behaviour. It has been equated with the *Sun* as representative of ultimate power; but some ancients saw the *stars*, too, as a myriad watching eyes. When the early Christians built their cathedrals they often left a hole in the very centre of the dome, representing the eye through which God could see into men's hearts. For Buddhists, the 'third eye' of Buddha represents all-comprehensive wisdom; the Chinese and Japanese see the right eye as the Sun, the left as the Moon. For the Egyptians the eye had an extremely complex symbolism, and in various ways it represented knowledge, power and strength. It can also be a symbol of evil, though possibly only to those with a troublesome conscience! As usual, everything depends on the context of the dream: sometimes one is being contemplated by an unblinking eye, which can be a frightening experience. The most obvious suggestion is that there is an unconscious indication that some part of one's current life needs very careful inspection or reappraisal, and this in turn suggests that one may be up to something less than respectable! In other circumstances it may be that someone actually does have their eye on you! Or it may be that you need to keep your eye on someone else (look for other references, if any, within the dream). Something in your eye? – then maybe someone is trying to *blind* you to their own motives or behaviour. Don't forget the possibility of a pun: could the *eye* be *I*?

Falling   Some dreams of falling, in which one wakes with a start, have a very simple explanation: we are literally falling asleep. But dreams are not often that simple-minded, and there may be other explanations. The difficulty is that the word has so many allusions: we fall in love, fall from grace; we fall over because we are in some way insecure; if you are female, you can be a fallen woman, and so on. A dream of falling may mean that you fear a metaphorical fall in waking life, a fall brought about by your own carelessness or slipshod work, for instance. There is also the possibility that this is a warning dream: if you dream you fell because of a rickety stair or a piece of loose carpet, check up on it. The unconscious may have spotted the danger before your waking mind had seen it.

Fan   The way in which a fan spreads out as you open it has been taken as representative of the growth of knowledge and experience – of the course of life itself – and a very beautiful and vivid symbol it is. The opening and closing of a fan has also suggested woman's menstrual cycle, and her changeability. The breeze created by a fan can represent the human spirit. Carried formally, a fan in some civilisations has been a symbol of royalty and power. All these things are worth keeping in mind. If you were struggling to open a fan, might this suggest that you want to get to the heart of some problem? If you were fanning someone was it to cool them (and perhaps their feelings towards you) or to ward off, maybe, an unpleasant odour? Fanning yourself, do you feel the (unconscious) need to 'cool it'?

The idea of a *fan* as an admirer is another matter: if you were one of a group of fans, to whom were you giving uncritical acclaim or support?

Father   A dream of your father could refer to your feelings about him or his feelings for you or to any personal circumstances between you. But the abstract idea of 'the father' should not be ignored; maybe the dream is not about your father as a man, a personality, but about the archetype, 'the father', as one of the most important symbols of power and order – the ultimate authority (for the idea of the father is connected with authority, law and order, while the mother on the other hand represents more instinctive feelings and actions). So if you were flouting your father's wishes or orders, could the dream really be about some rebellious streak in you directed at society at large?

The idea of Father Time is another one which should be recalled; he need not have appeared in a white robe and holding a sickle!

If the dream seems to be too concerned with your father himself, as a man, for him to be a symbolic figure, then of course you should look to your relationship with him for an interpretation (but do not forget that the ideas set out above may nevertheless apply in some way or another). Many women have dreams of their father when they first become conscious of their sexual feelings towards other men. Sometimes these dreams can have an uncomfortably guilty edge (Freud has much to say about the father-daughter relationship and its comment on female sexuality; and see **Incest**).

Feather The feather, with its beauty and lightness, can strongly suggest the idea of spiritual truth, and was often taken to represent the human soul rising to heaven. Feathered headdresses were worn in many civilisations to indicate the wisdom of ultimate authority. The white feather is a symbol of cowardice (the idea seemed to originate in the notion that a white feather among the black ones of a cock suggested that it was not likely to be the winner in a fight). The connection between feathers and flight led to the idea that the fairies commonly wore feathered gowns.

A dream in which feathers play a part may well, then, have something to do with aspiration. A feather soaring on a breeze could represent ambition (perhaps intellectual); on the other hand a feather wafted hither and thither on whatever wind is blowing may suggest you are too easily swayed by others' opinions or actions. A white feather? – are you failing to act firmly and decisively? Tousled feathers? – is something standing in the way of your ambition; are you being prevented from soaring?

Feet Unless your dream was clearly prompted by tired feet, a corn or in-growing toe-nails, and having dismissed any possible pun about 'finding your feet', 'putting your foot in it' or plunging into something 'feet first', it will be worth remembering the connection between feet and the ability to move – whether forward or backward! Not being able to move your feet may mean the inability to move in some other way – emotionally, maybe. Kissing the feet is a symbol of reverence or obeisance; but people sometimes speak of being 'trodden down'. Are you intent on subjugating someone to your wishes? See **Footprints**?

Fig   For centuries the fig has been the symbol of the female genitals, so this fruit has always suggested lust; there may well be a sexual connotation to your dream. The fig tree itself, through the same symbolism, can stand for the Tree of Life, while the fig-leaf can represent the phallus. Do these allusions suggest an interpretation? Remember that the consumption of food can often have a sexual undertone. Or is it that you 'don't care a fig' about someone or something – or are in some way 'in full fig'?

Film   See **Cinema**, **Picture**, **Photograph**.

Finger   Apart from using our fingers in the practical sense, we often use them to convey emotion, from the two-finger gestures which can mean either victory or contempt, to the finger pointed in accusation or lifted to the lips to enjoin silence. So what you were doing with your finger is obviously important. If not your own, whose was the finger involved? And what was it trying to convey to you, about what? Should you 'pull your finger out'?

Fire   Fire has been an enormously important symbol to almost every civilisation. But it is difficult to untangle the many allusions, for in different civilisations it has meant different things – death, to the Aztecs; wisdom, to Buddhists; knowledge, to the Hindus; the Holy Spirit, to Christians; anger, to the Chinese. Sometimes fire has represented purification (as it does scientifically); at other times its leaping flames have suggested the spirit leaping to meet God. One of the four basic elements, it seems psychologically to relate to our emotions and passions. If we channel our fiery emotions, they can work well for us, we can achieve much and get a great deal of satisfaction by expressing them in creative work. This can also apply to physical action and emotion, perhaps related to sexual passion. However, it is important to remember that fire can very easily get out of control, and that our fiery emotions should be controlled. We can be consumed by fiery passion, for our partner, for a cause or for power. Such fire can consume us. The old saying that fire is a good servant but a bad master is very relevant in this context. It is most likely that your dream of fire relates to some powerful and emotionally charged feelings – perhaps a sexually charged passion for someone. Rather differently, maybe you are extremely angry about something in your waking life. Most importantly, you must consider your attitude to the fire and how you were responding to it. Were you fearful, enjoying a warm glow or trying desperately to extinguish the fire? Or perhaps you were encouraging the fire to burn more brightly, more strongly. The fire itself is another factor for consideration: did it crackle and spark unexpectedly? Was there 'smoke without fire'? Were you in control of the situation, or did the fire consume you? If you were running away from the flames, are you afraid of your present feelings? Or are you trying to smother them?

Fish/Fishing Though the fish has ·been associated with Christianity since the inception of that religion (it was scrawled on the walls of the catacombs as a secret symbol to show where the early Christians might worship or hear Jesus' teachings in comparative safety), it has also always been a phallic symbol. It is not impossible that the two meanings are connected, in the sense that the first Christians were much concerned with 'sowing the seed' and seeing their numbers increase. Fish as a food has been associated with many religions – eaten often on Friday, a day associated with Venus, Isis and Ishtar, among other gods. Fish seemed to swim in the waters of life (*see*, very importantly, **Water**) – like the two fishes swimming in opposite directions, a cord joining their mouths, which represent the twelfth Zodiac sign, Pisces, a water sign, whose subjects are usually sensitive, intuitive and emotional, often deceptive, taking the apparently easy way out of difficult situations, usually in order not to hurt others. Here too is creativity and marvellous potential, often underestimated by the individual. It may be that your dream fish is saying something about your emotional reactions; perhaps you are undecided or feel you are being pulled in two directions and are uncertain – maybe about your feeling for a loved one, or about your sexuality. But there is a possibility that the dream was warning you that something 'fishy' is going on (note the deception hinted at above). On a practical level perhaps you have eaten fish that doesn't agree with you, or maybe the dream fish represents a Piscean known to you or is saying that you are behaving in a somewhat 'Piscean' manner at present. If you were *fishing* – for what? Compliments?

Flag   See **Banner**.

Floating   Any dream in which *water* occurs usually relates to our emotional reactions; in this case a logical line of interpretation would be the obvious, basic one. Are you trying to keep your head above water, emotionally? Or are you skimming the surface of a problem that you should consider in greater depth? If your mood in the dream was calm and placid, and you were enjoying your floating experience, probably all is well; but if you were fearful, maybe you are in a difficult 'sink-or-swim' situation. Perhaps you were floating with the tide or the current – if so, are you going along with what others expect of you, maybe a little too readily? Another obvious allusion is to 'doing nothing' – just lying there!

Flogging   Perhaps we should first note the possibility that this was merely a sexual dream, prompted by wish-fulfilment. If this seems to be the case, remember that masochism is not a sin – though if the dream recurs frequently, and is deeply worrying to you, maybe you should consider some therapy or professional help. In other contexts, much depends on whether you were doing the flogging or being flogged. Remember that in dreams you yourself can be represented by any of the symbols, so consider that while you could certainly have been the flogger or the flogged, you might also have been the instrument – the whip itself. Is someone using you as an instrument to castigate someone else? Are you feeling guilty about something, and punishing yourself? Or desperately wanting to punish someone else? Were you enjoying the situation? Did you feel pity or shame? Perhaps you have behaved recently in a way which was 'naughty' – most likely if a school context was involved.

Flowers   Flowers have usually been thought of as particularly feminine, partly because so many of them are cup-shaped, and must be entered by the *bee* before they can be pollinated. If your dream involved a bee, the inference is obvious! Who was the bee? – and if you were, which flower were you making for? The lotus (in the East) and the rose and lily (in the West) have represented self-knowledge and the urge to attain it. Flowers sometimes represent childhood; and planted in banks or beds, the idea of paradise – the heavenly garden. In many civilisations flowers are supposed to comfort and aid the dead (hence the tradition of sending them to funerals). If your dream flowers were particularly beautiful, and you were holding them as a bouquet or perhaps picking them, your dream was probably positive and reassuring – saying that you are at your best and that life is good; you are expressing yourself fully and rewardingly. If your flowers were in bud, might they suggest that you too are about to blossom in some way – or should blossom? Spring flowers suggest hope and confidence in the future. But were there prickles or thorns, or were your flowers out of reach? If so, are obstacles preventing you from achieving your desires? If your flowers faded, are you feeling somewhat hopeless about some aspect of your life?

Fly   Flies have never had a good press, usually being considered as dirty, spreading disease; the original Lord of the Flies was Beelzebub, Lord of Death. Your dream need not be as fierce as that, but it will worth considering whether you or someone else is 'spreading the dirt' or buzzing too impertinently and insistently around someone else's business.

Flying   Almost everyone, at one time or another, has dreamed that s/he is flying; it has been suggested that elderly people, in particular, frequently have such dreams. It is often said they have sexual connotations, but this is by no means invariably the case, though the feeling of soaring and freedom involved can be equated with sexual satisfaction, and on waking we usually feel elated or at least satisfied. If the dream involves our looking down on a landscape, it may be trying to help us to look at our problems from a new perspective – to get a fresh perspective on them. Rather differently, the dream may suggest that we need to escape, get away from the more mundane aspects of life. Sometimes flying dreams are telling us we are ready to 'take off' – on some important project, perhaps – or that we should spread our wings. Do you want to branch out in some way, or get away from it all? Was your dream reassuring you that you can achieve what you want? We should not, of course, ignore the possible sexual implications; was anyone else involved? By giving you such an intense, delightful experience was your dream suggesting that your sex-life needs enhancement? Are you sexually frustrated, maybe lacking in self-confidence? The dream could well be telling you that you need have no fears in this respect, that you can soar as rewardingly and easily as the next man or woman provided you 'let go' of any inhibitions which might keep you earthbound.

Food Dreams of eating and drinking are only exceptionally – and perhaps if we are very greedy! – concerned with our enjoyment of food; they refer much more often, indeed almost invariably, to our emotional, or sometimes sexual, life. So if we are hungry, it is for something lacking in that area: perhaps sex, or sensuality (for instance in our appreciation of the sense of touch), or simple affection. The kind of food we are eating, or craving, is clearly important: it will often be a clue to the meaning of the dream. Consider your feeling towards its taste (sweet or sour, enjoyable or not) and not least its shape. A man eating a fig, a woman eating a banana, need not think too hard to come to the proper, or improper, reference. The dream may be an enjoyable one, and a reflection of a happy and contented emotional life; but it may also be a hint that there is something lacking – perhaps something of which you are not consciously aware.

Footprints Whose footprints? Were you leaving footprints behind you? If so, perhaps you are concerned about the effect a present waking activity may have on future generations – maybe on your children. If you are following in someone's footsteps, are you doing so slavishly or in genuine admiration? Some ancient peoples thought that unexplained footprints were the mark of a supernatural visitor; were your dream footprints made by someone intangible. If so, could they represent some unfulfilled ambition or desire?

Forest See, of course, **Tree**, with all the implications of the symbol being much multiplied. But apart from that, a forest has traditionally been a place of initiation and trial, in which you can get lost, or from which you can emerge triumphant. Men and women of most religions have at some time seen a thick forest as lying between earth and heaven; inside it are sometimes the sins of the world, sometimes the secrets of life and death. The dream seems most likely to allude to confusion: so try to equate it with any current problems, and then to relate your adventures in the forest to those problems – were you afraid (if so, of what?) or confident (*over*-confident?) or merely lost?

Fountain See **Water**, in this case usually flowing delightfully and giving much pleasure. 'The fountain of life' offers the suggestion that you yourself want to be pleasant and useful to others; if the fountain was blocked, the inference is obvious. Freudians would point to the spurting waters and suggest parallels with the male ejaculation; this might not be impossible. Flowing water can sometimes represent an outpouring of knowledge (remember *Aquarius*, though his water was flowing rather than being positively propelled). Is there some knowledge, some teaching you want to make available to others?

Fruit Fruit usually represents abundance of some quality or other – 'first fruit' was particularly valuable. Remember the fruit of knowledge: the *apple* of course would be specially meaningful. For Christians the fruit of the tree of life was immortality; for earlier people, the fruit carried by Priapus suggested the fruit of sexual activity – there may be a suggestion here of wish-fulfilment.

Furnace See **Fire**.

Game What sort of game? Is it a game you often play and are good at, one you are forced to join and which you cannot play well or a game you are intent on winning or afraid of losing? It is almost certainly not a reference to an actual game, unless you are a professional player, when it may be the kind of anxiety dream connected with all professions and occupations. It is more likely to be a symbol of some situation in your waking life, one of the 'games people play'. So watch for a comment on, say, your current relationship or some manoeuvering at work. There should be other clues in the dream which will direct you: if not, ask (see p.45–6) for more help.

Garden What your garden means to you will be important, but more generally, there has usually been a parallel between a garden and life itself – in particular, the soul – about the cultivation of

which most societies have had strong views. So if you were cultivating it yourself, self-improvement is suggested; while a wild,
overgrown, garden choked with weeds might suggest that your life
and personality are in less than good order. A walled garden
traditionally represented femininity, chastity (sometimes invaded
by a predatory *unicorn*). Gardens (also see **Flowers**) have often
represented a happy afterworld, the Elysian fields. Do you want to
escape from mundane, everyday life? If so, for what sort of garden
are you bound?

Gate Like a *door*, a gate probably most commonly represents a way
in or out of some situation, perhaps of some form of behaviour,
some personal characteristic; an escape, maybe – but perhaps also
the entrance to a prison. What were your feelings about the gate?
Was it locked or wide open? Was it welcoming or the opposite?
What could you see between its bars? Gates, in various mythologies, had Guardians of one kind or another – sometimes welcoming,
but more often fierce or at least judgmental. Have you come to a
point where your next move may be severely judged by someone? If
you were slamming a gate, against whom? Or perhaps more importantly, against what? Who or what, was on the other side of the
gate?

Giant The idea of giants haunts us, usually, from our childhood,
and generally stands for something frightening or at lease awe-
inspiring; so look for the meaning of the symbol – does the giant of
your dreams stand for a frightening figure, or one whose stature
seems much greater than yours? Or for some personal characteristic you would like to cut down to size?

Globe A globe or *sphere* can stand for the world, or for the idea of
wholeness, self-containment; breaking one may mean that for better or worse you want to shatter your present image or circumstances, that you are tired of worldly things. See **Mandala**?

Glove Like all clothing, this can be a very personal symbol; Freudians relate it to sex. Inserting fingers into a glove may for men be
connected with sex, or with contraception. But on the contrary for
some civilisations the glove has been a symbol of purity; to take off a
glove was to show that one concealed nothing in one's hand and so
represented honesty and lack of deviousness. Throwing down the

glove was to offer a challenge. Be sure there is no simple reference to your hands being cold!

Gold   While many religions have been preoccupied with the idea of poverty, gold has found its place in most of them, often as a representation of a god, of the creator – literally, for the Egyptians, who believed their gods' flesh was made of it. Often there is some equivocation; for Christians gold could represent either spiritual treasure or false prophesy (the golden calf). For modern men and women, gold more probably represents possessions, riches, not necessarily concrete; but there may well be (as in all symbolism) hints of the past. What you were doing with the gold is vital: hoarding, gambling, spending? It most probably represents something you regard as very important – most likely a personal characteristic such as honesty, truth, beauty.

Grapes   The personal meaning is, as always, important. The grapes could certainly stand for alcohol but also (traditionally) wisdom ('*in vino veritas*'). Grapes are usually to the fore in any enjoyable orgy: there may be a sexual connotation – they are often depicted by artists in that sense, sometimes as symbols of enjoyment, sometimes of concealment.

Grass   Were you being told to Keep Off the Grass? If so, on to whose territory are you thinking of encroaching? Were you cutting the grass, making it neat? Is there a parallel here with waking life? What situation needs tidying up? Was the grass knee-high, and if so was this a symbol of freedom, of a happy running wild, or of waste and indiscipline?

Grave   See **Tomb**.

Guitar   Because of its shape, the guitar has always been the symbol of woman. So whose emotions do you want to play upon? With whom are you out of tune? Who do you want to lock away in a case, or hang about your neck? And so on.

Hair   Human hair is one of the most potent of symbols. Authority has always seen it as an indication of freedom and individualism, even of open sexuality, hence St Paul's fulminations against women's hair and the modern army's insistence on short haircuts (to mention only two manifestations). Hair has stood not only for freedom but for strength (remember Samson) and when shaved off, the lack of it indicates a positive frigidity, a devotion to the unworldly. All sorts of conclusions can therefore be drawn from a dream in which hair plays a prominent part; it is likely to have been an important dream, in one way or another. A dream in which your hair is flowing and free suggests that you want or need freedom in some sphere of your life (probably emotionally or sexually). If your hair was being cut, then you may either feel that you should put a bridle on your emotions, or (if it was being cut against your will) that someone is trying to censor you, or restrict your behaviour. There is also, for men, a well-documented possible reference to fear of castration. A dream of losing your hair may indicate insecurity in one form of another. A bald man dreaming of growing hair may of course indicate wish-fulfilment, but it might also mean that his emotions should be allowed freer rein.

Hammer   A male symbol, not specially phallic, but powerful and forceful. Who or what were you hammering away at? The hammer could be a manifestation of your own character – something you want to alter or change. Whatever you were striking could, however, represent the female principle in some way, so think about its significance as well as that of the hammer itself. There is a strong tradition in northern Europe of the hammer as the symbol of power wielded by Thor, for whom it was a sort of boomerang, usefully returning to his hand when thrown at some marauding stranger. If it represents some sort of weapon, it will certainly be a powerful one, if not necessarily physical.

Hand   Our hands are so important that any dream which emphasises them is likely to be important. Not only the dumb speak with their hands: we use them as extensions of our very personalities. On the whole, they have always been images of good: the means of rejecting the negative and embracing the positive. But the way in which we hold them is also significant: hands folded across the chest suggest resignation, peace (even the peace of death); a clenched fist represents passion (perhaps sexual) and protest. But we do not only lift our hands in anger – we lift them in surrender; clasped hands suggest a joining together of two people, or ideas. We cover our eyes to shut out evil, or in shame. We stretch out our hands to bless, but also to curse. We 'sit on our hands' to withhold applause, to prevent ourselves acting or to show others we don't intend to act! So think of the posture of your hands and what that may mean; then relate it to the context of the dream. Who else was in it? If no one, then what were you expressing to *yourself* by the way you held your hands? Were you blessing some enterprise of your own, or is your psyche protesting at some rash decision? Note also which hand was prominent in your dream: the right hand (even, oddly, for left-handed people) is the hand of action and strength; the left hand is more receptive – but also (perhaps because of the silly but pervasive symbolic significance of left-handedness as unusual and therefore sinister) suggests immorality, deceitfulness, dishonesty.

Hat 'The hat,' said Freud in one of his less sensible moments, 'is *always* a phallic symbol.' Well, almost anything no doubt *could* be a phallic symbol; but a hat seems much more likely to be a symbol of authority, these days of a perhaps rather old-fashioned paternalistic authority. For centuries a hat marked out a man of power; bare-headedness, on the contrary, was on the whole a sign of subjugation. Your dream may well bear such a reference. Similarly, to take off your hat is still a sign of admiration and respect: so whether you were doffing yours, or someone was saluting you, is obviously important. Remember, you may have been paying tribute to an idea rather than a man or woman. Buying or showing off an expensive hat? – self-appraisal?

Head First eliminate any possibility that your dream may have a physical reference – a headache; or perhaps you recently knocked your head. The head has always been the seat of understanding, of rationality, so a dream in which it is prominent may well bear that reference. A severed head may (while perhaps horrid) simply refer to a lack of understanding, probably wilful, of a situation. Was it a big head? If so, is conceit a problem for you or anyone else? Some gods were two-headed, representing choice, but also the beginning and end of life (or a project).

Heart   If the head has always been an important symbol of rational understanding, the heart has always been an equally important symbol of instinctive and emotional understanding. Long before it was recognised as the muscle which drives the blood, it was regarded as the very seat of life itself, in particular the centre of our emotional lives: we 'give our heart away' or experience a 'broken heart'. Such symbols may well appear in dreams; a dream of an open heart operation, for instance (unless you suffer from heart trouble) is likely to refer to the necessity to repair emotional damage or pay attention to an emotional trauma, or more simply that you are ready to open your heart to someone, or some emotion. There is much Christian religious symbolism which even in a largely irreligious age should not be forgotten, for it still holds a powerful place in our subconscious: so do not forget Christ's bleeding heart (sorrow) or the heart shot through with an arrow (repentence).

Heaven   See **Paradise**.

Helmet   Refer to **Hat**; but was this a ceremonial helmet or a practical, protective one? If the latter, which of your arguments is basically unsatisfactory and needs artificial protection? If the former, are you specially proud of something? (Why not a *crown* rather than a helmet? Are you as sure of yourself as all that?) Was it a crash-helmet? – and in what context?

Hero (or **Heroine**)   The traditional hero/heroine was usually an ordinary man or woman roused to heroism by extraordinary events, triumphing over temptation, evil or adverse circumstances more by the power of temperament, personality and natural goodness than by physical prowess (though that was also a part of the process). So if you were a hero in your dream, welcomed by acclamation, over what have you triumphed, or over what *should* you triumph? This may refer to anything from office politics to sexual flirtation. Was the triumph genuine or perhaps only ironic?

Was the hero someone else? If so – hero-worship on your part, or the suggestion that you should emulate him or her?

Hive   See **Bee**. But,if the dream focused on the hive, then it very possibly referred to society and your relationship to it. Recovering *honey* from a hive suggests an interest in money. Did the bees attack you? If so, are your motives sound?

Hole   What sort of hole was it? A damaging hole in some fabric or other obviously suggests a hole in an argument, or in some plan. A hole in the ground has darker connotations, suggesting a trap, even the entrance to the underworld, to Hell (see **Abyss**?). Were you falling into it or entering it purposefully? Was there treasure hidden in it? If so, is courage needed to achieve an aim?

Holly   Christmas? Certainly – and therefore an association with whatever your feelings are about that season: happy, bored, apprehensive, whatever. For the same reason, holly is associated with general pleasure, though it also *pricks*; so maybe a warning that present pleasure may have its prickly side? Remember that Christ was sometimes shown as crowned with holly, but so was Father Christmas.

Honey   See, if applicable, **Bee** and **Hive**. Honey itself is perhaps over-sweet; can you relate it to a present experience or ambition? Are you too sanguine about it, expecting too much? Honey is believed to bring health. In earlier times it was associated with virility, even lust: some religions made honey a forbidden food because of that association. Could there be a comment there? It has also been associated with sweet-talk: someone has 'a honeyed tongue'. Are you promising someone too much, or they you? If you were giving or feeding someone honey (or they you) it sounds probable. but it is also a very *pure* food; look for that association, too.

Hook   A hook can be an instrument of punishment; but more often is used to catch something or pull it towards one. What do you seek, then? How easily did your hook accomplish its purpose? Did the line break? See **Fish**, if relevant. Are you out to 'hook' someone? Or are you 'hooked' on something, or someone?

Horns For untold generations, the idea of horns on a man's head alleged that he was cuckold, and this symbol may by no means be dead yet. But horns were often a symbol of divinity: many ancient gods had horns and they can still represent power, even violence (particularly the horns of the *bull*). Did the horns seem potentially damaging to you, or were you wearing them (and if so, for what purpose?). Are you 'on the horns of a dilemma'? 'The horn' or 'horny' is still sometimes a synonym for the male erection; women should consider this. With men there may be a reference to their virility or fear of impotence.

Horseshoe See **Horse**, if apposite (were you shoeing a horse?). Horseshoes are associated with luck; a dream of losing one may therefore express a very simple emotion. Remember that a horseshoe turned downwards traditionally means bad luck.

House A complex symbol, which can simply represent home and family but which can represent the personality, the psyche, the intellect. To dream (and this is not uncommon) that one is exploring a known house and discovering previously unknown rooms is a classic indication of an expanding mind in search of new ideas. A house damaged in some way suggests psychological damage to the individual; house repairs, the opposite – the repairing of damage already done. On the whole, emotions towards a dream house are likely in waking life to relate to the self, especially if the dream house is one with which the dreamer is or has been closely associated. Revisiting a childhood home may refer to regrets about childhood, or to lost joys.

Ice A symbol of frigidity or of emotional coldness; but when it is melting, of the release of emotion (remember melting ice as the harbinger of Spring). The reference could be to a situation rather than a person: perhaps your feelings about some aspect of your life are changing – you are feeling less rigid, easier, warmer or more forgiving. If the ice was getting thicker or you were trapped in it, your dream could well be suggesting that your emotions are blocked or that your behaviour is cold. Was the suggestion that you are brittle or cold hearted? Remember, whatever your conclusions, most ice isn't permanent – it melts with the Sun; you could certainly instigate a thaw. This could be signalled by sunshine or bright daylight in your dream.

Icon If the symbol isn't religious (and this will depend on your attitude to religion) it will probably refer to some important spiritual aspect of your life, commenting on your attitude to spiritual matters and perhaps encouraging you to concentrate on them and on the more esoteric aspects of life. The icon, in religious symbolism, marks the boundary between the sacred and the profane, and in focusing attention on it your dream may seek to help you transfer your attention from the sterility of day to day problems and living into other purer and more rewarding realms of belief, thought and attitude. Think about the face on the icon – was it that of some saintly person with whom you identify, or perhaps love? Your father? Was the expression stern or kind? Do you need to do some 'soul-searching' at present?

Idol Your dream idol is probably making a statement about someone or something that you idolise in some way. But there could be an element of mistrust here, for idols can let us down – they may not be exactly what they seem. So was your dream warning you that you are pinning too much faith, trust or love to someone who, in the final analysis, may not be worth it? Perhaps your dream idol was a film actor or pop star (and see **Hero**) – if so, and the dream was pleasant, there could have been an element of wish-fulfilment (hopefully you enjoyed the experience!). But it might be advisable to consider whether the dream was suggesting caution.

Illness While it is unnecessary to be frightened by a dream of illness, it is always advisable to check with your doctor if in the dream you yourself were ill, or if any specific area of your body was distressed. The unconscious is capable of realising that something is wrong well before we are consciously aware of any negative symptoms, so it is obviously sensible to act on your dream so that should anything be wrong early treatment can correct it. Modern doctors are aware of this, so do not fear ridicule. Should another person have been ill in your dream, you must consider what he or she represents to you, and try to see the connection to yourself, maybe some characteristic in them which you are marking in yourself, and which is in some way 'sick'.

Incense If there is a religious connotation, a dream in which you are swinging the censor may suggest that you should concentrate more on the nature of your belief; but there is the possibility that the dream has something to do with your resistance to 'evil' – this was one of the purposes of incense. Was the incense positively Christian? Many people now burn joss-sticks merely for their odour, in which case, are you trying to disguise a 'bad smell' – not necessarily physical?

Incest Dreams are messages from ourselves to ourselves – you must know this if you have read other chapters of this book. If your dream disgusted or distressed you, remember that no one else is inflicting this distress upon you: it is rooted within your nature, and you can deal with it provided you understand it. Traditionally, incest (though condemned in some societies) was connected with refinement. The Pharoahs, for instance, considered that it maintained and increased their power, spiritual and intellectual as well as physical; your dream may not be purely a sexual one, though it may be saying something about your relationship with your parent or child. Needless to say, if you are deeply concerned about this dream, and certainly if it regularly recurs, you should seek professional help in dealing with it.

Income The dream focus on your income is probably making some kind of statement about your security – perhaps financial but possibly emotional (see **Money**) – referring specifically to what you are getting out of a relationship, or your emotional life in general: if you were bankrupt in your dream, the inference is obvious; if you were frittering away your income, are you spending your emotions too freely, without yourself benefiting?

Incubus An incubus is a masculine spirit which, impersonating a man, makes love to women in their sleep; as a result, demons are born. At least, that was the common belief in the Middle Ages. A female spirit which similarly visits a man was known as a *succubus*. Today, dreaming that someone is making love to one is simply a means of sexual relief; the identity of the person concerned is most likely to be the result of wish-fulfilment – unless rape is concerned, or a positively unpleasant sexual relationship, in which case a warning of some kind may be involved.

Infant   Dreaming of a young child or baby suggests many possible interpretations. If we think of the helplessness of the young child and its dependence on older people, the dream could be making a simple statement about your present feelings. Perhaps you very much want to have a child and the dream is the result of wish-fulfilment; but otherwise the child could represent some new talent or idea that needs nurturing and developing. You may be longing, maybe more than you consciously realise, to develop something that will grow and become important to you. Perhaps your dream infant was someone you know who, in your dream, was a child again. If so, can you see any possible identification with that person's behaviour (being childish perhaps) and your own?

Injection   Your dream injection may well have sexual connotations – the Freudians would undoubtedly suggest that, and not without reason. But your attitude and reaction to it – and whatever you were being injected with, or protected against – is obviously most important. Maybe the dream was making some kind of statement about your attitude to drugs? If so, are you leaning towards escapism at present? Perhaps you need some kind of injection in your waking life – of liveliness, energy or the will to get on with life in a more rewarding and positive way.

Injury   The dream may well be commenting on your present state – maybe someone has hurt you, physically or emotionally. Or have you hurt someone else? Could your dream be warning you that you are hurting someone, or about to do so? But the type of injury may be important, too. Have you been 'stabbed in the back', for instance?

Ink   Usually ink is either black or at least very dark, and often very dark colours represent a tendency to depression and negativity of outlook, so that your dream ink may be making a statement about your present feelings. But perhaps you are trying to forget about something – to blot it out of your life, or to cover it up. Symbolically there is a connection between ink and potential; were you keen to write or draw in your dream? Perhaps you have some latent potential that needs development. And what of invisible ink? Are you keeping a secret at present or are you fearful of someone finding out something about you? If the ink was coloured, see **Colour**?

Insects Some are frightening, some are hardworking (ants, for instance). Most are, in their own way, very determined and active creatures, whose survival rate is remarkable. Can you identify with your particular dream insect? Were you stung or bitten? If so, your dream insect may represent someone at least hostile to you, at worst an enemy. Perhaps there were swarms of insects in your dream and you were among them – do you think that, crowd-like, they represented problems, or that you are simply going along with what everyone else is saying or doing?

Insult Did you feel angry or hurt in your dream? It is important to decide whether the dream insult was encouraging you to be bold or warning you against a line of action which could hurt someone else. But the symbol may have been summing up present feelings which result from another person's attitude towards you.

Invalid See **Illness**. Your dream invalid may represent yourself; or perhaps our unconscious is noting some subtle sign that something is wrong with the person in the dream, in which case you might tactfully enquire whether they are entirely well, or need a check-up of some kind. But perhaps the dream invalid represented some task or hobby which is not going well and needs more attention? There may be a clue elsewhere in the dream, or you could ask (see p. 45–6) for further explanation. Could there be some area of your life that is 'dying', or conversely 'getting better'.

Invisibility If, in your dream, you were invisible, the symbol could well be reflecting a deep-rooted need not to be noticed or the desire to conceal something, maybe some aspect of your personality. If you disliked being invisible, perhaps you are seeking attention or are disappointed that you, or some plan of yours, are in some way being discounted or ignored.

Iron Iron is hard, strong and long-lasting; but we must not forget that it is prone to rust. It can be made into warlike weapons or ploughshares. Fetters and chains are of iron, but we need a certain amount of iron to keep our blood in good order. So was iron giving you support of some kind, representing psychological or physical strength? Are you burdened down by restricting chains? Should you break free? Perhaps your dream was suggesting that you take up arms or do battle? Is something gnawing away – at your security, for instance? This could be so if, for instance, you found rust on your iron. Was the dream a pun on a very great deal of ironing you may have to do? If you were using an iron in your dream, are you trying to smooth out problems, which may have been represented by creases in the fabric you were ironing?

Island Symbolically, an island represents isolation and loneliness; islands are surrounded by *water*, which is almost always symbolic of emotion. So there seems a strong suggestion that you are in some way isolated emotionally; you are standing above your emotions, or feel in some way isolated and even trapped by them. But an island can also save you from the water and if you swam to it, or were wrecked upon it, you may need some kind of refuge from an over-emotional situation. What you have to decide is whether you merely put a message in a bottle and wait to be rescued, or construct a raft and try to subdue the sea of emotion, accepting it and using it as a means of escape, or perhaps a return to reality. A dream of an idyllic dream island may simply be a matter of wish-fulfilment. Perhaps you need a good, relaxing holiday.

Jar Like all containers, a jar is a feminine symbol, and the Freudian implication that this may be a sexual dream should be heeded. Were you pouring something from a jar? If you are a woman, are you giving yourself to someone (not necessarily in the sexual sense)? And remember Aquarius, the water-carrier, in the Zodiac. Could there be an association with an Aquarian? Were you hoarding something, and if so, what? Admiring a jar as an object may suggest admiration of a particular woman: look for the association.

Jaw As with other anatomical dreams, there may be a physical association, or indeed a punning one: have you been giving someone 'too much jaw'? A monster's jaws can symbolise attack – by whom, or what? Look for other clues.

Jealousy   As with all dreams of abstract emotion, this may be entirely literal, along the lines of wish-fulfilment, simply transferring a waking emotion into dream form, or maybe showing you an emotion of which your waking self is not aware. If someone is jealous of you, remember that s/he could represent you, yourself. If so you should consider whether you are making enough of the attribute of which your dream admirer was jealous.

Jewels   Riches of any kind, in dreams, should not be taken literally: they more often than not represent emotional, intellectual or spiritual riches, and you should look for the connection: lost jewels may represent forgetfulness of the true value of things; seeking jewels may mean that you need to find yourself, or something of yourself. But look too at the jewels themselves, and keep in mind their traditional meanings:

   agate   symbolises bravery, virility, health, peace.
   amethyst   symbolises humility.
   aquamarine   symbolises youth and hope.
   beryl   symbolises married love.
   bloodstone   symbolises understanding.
   cat's-eye   symbolises long life.
   diamond   symbolises life itself, eternity, innocence.
   emerald   symbolises faithfulness, hope, immortality.
   garnet   symbolises loyalty.
   jade   symbolises excellence.
   jet   symbolises mourning.
   lapis lazuli   symbolises success.
   moonstone   symbolises tenderness and love.
   opal   symbolises faithfulness.
   pearl   symbolises femininity, chastity.
   ruby   symbolises passion, power.
   sapphire   symbolises truth.
   sardonyx   symbolises honour, vivaciousness.
   topaz   symbolises friendship.
   turquoise   symbolises courage.
   zircon   symbolises wisdom.

Though many people are not aware of these definitions, the unconscious does sometimes, remarkably, make the association.

Journey A journey may well symbolise life itself, or part of it. In ancient legends the adventures of heros – the Odyssey, for instance, or the adventures of Ulysses, to say nothing of the many fairy stories and legends – represented the life of man, the difficulties he must overcome to reach the next life with a satisfactory reputation. So try to relate your dream journey to your life, and any incidents in it to particular incidents in your waking days, weeks, months. If you found yourself at a *crossroads*, for instance, this will almost certainly be a reference to some decision you must make. Note anyone who accompanied you, or who you encountered, and the part they played in the dream.

Judge Were you the judge or the judged: and who were you judging or who was judging you? This may be a dream about a specific person whose opinion is important to you or of someone on whom you wish to impose your will, if not by persuasion then by 'laying down the law'. There could be a reference to some 'crime' you have committed – which may be a crime only in your own mind; in other words, are you feeling guilty about something? If you were judged to be innocent, then maybe you are worrying unnecessarily. A guilty verdict should persuade you to think again. Wish-fulfilment could be involved: was your vegetable marrow judged to be the Best in Show?

Juggling A juggler keeps a good many balls, sometimes too many, in the air at the same time. How does this refer to your present waking life? What do the balls represent? Have you simply taken on too much? Are you trying, in waking life, to juggle your finances? Was your juggling act successful or not? Jugglers are associated somewhat with a certain trickiness: they are too clever by half. And you? This may be the implied comment.

Jumping Over what? Successfully, or did you fall? What obstacle must you surmount in your waking life? Or were you jumping for joy? Again, look for the association.

Jungle A jungle is quite different from a *wood*; for most people, it is somewhat forbidding – dark, almost impenetrable, full of strange sounds and probably strange and dangerous animals or men. Your state of mind will be important: if you were confident, then your dream will be encouraging you to stride purposefully through whatever waking jungle confronts you – thickets of difficulty, or tribes of antagonistic competitors. If you were terrified, then the waking prospect probably frightens you, and perhaps should do so. The incidents in the dream will also be important, and will suggest to what waking events the dream refers. If you were entirely happy, enjoying the discovery of new sounds, scents, trees and animals, then you are perhaps enjoying – or, certainly, should enjoy – exploring new experiences in your waking life. See **Wood**? But in general if you wake thinking jungle, then the inference will be quite different.

Jury   Much depends on whether you were judging or being judged (and see, perhaps, **Judge**, above). A jury however is probably more likely to represent public opinion than your own conscience. If you were a member of it, then you are perhaps concerned that you should seem a regular member of society, or even (if you were foreman) the leader of it. Your dream may be questioning whether you should not be more individual (especially if you were of a minority opinion). Found guilty by a jury, you are in some way making a stand against public opinion; remember that juries have been known to make mistakes – your unconscious seems likely to be prompting you at least to reconsider.

Key   The function of a key is to unlock a door: to let you in, or let you out? Are you looking for the key which will solve some problem and release you from a particular situation? – or are you looking for the key which will let you into the heart of a problem, or indeed into someone's heart? The search for a key and the use to which you put it is significant; and what you did with it when you found it. If it was lost, perhaps you have not really realised that a simple solution to a waking problem exists. A key can often be a phallic symbol, as any thought of its purpose must suggest. See **Lock**?

Killing   Who or what were you killing? – and what does it symbolise? Look for a connection. Is there an instinct, a behavioural trait, which you wish to kill in yourself? As always, if another person is involved, he or she may be your shadow (see p. 37); look for the trait in him or her which you wish to kill in yourself. Murder as a simple expression of waking dislike of someone else is unlikely: it is much more likely that the reference is to some aspect of your own personality.

King See **Royalty**.

Kiss To dream of kissing or being kissed may be a matter of wish-fulfilment, but there are other implications. Judas betrayed with a kiss, after all, and even if you are not a Christian that symbolism is still potent. More generally, however, the kiss is a sign of goodwill; the Pope kissing the ground of a country he is visiting, or heads of state greeting each other with a kiss on the cheek. So if the dream does not seem particularly sexual, look for these other implications.

Kitchen We associate a kitchen with creativity – but it is also a place of frenetic activity, displays of temperament, and consider-able heat. So there may be a reference to some activity in which you are engaged in waking life: some contretemps associated with work, or even with your emotional life. Were you unconsciously thinking of Harry Truman's advice – 'If you don't like the heat, get out of the kitchen'? Was the *food* you were producing well-cooked, well-presented and enjoyed? Food is often a symbol for emotion; so are you presenting your case well to someone you need to impress, or want to like or love you?

Kite In medieval times kites were signs of peace: they were flown to signal the conclusion of a treaty or agreement between warring factions. They are also flown at times of celebration and carnival. They seem likely, then, to be positive symbols. But since their flight is so dependent on human guidance, they may also be an extension of yourself and a current preoccupation. So how skilfully were you flying the kite? Were you entirely in control? Were you flying it high and proud, or merely attempting to prevent it from crashing to the ground? Were you, perhaps, the kite, seeking to break away, to be free?

Knee As with any other part of the anatomy there may be a prac-tical reference (to injury or discomfort); but remember bending the knee, as in subjugating yourself to someone. Housemaid's knee suggests that you may be fed up with menial work of some kind.

Knife   A knife is usually a terrifying symbol (most people would rather be shot or hanged than knifed) – and it seems most likely to carry an unpleasant meaning, perhaps of vengeance or of the death-wish. But it can also release you from bonds (the Buddhists would see it in that light). However, the first consideration must be whether you 'have it in' for someone – are you about to stab them in the back (or they you)? Carrying a concealed knife may hint that you, or someone else, is concealing feelings of antipathy. If you are cutting something, what does that something represent? Are you trying to dissect a problem, or merely cut the head off one? Freud insisted that all weapons were phallic symbols, and this possibility should not be dismissed. It is difficult to conceive of a knife as a benevolent phallic symbol, and such a dream seems likely to be reflecting sexual aggression of some kind.

Knight   Classically, the knight represents honour; but in the ancient stories, also a questing spirit. The *horse* (if you were mounted) is also possibly important. If you were the knight, whose honour are you protecting? If a knight was rescuing you, is this wish-fulfilment or do you really see someone as your protector, or wish that he might be? If you were wearing armour, was it restrictive – and if so, against who are you protecting yourself, and is that necessary? Or were arrows and swords glancing off it? In that case, should you rest assured that you are in the right, and that allegations cannot injure you?

Knitting   If you are a woman who commonly does a lot of knitting, the image may stand for your working life in general: so speed, tangles, the dropping of stitches will have a significance in that area – are you in a tangle about something, prone to carelessness, or shaping a beautiful garment which will satisfy you and please others? Knitting, for men, is a more domestic symbol, and may suggest that you feel your partner (if she was the knitter) is too preoccupied with domesticity. Though if you were holding the wool, the suggestion might be of a particularly happy union.

Knock   Someone knocking at the door? Who (what) should you let into your life? Did you knock your head? If so, what needs knocking into it? Or are you thinking of knocking heads together?

Knot   Tying or untying a knot? An intransigent knot could represent an intransigent waking problem; look for hints, in the dream, of how you should approach it. A knot which comes undone beneath your fingers may represent, on the other hand, a problem which is far less difficult than you think. A knot can hold, restrain: does that suggest that you need to hold back in some way? Look for other clues. Remember the pun: 'I do *not* want to do this!'

Label   Labels can be honest – but they can also be dishonest: labelling something in your dream, could you be applying a label to yourself? What did it say on the label? Or were you trying to remove one, disapproving perhaps of the image other people have imposed on you, or which you have been forced in some way to adopt? Were you putting a price on yourself? Warning yourself about someone else?

Laboratory   What is important is what was going on in the laboratory, the sort of work in which you were involved. These are places of exploration, so it is possible that some self-examination is needed, whether of your motivation or your motives. Or were you trying to dissect something, and if so, who or what did it represent? Maybe someone's reputation? Were you making a Frankenstein – creating a monster? What reference could there be to your waking life? Some kind of plot seems likely.

Labyrinth   Labyrinths or mazes played an important part in ancient myth and legend: they have an air of mystery, set a problem, hold out the promise of treasure at their centre – but sometimes also of threat. The most famous labyrinth was that which Theseus explored, with a maiden-eating monster at its heart. Over the centuries, the symbol became an extremely complicated one: a labyrinth could represent the life of man; a mystery few could master – or could simply be a complex game. Again, it could represent a path from which no one could escape, leading in a convoluted way to one central goal – or it could be a puzzle which took wit and immense patience to unravel. A dream of a labyrinth seems most likely to mirror uncertainty and perplexity in waking life – some puzzle which confronts you (it may be one of which you are unconscious: a situation could be much more complicated than you think). Think about your attitude, in the dream: were you confident of finding your way, or merely wandering in complete perplexity? What was at the centre of your maze: were you being forced towards an uncertain or even dreadful fate, or sure that some kind of reward awaited you? Were you trying to break out of a predetermined path, or following it slavishly? Did you carry some kind of a *map*? And if so, was it accurate or misleading? All these attitudes no doubt comment on whatever problem you are facing in your waking life.

Lace   Lace is beautiful but complex: almost like a *web*. A dream that one is lace-making seems likely to refer to some complex task facing one in waking life. So was it going well? Or were you getting in a fearful tangle? If the latter, how did you feel about it? Or were you examining a piece of beautiful lace, handsomely presented? What situation might this have represented? Are you about to get into someone else's problem, trying to 'rescue' them? See **Knitting**?

Ladder   A means of climbing, and therefore of aspiration, of progress – look to your waking life for the aim, whether material or spiritual. In religious symbolism, the ladder progressed from hell to heaven, but this may not be the case for you. We climb a ladder hoping to reach the top, but also often quite fearfully; were you confident, in your dream, or terrified of falling? The dream may be giving you more confidence, or warning you to be careful.

Lake   Lakes are deep, calm, unruffled, in the main; and (see **Water**) this is most likely to be a dream about your emotional life, or about your unconscious itself. Was there something lurking in the depths? A monster, or a female water-spirit are common in the myths of the northern countries. Were you swimming in the lake, or riding on its surface in a boat? Should you take a confident dive, expressing your emotions more deeply? Or are you afraid of them?

Lameness   If not a reference to a physical disability, then perhaps to material progress: is something impeding your strides forward? Are you in some way being prevented from progressing towards a goal? But perhaps you should be more cautious. How you felt about your lameness is obviously important; most likely you were irritated, perhaps ashamed. Should you throw away your (psychological) crutches?

Lamp A dream of a torch or an electric light may suggest a search for something, perhaps the way forward. An oil lamp is a more old-fashioned symbol, and is more likely to have a psychological reference, maybe to the affections. Perhaps you are not clear about them, and how they should be disposed?

Landlord An authority figure. Money being so often associated with emotions, is someone taking from you, emotionally, and giving you mere house-room in exchange? Or do you owe someone an emotional debt? Were you under notice to quit? If you were the landlord, should you be putting up the (emotional) rent to someone in your life? We do not generally love our landlords, so the reference may well be to someone to whom you feel you owe something, emotionally, but with whom your relationship is rather cool. Not an easy dream to untangle, unless there are obvious clues elsewhere.

Language Probably a dream about communication: if you were gabbling away in a foreign language, maybe one you don't actually know in waking life, this can be nothing but a compliment. If you were failing to communicate with someone in their own language, maybe someone you know well, then there is very much an implied criticism. A dream about learning a foreign language is a hint to enlarge your means of communication, perhaps with the human race in general, perhaps with one particular person.

Laughter A specifically funny dream is a relatively rare event; on the other hand most of us have wakened laughing at the apparently ludicrous situations about which we have dreamed. The thing to remember is that however silly a dream seems, it will rarely be entirely meaningless, just a joke. So even a comic dream should be thought about with some care; there may be a serious message there.

Lead Were you being led; if so, by whom? A dream in which your own dog appeared may well be about you; we often identify very thoroughly with our pets. So are you being too easily led in waking life? – if in your dream you were a reluctant dog, then think about the possibility. If you were leading someone else, then consider your attitude to them.

If your dream was of the metal *lead*, the symbolism seems, to coin a phrase, rather heavy; are your spirits as heavy as lead, your outlook leaden? Are you trying to lift a heavy problem, live through a heavy situation? Remember that lead is a base metal, yet is rather valuable. The load may be worth carrying.

Leaf   A new, young leaf is a symbol of birth, fresh ideas; falling leaves represent autumn, an approaching end; they are swept up and burned – so, old ideas being rejected in favour of new, or being cleared away in preparation for something new? Falling leaves may also symbolise regret; young leaves, burgeoning hope.

Leek   An enormous, prize leek? Surely a phallic symbol of generous proportions, and simple wish-fulfilment?

Lemon   Lemons are used in cooking to give zest to a dish, but can sometimes be too bitter, so the interpretation of your dream may depend on your reaction – whether your lips were puckered in horror, or you were welcoming a refreshing tartness. In turn, this may be applied to some waking situation or decision: is it bitter to you, or unusually pleasant? If someone else was reacting to the lemon, then their reaction may be to some action or attitude of yours.

Letter   A means of communication: so, if writing a letter, to whom was it addressed and what was it saying? Perhaps you need to communicate with them in waking life. Receiving a letter from someone else may suggest you need to listen to them more closely, respect their opinion. Opening a letter with pleasure or in horror may relate to your attitude to some recent news, perhaps a mistaken attitude.

Leper   In the past, when leprosy was a fearsome scourge, a leper was an outcast; these days there may be a reference to that symbolism – a feeling that you are set apart in some way, that others fear or dislike you; or if another person is the leper, that in an obscure way you fear or mistrust them. This seems more likely to be a rather unpleasant dream than not – perhaps a warning – though a dream that you were tending a leper may be a suggestion that you should be more tolerant towards someone or some attitude, more likely to be personal then otherwise (unless there were many lepers, in which case the reference may be to society at large).

Library   In some ways this is likely to be rather similar to a dream of a *house* in which there are many rooms; the reference is likely to be to knowledge, and the necessity to extend it; or to new ideas waiting to be explored. Were you searching for a particular book (idea)? If so, did you find it? Try to remember particulars about the book in question; there may be a valuable hint here. If you were dusting books, maybe you need to dust up your ideas. Cataloguing them? Perhaps your notions need to be set in order.

Lie   If you were lying in your dream, look for the parallel in waking life; and the same is true if you were sure someone else was lying to you. Most likely, this will be a warning dream – remember, you may be deceiving *yourself*.

Light   Light represents knowledge, ultimate truth, good as opposed to the darkness of evil – so there is more likely to be a positive meaning than not. It may simply be confirmation that you are on the right track; but only the context of the dream can tell you in what sense. You may have to ask for more clues (see p. 45–6). Are you feeling light-hearted? Have you just successfully completed a diet?

Lightning   A sudden flash of lightning reveals an unsuspected truth: something or someone seen in a lightning flash is instantly made clear, and may represent a situation, an argument, a solution to that argument. What was seen in such a way? And what does that thing symbolise? It is highly likely that the dream is telling you something important, for it presents the picture with considerable drama, and in a manner which is very striking. If you are struck by lightning in a more literal sense this too may be the strongest hint of some kind: maybe a warning, maybe the symbol of a brilliant idea.

Linen   Dirty linen? Were you washing it in public? Hanging clean linen on a line? Did it fall into the mud? We associate linen very strongly with ourselves and our character; so its state probably reflects our current idea of the state of our lives or our psyche. There may be a sexual application, especially if underclothes or bed-linen is concerned (changing the latter? – should you end an affair?).

Litter   Detritus which we drop because we no longer want it or, if we are tidy-minded, which we put in a litter-bin. So uncharacter-istically dropping litter, we may be throwing our emotions about rather too ostentatiously. Carefully hiding it from public view suggests a tidy emotional life. The same notions can be applied to other people throwing their litter about. The nature of the litter may be quite important, of course; what might it represent?

Loaf   See **Bread**.

Lock   The Freudians would claim that a lock is almost always a sexual symbol, and indeed this is quite likely. A man who dreams of picking a lock, or turning his *key* in one, may well be engaging in a wish-fulfilment dream. A woman with the same kind of dream may be dreaming of coitus, or perhaps of losing her virginity; even, if the lock is being forced, of rape. Look for the other person in the dream: to whom does the lock belong? But there may be another interpre-tation: you may be unlocking the door to a new idea, a new phase of life. See **Door?**, **Gate?**

Lotus   A dream of this mysterious and beautiful flower is most likely to occur to someone who is familiar with the eastern religions in which it is particularly significant. Growing out of muddy waters, it represents purity and truth, both birth and death, Nirvana to the Buddhist, perfection to the Chinese, immortality to the Egyptian, spirituality to the Hindu, the heart of man to the Taoists. Those for whom eastern religions are significant should consider the symbol in this way.

Luggage   We carry luggage around as we carry other burdens that we need: so luggage in a dream can refer to our families, but also to the burden of our personality and the various traits of which we may be either proud or ashamed. Lost luggage might suggest that we have in some way lost ourself – or perhaps want to lose ourselves, or some other burden (were you desperately seeking it, or rather pleased that it had gone)? Seeking among other people's luggage for your own may symbolise your quest for a personal identity.

Machinery   The machinery in your dream could be a reference to the condition of your body, which is in essence a machine. So consider the state of your dream machinery: was it well-oiled and performing well or rusty and grinding to a halt? Perhaps you have stiff joints and need more exercise. Or are you coping with too much stress in your life? Is your life at present too routine, too predictable? Are you too caught up in the rat-race? – or a small cog in a big wheel? Maybe you need to open life out, in some way.

Madness   If your behaviour was 'sheer madness', you must decide whether the dream was wish-fulfilment or a timely warning. But it is also necessary to consider whether the dream madness was suggesting that you are under stress or very bored, needing to break away from whatever is holding you back.

Madonna   The symbol will be of greatest importance to Roman Catholics, but generally the Madonna is to be revered and admired. She represents transforming power and is the bearer of light. Your dream woman, whether simply a Madonna-like figure – someone demanding respect – or the Virgin Mary herself, was probably reassuring you. If she gave you guidance and advice, you should heed very carefully what she said, because the message will probably emanate from your feminine, intuitive and instinctive self, and it seems likely that 'deep down' you know that she is right.

Magic   Magic can represent transformation or trickery. If the former, were you amazed at what happened in your dream? If so, perhaps you are about to be transformed in some way. Is this what you wish? Or were you watching some clever, crafty conjurer, and were taken in by his actions? In that case, the dream could be a warning, or a summing-up of your own present behaviour.

Man   Masculine, assertive action – the *anima*. Was your man bold and noble, aggressive and violent, kind, protective or benevolent? Presumably you did not recognise him as someone you know: he was just a masculine figure. Whether you are a male or female it is possible that your dream man represented the masculine side of your personality. You could be receiving encouragement to express this more positively, or a warning that it is too dominant. In the broadest terms, you should consider whether the dream was relating to the Family of Man – to your place in it, and the contribution you are making to the good of mankind. You may need to think in this context, and take some kind of action along these lines. See **Old Man**?

Mandala   A mandala was originally a mythical symbol of the universe, a circle enclosing a square, sometimes with a figure at its centre. In psychological terms it represents the whole man or woman, the soul on its pilgrimage towards completeness. Hindu temples are built on this pattern, and the mandala has great symbolic meaning for Buddhists. It may be difficult to recognise a mandala in your dreams, but basically the appearance of a circle or square, containing something, should be noted. A dream mandala probably represents security – if you were enclosed in it, this need not represent imprisonment of any kind; it is usually a reassuring symbol, suggesting that you are at one with youself and on your way to achieving psychological wholeness. It would be rewarding to recall your mandala in a drawing or painting: the action of doing so will centre you, and the inner meaning of the symbol, which will be very personal to you, should reveal itself with greater clarity.

Maniac   A warning: are you over-reacting in some way? Or repressing some emotion which needs to be released? Is there some imbalance in your life (not necessarily psychological)? See **Madness**?

Map   Maybe you are making plans, in your waking life, and your dream map was subtly showing you the way (what was it a map of? were you able to read it properly?). Or are you uncertain and lost (was the map confusing rather than helpful?). Do you need direction in life?

Market   Your dream market might suggest that you have a variety of choices in your waking life – so how decisive you were, whether you made purchases or not, could well have a bearing on your attitude. If the market was crowded, consider too how others behaved – the atmosphere is probably significant, as was your mood in the dream, i.e., positive, fearful, happy or wary. See **Money**: were you spending freely? Remember the connection between spending money and spending emotion. See **Shopping?**

Marriage   Most obviously, this could have been a statement about a current relationship. But perhaps two areas of your life are coming together, for here is a symbol of joining, of combination. Marriage was sometimes symbolically seen as the joining of opposites, and in some cultures symbolised the marriage of earth and sky – in Egypt the bull which represented the masculine principle and the cow which represented the female. If you were getting married, are you about to make a serious commitment of some kind (not necessarily emotional or sexual)? If you are single and long to be married, the dream, while hopefully enjoyable, was more than likely wish-fulfilment.

Mask   A mask is worn as a disguise, sometimes for fun but sometimes very seriously. Sometimes too it has been worn as a protection against discovery (the highwayman's mask, for instance). Much will depend on your motive, in the dream, for wearing the mask – or someone else's motive for being masked. Note, too, the kind of mask you were wearing: had it a face? – perhaps an animal face? If so, what sort of *animal*? It might suggest that you are in some way pretending an emotion you do not feel, or hiding your true feelings. You may need to unmask in some way, to be yourself.

Massage   The most obvious suggestion is that you feel a need for physical human contact, which recent research has shown to be important to health. It may also have suggested that you need to relax a little more. Or was it referring to some area of your body which may need cosseting? It would certainly not hurt you to consider having a series of massage treatments.

Match   Striking a match could relate to a sudden passion – was your dream match a phallic symbol? It could also represent enthusiasm. But were you matchmaking in your dream? Or are you, in real life? There could be a pun here. Perhaps you have just matched two garments, or some colours.

Mattress: A mattress is lain on: and it is entirely possible that there may be a reference to some feeling that you are being used, subjugated, in your waking life. A dream of turning a mattress may refer to the desirability of your turning your life about in some way, showing a new side of your personality, perhaps. A broken-down, uncomfortable mattress (provided you are not actually sleeping on one!) may refer to something which is simply making life uncomfortable for you (not necessarily physically).

Maypole   For the Freudians, so obviously a phallic symbol that it scarcely needs saying: and moreover a celebration – so, whether you are a man or a woman, you may simply be enjoying yourself sexually. Was there one prominent person dancing around the maypole? But traditionally the maypole represented the Tree of Life (a phallic reference, again) – there used to be a disc at the top of each maypole, which represented Woman. It is associated with spring and rebirth: there could be a reference here.

Maze   See **Labyrinth**.

Mermaid   A mythical woman with something special about her. The presence, or reference to, the *sea* and *water* suggests that your emotions are much engaged. A mermaid is fish below the waist: is there a reference to coldness, frigidity? If you are a woman, and were the mermaid, this is something to think about. If you are a man, this may be a dream of rejection and regret.

Message   A hint, probably, that someone is trying to 'get through to you' – or that your unconscious has an important message. So keep eyes and ears open; if nothing occurs to you, ask your dreams (see p. 45–6) for further elucidation.

Microscope   An instrument for looking at detail, for seeing what cannot be seen by the naked eye, and so quite possibly a hint that you are missing something, somewhere: look to the context of the dream for a suggestion as to which area this might refer to (what was under the microscope – is there a connection with someone you know? – was it at home or at your office, and thus a connection with domestic or work conditions). See **Laboratory**?

Milk   One of the basic foods and therefore representing something which we need and must have in order to survive, physically or psychologically. In most societies, milk has been a symbol of divine food; so there may be a reference to a deep-seated spiritual need. If you are a woman and were giving milk, feeding a child, there could be a reference in wish-fulfilment to an unborn child, an early signal that you are pregnant. But perhaps you need to feed and nurture a new idea, give more attention to a new situation, a new job.

Millstone   Millstones not now being common, there is probably an echo of the Biblical text about the punishment of those who offend against children. Could this be a reference to your treatment of your own children? Millstones also 'grind exceeding small': should you look at something in extreme detail? Have you a millstone round your neck? – some heavy burden you could well do without?

Mirror   A potent image for all sorts of reasons, but mainly because in it, you see yourself; and the kind of reflection you see is vital. Were you particularly ugly, or particularly handsome? Pleased with yourself, or conscious that you are not quite at your best? Things are reversed in mirrors: a reference to something which is topsy-turvy, and needs turning the right way up? Are you presenting an inaccurate picture to the world? The Chinese philosophers held that if one saw one's true reflection, the evil in one's soul would be killed by the horror of the vision. Those who sold their souls to the Devil had no reflection. Were you climbing, like Alice, through the mirror? – and if so, have you perhaps the wrong slant, at the moment, on the world around you? Mirrors, apart from their reversal of the picture, tell the truth – cannot be deceived; the ancients gazed into them hoping to see a vision of the eternal. Are you looking for something better than your present condition, physically or psychologically?

Miscarriage   Not necessarily a warning, or even an unpleasant dream, though if you are pregnant it could simply reflect a fear (*not* by any means a prediction!). But there could be a reference to a scheme, or even a letter or parcel, that has miscarried.

Misery   One can sometimes have a dream in which one is miserable, without good reason; and such dreams can cloud a whole day. Unless something is making you miserable in real life, an unfocused dream of this sort may be a steadying influence of some kind, especially if life is particularly good at present. But if it is really worrying, be brave enough to ask your dreams (see p. 45–6) to focus up and tell you more.

Mist   Mist suggests the inability to see clearly; so perhaps you are unable to see the consequences of present circumstances or actions, or are simply confused about them. The context should refer you to the meaning and purpose of the dream.

Mistletoe   Wish-fulfilment? Quite possibly. But remember that though it is now almost exclusively regarded as an invitation to a kiss (or, who knows, something more: so who was under the mistletoe, or approaching you as you stood beneath it; and were your/their attentions welcome?), traditionally mistletoe (the Golden Bough of the ancients) stood for the female principle in life, just as the oak stood for the male; there may, even now, be a recognisable allusion there.

Mockery   Don't lose sight of the fact that your dream may be mocking *you*, even if in the person of someone else. Mockery is not a particularly pleasant form of expressing emotion, so there may be a warning here.

Model   A model is a representation in miniature; so it may either be scaling down a problem, or trying to simplify one in order to suggest the solution. Model-making is a painstaking occupation: is there a suggestion that you need to take more care about something? If the model was human, then there may be a suggestion of vanity, of showing-off (if you were the model) – or that you need to smarten up your image (if you were admiring a model). For young people, dreaming of being a model may be a form of wish-fulfilment.

Monastery   An exclusively male preserve, a place where the emotions are strictly under control and sexuality is severely restrained. So: a suggestion that it is a time to examine your sexual life, or perhaps merely to enquire whether you may not need to withdraw somewhat from society and devote a little time to self-examination and thought. If you were aching to escape from the monastery, the opposite is true. For a woman, dreaming of a monastery may suggest that you want to regard men as friends rather than sexual partners; or, if an individual is concerned, there may be a comment about him and your attitude to him. And see **Monk**?

Money An important symbol and like most dream symbols the obvious interpretation is by no means always the one to go for. It is very often the case that money equates with emotion: in waking life people who are very concerned with worldly wealth, and are over-careful about spending it, find it equally difficult to give their emotions generously; it is even sometimes true that there are sexual problems – frigidity in women, impotence in men (it is no mere coincidence that one of the synonyms for male ejaculation is to *spend*). So think very carefully about your attitude to money in your dream, what you were doing with it, who you were spending it on and with what attitude or object; then look to your emotional relationships or your attitude to your emotional life, and try to draw the moral. Very often there will be a parallel.

It is possible that waking worry about finances may be at the root of your dream; it may have been advising you about a financial problem, or even pointing you in the direction of a good invest-ment. It has been known. But nine times out of ten there seems to be an emotional reference.

Monk A monk seems largely a figure of mystery, someone separate from common humanity; dreaming of yourself as a monk may well suggest that you need to withdraw and look at your life, your motives, your morality. Someone else as a monk? – were you admiring, reverential, scornful, envious? The relationship may be a rather important one. See **Monastery**?

Monster Monsters, often not very clearly delineated, usually appear in nightmares (see p. 49). The important thing to do is face them, even invite them into subsequent dreams and ask them to show themselves openly; to get to know them, to make them your friends. Like problems in waking life, when looked full in the face they often seem far less frightening than if you allow them to skulk in the shadows. So be courageous, and try not to allow irrational fear to rob you of sleep. Remember that this is *your* monster. Consider what, within your mind, your character, your perso-nality, is as frightening as the thing which haunts your dream. There is certainly something, for no one is forcing you to dream this – or any other – dream. Your unconscious is presenting you with a view of this monster, and if you work out the reason why, it may well turn into a cuddly toy! Free association might be the answer: take a pencil and scribble down the first half-dozen words or so that come to mind when you think about your dream monster, or draw him. Wipe out the motive for his appearance, and all will be well. Sometimes merely recognising the motive is enough.

Moon   The moon has always been a very potent symbol for human- ity, partly because of its overwhelming presence in the night sky – only the sun was more remarkable to primitive man; and the moon was more approachable – one could look it in the face. Yet it seemed also more mysterious, sometimes veiled in cloud, waxing and waning, affecting the tides and women's menstrual cycle. Unsur- prisingly it became strongly associated with femininity, while the sun remained robustly masculine (though there are were a few exceptions: the Japanese and the Maori people regarded the moon as potently male, and associated it with fertilisation). Its mystery has always been stressed: it has represented magic, witchcraft, destiny, the intuition. In astrology the moon is associated with instinct, emotion, birth, response, the memory, one's ancestors, suggesting someone both imaginative and moody, patient and unreliable, shrewd and with weak reasoning powers. So even if your dream is merely of a beautiful, moonlit walk, there are probably other ramifications. Look carefully at the other symbols in the dream, consider your emotions in the dream and any waking emotional problems; and consult the dreams of the night before and the night after this one. The symbolism is likely to be diffuse, but at the same time important; you may have to ask (see p. 45–6) for further help.

Mother   Dreams of parents (see **Father**) are always important. At the simplest level this dream may relate to your feelings about your mother. A dream of a deceased parent may be a reassuring 'mes- sage': you can take it as a confirmation of immortality, or of your parent's continued life within your own mind and memory, accord- ing to your convictions about death. On the other hand, we must remember that from the very earliest times the figure of the Mother has stood for the female principle itself, at its most basic: from the Mother of God (see **Madonna**) to Isis, Hathor, Lakshmi, Parvati and Demeter she has been a reassuring and loving figure – yet in other guises a figure of fear and punishment: Astarte, Kali, Lilith and Hecate. Many other symbols surround and represent her, as other entries in this section suggest: the *Moon* and the crown of *stars*, the colour *blue*, *caves* and *wells*, the *lotus*, all hollow vessels. So, with this plethora of references, this is likely to be an extremely difficult and complex dream to unravel unless, thinking of your mother herself and your relationship with her, the meaning is immediately obvious to you. You may well have to look at other dreams in series – those of the night before, the night after, or even several more – for elucidation; or you could (see p. 45–6) ask for further symbols in the hope of clarification. Do not be concerned or anxious if, in your dream, you are expressing dislike for your mother, or she appears in some threatening guise. In all human relationships there is pleasure and pain, love and what can sometimes almost amount to hatred. It is the balance that is important; your dream may be an attempt to help you attain or keep that balance.

Mountain Mountains have always awed man. Moses descended from the mountain with the Tablets of the Law, the Greek gods lived on Mount Olympus, temples were often built as representations of mountains. If you were mountaineering, towards what were you climbing? Some spiritual or psychological goal? Though the climb could represent some entirely material waking ambition, this is perhaps less likely than a reference to some less corporeal goal. Was the climb easy, or were there obstacles: and what sort of obstacles? If you surmounted them, there is obvious encouragement to you to surmount waking obstacles too. Descending a mountain, perhaps skiing or tobogganing, suggests an easy ride. This may be wish-fulfilment, or the suggestion that you are having a free run at the moment, and need not fear to enjoy it.

Mourning It is important to decide what the person you were mourning represents to you. If this was unclear, your dream may well be summing up present feelings of depression, sadness that the past is not the present, or a wish that elements of your life hadn't changed.

Mouth It may be that your dream was telling you that you have been speaking up rather too vehemently, or perhaps you are down in the mouth about something. But it is always worth remembering that any dream about a specific area of our bodies can be a warning of some disorder, so it might be as well to get a medical check-up, or a dental examination. On another level this dream of your mouth could be connected with snoring (did you wake up with an extremely dry mouth and throat?). But there may have been a statement about your sexuality: the mouth in your dream may have represented a vagina. In which case were you putting anything in your mouth?

Mud It may be that you are being dragged through the mud at present; is your name mud? But perhaps you feel that life is particularly heavy going and that you are not making any progress. Perhaps you were searching for something in the mud; if so, what? – the item or what it represents could be very important. The mud, especially if it was particularly black or murky, may well be making a statement about your present state of mind and suggesting that you are depressed. Consider, too, your self-esteem, which may be rather low; perhaps you do not like yourself very much.

Murder If you were committing the murder it seems likely that there is an element of your life, or perhaps a characteristic or personality trait, you want to eradicate. Jealousy, perhaps? You will get a clue from the identity of the victim. Remember that even if you were witnessing the murder, you would still be the murderer. Your attitude to the incident is also extremely important – if you were fearful is there something you are afraid of facing up to in waking life? If you were brave and tried to prevent the murder, was your dream telling you to be brave and assertive? Perhaps you were very angry before you went to bed, and metaphorically wanted to kill someone or something. See **Killing**?

Museum Your dream museum probably represented the past – maybe some elements of your own personal past. What you were looking at, and how you felt about it, will be important. Perhaps you are in a rather nostalgic mood at present (were there toys on display?). Did what you saw fill you with horror? Did you simply long to own the exhibits or to steal them? Were you unable to reach what you desired?

Music See **Orchestra**, or if you were performing on a musical instrument, **Actor**.

Nail   Were you attempting to hammer a nail home? If so, perhaps you are in waking life trying desperately hard to make some point or to express your opinions or desires to other people. The nail could have been a phallic symbol, making a statement about your sexuality (men) or your attitude towards the penis (women). Perhaps you broke or tore your finger-nail: if so, the dream could well be a statement about your self-esteem. Did you bite your nails in your dream? If so perhaps you are feeling tense in real life. On the other hand if in waking life you bite your nails, do you think your dream was encouraging you to stop doing so? Were you varnishing them in your dream? Are you trying to cover up or disguise something – have you been deceptive recently?

Nakedness   See **Nudity**.

Navel   The human navel was anciently seen as a symbol of the 'cosmic centre', the centre of the Universe. It may be that your dream was representing your attitude not only to yourself in relation to the Universe, but also concentrating on your psychological wholeness. You may find it interesting and revealing to refer to **Mandala**, which represents a similar symbolism. You may be in a somewhat contemplative mood at present, or your unconscious is suggesting that you should become meditative and less materialisic.

Necklace   This on the whole is a very positive symbol. If someone was giving you a necklace, the chances are that you felt pretty good about it in your dream, so it seems to follow that your self-esteem is high – that either you are giving yourself well-earned praise, or others are doing so; the necklace, rather like a *crown*, is an accolade. But is there something you really desire and are striving for? Your dream necklace might represent that: you need more money perhaps, or is there an element of wish-fulfilment in your dream?

Needle   See **Pin**; a dream needle should be considered in much the same way, unless you 'have the needle' about something. If you were *sewing*, then consult that entry, but consider carefully whether the focus was on the needle or the actual work you were doing. See, if relevant, **Prick**.

Neighbours   Your dream neighbours may well represent some problem which may be too close for comfort. Was it warning you about your reaction to such a situation? If you were quarrelling with your neighbours in your dream it may be that in some respects you are at odds with yourself, trying to resolve some deep-rooted psychological problem. You may need to ask your dreams for greater clarification. But perhaps you are a fan of the soap-opera *Neighbours*, and identify with one of its characters. If so ask yourself what could prompt your unconscious to quote, as it were, from that character: most soap opera characters are archetypes.

Nest   The dream may well be making a statement about your emotional or physical security, suggesting that you should 'feather your nest' (i.e., make provision for the future and add to your creature comforts) or even 'fly the nest', if you are young and ready to leave home. Your emotional security, your relationship with and attitude to your partner, for instance, may be in question.

Net   This is a symbol of ensnarement or entanglement, often with emotional and/or sexual connotations. Were you caught up in a net, or casting it? Here is surely a statement about your present waking situation. Perhaps you are plotting something? – if so the dream could be warning you that you might be about to be trapped by your own machinations.

Newspaper   If you were reading a newspaper your dream could be suggesting that you are out of touch in some way. This could be a 'message' dream in which your unconscious is trying to point out something to you. A great deal will depend on your attitude towards newspapers in real life. Perhaps you enjoy them for the gossip, perhaps you take them seriously, perhaps you merely think of them as trash. What you actually read or saw in the paper is extremely relevant, if you remember it.

Night   If your dream night was very dark and you were trying to find your way – almost as though you were in a wartime blackout – it may be that this symbol is summing up feelings of depression or loss of direction, even hopelessness, which are troubling you in your waking life. You may be trying to hide from a problem, or even from elements of your own personality which you may not altogether like. But maybe your dream was marvellously romantic – it was a clear *starry* night with a full *moon*, and you felt good in your dream. Such symbols represent hope and contentment, perhaps romance, a suggestion that you are achieving psychological wholeness.

Noise Provided it wasn't prompted by some external noise, and there is no indication of trouble with your hearing, a dream of some persistent and unpleasant noise might indicate that you are suffering from stress or tension. If your dream noise was shouting and you were joining in and helping to make a din, have you something to shout about? Was your dream suggesting that you are not being assertive enough?

Nudity This is an extremely common dream symbol which all too often is glibly interpreted as having sexual overtones. While this is a possibility not to be ignored, it is by no means the only one. A great deal depends on how you felt in your dream. Were you simply showing off your body? Or were people laughing at you? Did you feel ashamed? If so, how do you feel about your body in waking life? Could you be in better shape? There could simply be an encouragement to diet or exercise. Revealing yourself quite naturally, without either pride or shame, could be a suggestion that you should be more frank and open with others. Who else was in your dream; what was the context? Perhaps you are ready to strip off layers of your personality – old inhibitions, habits, opinions – that you feel are outmoded or that you have outgrown. Extreme anxiety about being naked could relate to your desire (we all have it) to keep certain aspects of your personality, your self, concealed; the dream may reflect some anxiety about being 'exposed' in some way. This is equally, perhaps specially, true of the classic dream in which we find ourselves naked in a public place – though this may relate to a certain nervousness we feel about our relationship with other people, with strangers; a hint that we should be more open and relaxed. There could even be a simple allusion to your clothes – perhaps you need to throw out, or cast off, outmoded garments, and create a new and more fashionable image. If the dream does seem to you to be sexual (and if your instinct tells you that this was so, believe it), there may be a suggestion that you are less free and relaxed with your lover than you should, or would like to be. In many civilisations nakedness, far from being sexual, is an indication of simplicity and innocence – Adam and Eve before the fall. Witches speak of being 'sky-clad' – open to the elements – once more an allusion to openness, frankness.

Numbers Look first for an obvious connection with your waking life: are you worried about your bank statement, or some other purely practical matter? Muddle with numbers in a dream may reflect muddle in some area of your waking life, for numbers are by nature orderly and logical – so the allusion may be a slanting one, pointing at illogicality or disorder. If the dream is of a specific number, once more look for an allusion to waking life – perhaps a pun (one = won, eight = hate, and so on). Individual numbers howevei do have a symbolic life of their own: *even* numbers are considered feminine, *odd* numbers masculine, for instance; *zero* represents oblivion, nothingness. *One* – unity; loneliness; sometimes God or a god. *Two* – duality; length; opposites; the Sun and Moon; male and female; in Islam the Spirit. *Three* – creation; birth (the beginning of life: two is static, three begins to move); in Christianity the Father, Son and Holy Ghost; to the Chinese the first *yang* number; to the ancient Greeks, Fate. *Four* – the four elements and seasons; the four points of the compass; the four quarters of the earth; solidity and order. For the Chinese, the number of the earth; for the ancient Egyptians the number of Time; for the Hindus, perfection. *Five* – the number which represents man (stretched out, showing his four limbs and head). Again a representation of wholeness, which for some civilisations has represented the partnership of man and woman – (*two* is even, therefore feminine, plus *three*, odd, therefore masculine); both Greeks and Romans took five as the number of love, of Venus. The Buddhists allude to the heart at the centre of man, plus his four limbs – another sign of wholeness. *Six* – a perfect number, summing up the previous ones (1 + 2 + 3). As the highest figure on the dice, the number is regarded as lucky; the Christians related it to the Creation, God having made the world in six days. Shown as two superimposed triangles, it represents bisexuality (the female triangle pointing down, the male triangle pointing upwards). *Seven* – yet another number representing wholeness, found both in world myths and in nature – seven pillars of wisdom, seven colours in the rainbow; seven days of the week; seven strings in Apollo's lyre.

There are also seven notes in the musical scale. Buddhists climb through seven stages to heaven; Egyptian myth often uses the number – seven cows, with a bull, represent fertility, for instance. *Eight* – as seven represents in many religions the number of steps to heaven, so eight represents heaven itself; new beginnings, then – for Buddhists, perfection; for the Hindus the basis of the *mandala*. *Nine* – a highly mystical number, which for the Buddhists symbolises spirituality, for the Chinese ultimate spiritual power, for the Greeks art (nine muses). *Ten* – creation itself; the Chinese spoke of ten thousand things as being the mysterious basis of the universe; and ten is the perfect number to the Hindus. Ten appears often in the Bible (ten virgins, ten commandments, ten talents, ten lamps). *Thirteen* is unlucky, though only in the West; *666* is the Mark of the Beast, much used by diabolists; *888* is the Mark of Jesus.

Nun/Nunnery A nun is certainly a female image, but one removed from the general idea of femininity, with its strong overtones of virginity and removal from everyday society as we understand it. Symbolic of 'goodness', such a figure might be expected to embody your best instincts; if your dream nun proffered advice, you will do well to listen. Whether you are a man or a woman, remember that the feminine side of your personality was speaking to you. But it may also be that your dream nun was the voice of your conscience, so the dream may have offered a warning. There is an element of 'separateness' too, for nuns live their lives in nunneries or convents; yet while they seem to be other-worldly, they are very often surprisingly worldly-wise. If you are a woman do you tend to distance yourself from the opposite sex? If you are a Christian you should consider your dream within the context of your beliefs – perhaps even more so if you are a Roman Catholic. If your dream was of a nunnery and you were entering it, there could be identification with some sacrifice (of your freedom?) you may be going to make in your waking life. You may have a great desire for peace and quiet, or simply to be by yourself. You may be in need of some kind of spiritual uplift, not necessarily of religious nature, but something to distract you from the problems of day-to-day living. Or was your dream suggesting that you should 'live by the rule', pointing a finger at recent behaviour?

Nursery Was your dream a nostalgic reference to your own childhood? If so there is a possibility that you may be tending to look too much to the past. If you were a child again, might this reflect insecurity, or a wish to get away from a difficult situation or problem in your waking life? The dream could be making a statement about your attitude to parenthood. Perhaps you are ready to start a family. Or do you think that the nursery represented some new ideas which are formulating in your mind, and need to grow and mature? You may simply have behaved rather childishly recently!

Nuts Nuts are really seeds, so your dream nuts could have been referring to the genesis of some idea. If we think of nuts in the context of the beginning of life, do you think that the dream is a comment on you wanting to conceive a child? The food value of nuts is considerable, so there could have been some oblique reference to your dietary needs – more fibre or wholefood?

Your dream nuts could have been the other kind – those which pair up with bolts! If so are you getting down to the nuts and bolts of a project or some demanding work? Or are you just saying 'Nuts!' to someone or something? (A nut is feminine, remember, while a bolt is masculine – though 'nuts' has also been, since the eighteenth century, slang for the testicles; don't ignore a possible sexual allusion.)

Nymph We think of nymphs – the guardian spirits of glades and woodlands – as happy and uninhibited, so perhaps your dream nymph was mirroring your present mood – is an air of slight naughtiness pervading you? Or was your dream nymph a nymphet? This could well be making a potent statement about your sexuality – an inner attraction to young girls? Seriously consider the possibility, especially if some young teenager is flirting with you at present.

Oar This symbol seems to be making some kind of suggestion about pulling your weight, certainly if you were rowing. But there is also a connection with *water*, hence perhaps a reference to your emotional state. Did you lose your oar? Were you in deep choppy water? If you were using an oar for any other purpose than that for which it was made, or if you were making one, might it have been a phallic symbol?

Obscenity   If your dream was obscene, we can only repeat that dreams are messages from yourself to yourself, and that you must interpret with this in mind. Even if you were revolted by your dream on waking, take it seriously. Perhaps you should face up to certain elements of your sexuality which you are repressing. If distressed, we suggest that you consider seeking professional counselling.

Ocean   See **Sea**.

Office   If you work in an office, you should also see **Room**, because your office is extremely personal to you and could well represent some element of your personality. In addition, what sort of an office was it? Busy? Tidy? A mess? Noisy? Are these statements you could apply to yourself, or perhaps to your attitude towards work, wherever you work or whatever you do? Was your dream referring to your schedule or life-style? Perhaps your routine is rather boring at present, and you need to make changes. Perhaps you are a young mother at home with a toddler, and your dream was suggesting that you should get back to work. Why not consider doing so, if only part-time? It may well be that you need to expand your life in some way, and that way has been obliquely shown to you through your office dream: you probably need more to do with your time. If you were shutting the office door, the reverse could be true: you simply want to get away from the bustle and relax.

Officer   Your dream officer was an authority figure, probably representing the masculine, assertive side of your personality. If he was issuing commands, take heed of what he said, of any warning he gave. However, if he was bullying or over-assertive, can you relate those feelings to your waking life, and do you need to fight them? No doubt a future dream will give you greater help. Were there aggressive elements in your dream? Do you feel as if you are being bossed around in waking life?

Oil   This is very likely to be a pun. We think of pouring oil on troubled waters, of oiling the *machinery*. But perhaps you were using oil for *cooking* or *eating*? If so, some kind of sustenance seems to be suggested: emotional or sexual, as much as nutritional. Or was your oil polluting a *river* or the *sea*? Consider whether your dream oil was making a statement about your emotions and their expression. If it was preventing you from reaching clear water, for instance, something could well be preventing the flow of your emotional energy and its free and positive expression. If the *water* was seriously polluted, perhaps your emotions are stained by some wilful, ugly element? On the other hand there are the lovely essential oils used in massage – if they featured in your dream surely they were a positive reference to your own sensuality.

Ointment   If you were using ointment to heal a wound, here is beautiful symbolism: the dream is probably making a reference to some kind of healing process that you are going through, either emotional (are you, for instance trying to heal some hurt done to you by a loved one, or have you suffered a loss and are grieving?) or physical. Or you may be helping to heal someone else. It is always worth remembering that dreams which focus on a physical area or organ can be pointing to a problem which, if it is treated early, can be easily cured. The unconscious is an excellent guide in this respect. But maybe you were making ointment, mixing various ingredients: are you trying to gather your thoughts together or about to reach some definite conclusions? The healing process in all its facets seems to dominate the line of interpretation of this particular symbol.

Old Man   You must first decide who your old man represents. He could have been a pleasant grandfather or Santa Claus figure, or an old fool; he could have been stern and God-like, or some old man actually known to you. In any case you must come to some conclusion about what he represents to you, and what you identify with him. But in many ways there is an 'old man' in all of us – our own inner, archetypal father. He can represent the voice of authority – stern, repressive, restrictive – or he can be the sort of father everyone would like to have. You must decide whether you should take his message or actions seriously, whether he is inhibiting you, or trying to repress you or sap your confidence. There are a lot of very old men and god figures in mythology, Cronus, for instance, who ate his children because he felt threatened by them – a fearful old man, perhaps envious of youth. Then there is Father Time, the grim reaper. It might be this character who featured in your dream, especially if you are at the moment particularly concerned about your age (have you just turned thirty or forty?). Zeus in the Greek pantheon and Jupiter in the Roman are identical personalities – jolly, rakish old men, not unlike Shakespeare's Falstaff. You might care to consider these and others to see if your old man shares any of their characteristics. This is an intriguing symbol, and its interpretation is likely to be very complex; we can only suggest some avenues through which to channel your thoughts and ideas.

Olive   The olive branch is a symbol of peace, of war concluded and enmity resolved. Have you recently patched up a quarrel with someone, made your peace, in other words? But perhaps you were eating olives. Think of their luscious texture: was that making a statement about your sensuality? Did the olive stone feature? It is extremely hard, and might represent some difficult problem – a hard *nut* to crack? – or perhaps a hard streak in your own, or someone else's outwardly pleasant personality, or a difficult patch in some situation or discussion which seems to be going well. But remember too, that the stone is a seed from which an olive tree will eventually grow – so have you an inkling of an idea which could, if nurtured, bear fruit?

Onion   If you were peeling the layers of the onion, were you trying to reach the heart of a problem? If your dream onion was making you cry, remember that they are never worth tears, and that the suggestion may be that you are too worried or upset about a current difficulty – that the tears really aren't warranted.

Operation   At its simplest, most basic level your dream operation could well be a pun on some task or project on which you are about to embark – another kind of operation. But if this is not the case, the dream could be commenting on something of which you wish to rid yourself – a personality trait you dislike or some characteristic you know to be undesirable? Perhaps you are trying to give up something like smoking? All this could apply whether you were being operated on or performing the operation. On another level, take heed of your dream from the purely physical point of view. You could be receiving a warning from your unconscious that you have the early symptoms of a complaint, so get the appropriate medical check-up. If the operation was on your eye, while that too could be a physical warning, your dream could be suggesting that you are not seeing some problem, something or someone, as clearly as you need to.

Orange   See **Colours** also. If your dream was of the fruit, was it bitter when you expected it to be sweet and delicious? If so, there could be a warning that you are being deceived or self-deceptive. Could there be a suggestion that someone is about to hurt you in some way? Reflect on the word bitter: could this apply to you in waking life? Very differently, perhaps your orange was particularly juicy – that conjures up a very different picture!

Orchestra   Was your dream orchestra tuning up? Playing in tune? Out of tune? Were you conducting? If tuning up, are you tuning yourself up to get started on some important large-scale project? If out of tune, perhaps your dream was suggesting that you are simply out of tune in some area of your life – you aren't getting on well at work, or maybe aren't in harmony with your partner. If you were conducting it would seem that you are very much in charge of your life, and of other people – really taking the lead. This should be understood as an excellent boost to your confidence. But if you were conducting and the musicians were not taking a blind bit of notice of you, you will have to go in for a little soul-searching. Are you being unnecessarily bossy? Trying to exercise an authority which you do not possess? If so, you are being ineffectual, and should take some kind of action which will improve others' opinion of you. But perhaps you were actually playing an instrument in the orchestra. In such a case your dream was suggesting that you are going along with others' opinions, being supportive. If you were at a loss as to what to play while others were contributing in a satisfactory way, this was a classic anxiety dream, suggesting that you are unsure of yourself and are probably worried about some aspect of your life. You may need to try to develop greater self-confidence.

Organ   The conventional, traditional organ is surely the instrument most associated with grandeur and pomp, and with religion. It is indicative of ceremonial and all splendid occasions. Electronic organs on the other hand are identified with anything but grand occasions – a jolly evening at a club, pub or in someone's home. Obviously, a great deal will depend on your dream situation and the sort of organ in question. If it is a huge one – the sort we find in cathedrals or in the Albert Hall – could your unconscious be praising you for some recent action? If you were playing an organ the suggestion seems to be that you are in command and perhaps (rather as if you had dreamed you were playing a *trumpet*) showing off – but this could be justified.

We must remember the pun: your dream may have referred to one of the organs of your body – and considering the shape of the pipes, the dream could have sexual overtones for males, certainly if you were conscious of an enormous pipe giving forth a sonorous sound!

Orgy Hopefully you enjoyed yourself! But if you felt distaste or revulsion, or were apprehensive or nervous, the dream may have been commenting on your attitude towards sex in general. If you are normally shy and inhibited, it could have been mere wish-fulfilment, or may have been suggesting that you should become more relaxed in your attitude towards sex, even less prudish. If, on waking, you were shocked by your dream (how could someone like you have a dream like that?), you must accept that it was *your* dream, and must look for a way of reconciling your waking disapproval and your sleeping desires.

Orphan There could well have been an air of prevailing sadness or sympathy in your dream; did you feel lonely or lost? It may well be that you were the orphan, and even if you weren't, your dream orphan was probably making a statement about your present feelings. Do you feel alone, lost in some way, that you have no one to guide or look after you? There might have been another character in the dream who was giving advice or trying to help the orphan; if so concentrate on that symbol, for here was your inner authority-figure, your practical self.

Oven Most likely to be a pun. What's *cooking*? Have you a 'bun in the oven'? – in other words are you pregnant or think you might be? This might also be a reference to something you are cooking up.

Ox See **Bull**.

Oyster There are some interesting symbolic overtones in the oyster. It has been taken to represent the womb, but also related to the creative force, to birth and rebirth. Oysters are traditionally supposed to increase male virility; there could be an obvious sexual allusion there, for men who have unconscious fears in that area. There is also a connection with *water*, and as always your emotional life could be in question. Or do you particularly want a child? See **Pearl**?

Padlock   See **Lock**.

Pagoda   A dream of a pagoda will certainly carry personal implications for you, particularly if you are interested in eastern religion, in which the shape is particularly significant (representing the sacred mountain at the centre of the world, and offering a stairway to the infinite, to heaven). The dream may very possibly be commenting on some aspect of your spiritual life, perhaps urging you to think about or to concentrate on these areas rather more. There is also the possibility of wish-fulfilment: you may have a desire to travel to the Far East. If you have done so, the dream may be commenting on that experience, from almost any point of view; look for other clues.

Pain   If you dreamed of a pain in a particular area of your body, take it as a warning and get the offending area checked by your doctor. This is the sort of dream symbol that really can be extremely useful, for often our unconscious detects physical ailments or symptoms before they can be diagnosed. A dream of pain may reflect some kind of psychological pain; there may be the suggestion that someone close to you is simply being a pain – a 'a pain in the arse' even?

Paint   First see the relevant **Colour** of the paint. This will greatly influence your interpretation. But what were you painting – a portrait of the Queen, some magnificent landscape, graffiti, a wall? In your waking life are you trying to cover up something? a secret? Was your dream suggesting that you have a latent creative talent for painting, and that you should buy some paints and get busy? If you were painting a *room* or *house*, see those symbols. Should you paint the town red? Were you mixing paint? If so, are you 'stirring things up' or 'mixing it' in waking life? If you spilled paint, there could be a statement about your emotional life, in which case the *colour* will be especially important.

Paper A newspaper? A reference to your attitude to some matter currently in the news? There have been curious cases of people who have dreamed of headlines echoed by later events: make a note of any prominent headline if you are interested in following such matters up. If you were cutting paper or making models, the emphasis seems to be on fragility – could some waking plan or situation be less substantial than you think? Or were you 'papering over the cracks'? If the paper was a blank sheet, this may suggest that you realise you have the capacity to make your mark quite individually on a situation.

Parachute A safe recovery from danger: a parachute is a kind of insurance, so is there some circumstance in waking life which needs such back-up? Did your parachute fail? In that case you should check up on any safeguard to which you think your dream may refer – your unconscious may have spotted a flaw. See **Flying**, **Falling**?

Parade See also **Procession**; but parade has a slightly different connotation, suggesting display. Are you, or should you be, parading your emotions more obviously? Or are you doing so too flamboyantly? A military parade suggests a show of strength; a carnival parade, a celebration. Think in the abstract, and watch out for puns.

Paradise Every civilisation has had its idea of paradise – the Christian Heaven, the Elysian Fields, El Dorado, the Promised Land. Consider whether this means, to you, a real state to which you aspire, or merely 'pie in the sky', for the intepretation of your dream will probably rest on that. The dream could be wish-fulfilment – you long for a state of peaceful plenty; or it could be a strong hint that you need to relax. There may be other images: if your paradise is disturbed by the *serpent* or Eve offers you an *apple*, follow the suggestion up.

Paralysis As with all 'medical' dreams, do not hesitate to follow up any hint of possible disability. But dreaming that you are paralysed is more likely to allude to paralysis of the mind: you are not free to think as you wish, perhaps because you are inhibited by your childhood training, or your environment, and you should make a real effort to overcome the paralysis.

Parcel   The interpretation will depend, as always, mainly on the context: were you pleased to get the parcel, frightened to open it; did you want to pass it on, hide it away? Were you posting it? Receiving it? The idea of secrecy seems inevitable: the thing itself is hidden by its wrapping, so you may be trying to get rid of some character trait to which you do not wish to admit, even to yourself. Or there may be an allusion to some area of your life you want to amend by shifting responsibility; or you may be forced to accept it. The allusion will either be very obvious, or quite difficult to grasp – in which case, ask (see p. 45–6) for help.

Parents   See **Father**, **Mother**.   A dream in which both parents appear may be making a point about your relationship with them, or about the male and female sides of your character and the balance between them.

Park   A park is a cultivated piece of landscape, and the reference may be to some aspect of your personality which needs ordering, cultivating, encouraging. But what was the context: were you simply strolling, admiring the park (i.e., rather content with it), digging up some part of it (making some alterations), trying to get into, or out of, it? Any kind of landscape can represent the inner landscape of your personality, and your attempts to fathom the meaning of your dream should centre on this probability.

Parliament See **Politician**?   Parliament is often referred to as a 'talking shop', but there are also connotations of order, of a personification of the State; so the reference may be to your relationship to society, your view of it, your acceptance of, or rebellion against, its decrees. Then again any debate in which you were taking part could refer to any discussion in which you are presently engaged (in your own mind, or overtly). Were you defending the Government, the status quo, or speaking for the Opposition?

Party   For most people, a party is a pleasant and gregarious occasion, and the dream may be commenting on your relationship to other people, perhaps society in general, and your feelings about them. If the party was highly enjoyable, all seems well; if you or someone else was spoiling the party, questions must arise. Other symbols within the dream should give it a more particular context. If it was a political party of which you dreamed, there may be some criticism of your waking political or social stance or behaviour.

Passage   There is something of the feeling of a *cave* about a passage – with the important difference that a passage is assumed not to have a dead end, but to lead from A to B, sometimes securely, sometimes dangerously. So you have to look for two situations – two people – two positions – the connection between which is important to you. The concept may be very abstract: the connection beween right and wrong, even between life and death – or it may be as concrete as the passage from one job to another, and the necessity for the transition to be a smooth one.

Past   A dream about the past must be related to specifics – a memory, a person, a place, an object. We often dream that we are back in our first job, back with our family, back at home, and interpretation depends on the emotion we connect with those circumstances; the dream can be fulfilling our simple wish to lead life as uncomplicatedly as we did when we were a child, but there may be a reference to some incident of which we are ashamed, the effects of which we have not yet shaken off. At all events, the dream will have some reference to our present life; it will not be a simple reminiscence.

Path   See **Road**.

Pattern   Patterns have been of great importance in man's mystical life, and have been translated into corporeal form in architecture as well as art. Was the pattern whole and serene, a *mandala*, perhaps, or broken or disturbed? How does the dream pattern reflect the pattern of your present waking life? Had you lost a pattern? Were you drawing up a new one?

Pavement   A pavement should be a place of safety, but is not always so; were you treading it confidently, or being splattered with mud from passing traffic? The dream may allude to a careful path you are having to tread at the moment.

Pearl   Pearls have always been admired and precious, and have attracted many mythical meanings: they have been thought to embody the power of the *sea*, the marriage of *fire* and *water*; a pearl has been seen as the Heart of Buddha and his third eye; the Greeks and Roman thought of it as symbolic of love (Venus was the Lady of the Pearls); to Islam it represents the divine world. So this is clearly likely to be an important symbol in any dream. Had you bought pearls, being given them? Were you setting them in precious metal? Hoarding them? Had you lost them? The questions must all relate to some valuable aspect of your life, and probably of your spiritual life.

Pen/Pencil   Traditionally related to wisdom, the pen is an instrument of communication – but not as specific as a *letter*, perhaps. A pen through which ink is refusing to flow may allude to a blockage of your means of expression or emotion; a pen which floods and blots the paper may relate to undisciplined emotion, too readily expressed. Though 'pen' has been a synonym for the penis for three hundred years, these days a pencil is more likely to be phallic than a pen: remember the old saying about 'putting lead in your pencil?' However, the image of ink flowing through the pen is also potent, and a dry pen may suggest impotence, to 'have no more ink in the pen' was an image of impotence as early as the sixteenth century.

Penis   See **Phallus**.

Pepper   A dream of adding pepper to a dish (and see **Cooking**, if relevant) is most likely to be an invitation to put a little spice into your life; over-peppering may have just the opposite connotation. So do you need more flavour in your life? Have you met someone who might be described as 'hot stuff'?

Perfume   Presumably, a pleasant odour? Perfume is peculiarly feminine, so the association may be with a woman in your life. The context will be vital, as usual – as will your reaction: delighted or nauseated? Was the perfume over-sweet, very dry, somewhat unpleasant or heady?

Petrol   Given the possible phallic interpretation of *car* (and it is surprising how infrequently women dream of their cars!), running out of petrol or filling the tank has an implication too obvious to need explication. Danger from petrol, possible explosions, would seem to allude to some kind of over-expression of emotion, sexual or otherwise.

Phallus   If so many objects are phallic and represent the penis in dreams, does the phallus itself never represent anything else? It seems on the whole unlikely; it is such a strong image that it usually seems simply to be itself, though it may not always be peculiar to the dreamer − that is, it may not represent the phallus of the dreamer, but the general capacity of man to create; and there is no reason therefore why in principle it should not represent other means of creation, the creation of art, for instance. However, a dream of an actual phallus in action (as it were) is so specifically sexual that it is almost always to be regarded simply as an expression of sleeping sensuality.

Photograph   See **Picture**, but a photograph is not so clearly an imitation of reality: it is a record of reality. It may be reminding you of, or telling you something about, the person depicted. Is it suggesting that you have someone out of focus, are not seeing them clearly? What was depicted, and your waking attitude to it, will be important, but so may be the photographer, for s/he may represent someone with those vision of life you identify or disagree.

Piano   See **Music**; but your reaction to the piano in waking life will be important − whether you find it difficult, dislike practising it, admire someone's performance, and so on. A piano is more complex than some other instruments, and this may be significant, as may be the very word 'performance'. To what kind of waking performance might the dream refer?

Picnic   See **Eating**; but remember that a picnic is particularly informal.

Picture   To dream of looking at a picture suggests the idea of distancing yourself from reality (see **Cinema**, **Photograph**): you are not looking at reality, but at someone's (probably your own) idea of reality; so the dream may well be suggesting that you try to see things straight, not to invent other people's reactions but recognise the real ones; or to see a situation or a relationship clearly rather than allowing your own emotions to take over. What was in the picture? – there should be a hint somewhere of what the dream is alluding to.

Pie   On the whole, we associate a pie with home, with domestic cooking (and if you were making a pie, see **Cooking**). Were you dividing the pie, and if so was there an emphasis on fair shares for all? Remember that the simile is often used by politicians in a financial context; did the pie represent a pie-chart? Could there be an allusion to the family income? If the emphasis was on the contents of the pie, then the suggestion might be that a particular idea or scheme needs more cooking, more consideration; or perhaps should be served *now*, before it goes off!

Pilgrim   A pilgrim knows where s/he is going: there is no question of wandering aimlessly about. So was the dream confirming that you are right in your present actions, that you are making straight for the bull's-eye? It is a possibility. But if the atmosphere was extremely religious, is it possible that some kind of moral force is lacking in your life, and that you are unconsciously aware of the fact? It may be that in some way you are missing your goal or your aim in life. The context is, as always, important: whether you were eager to reach the place for which you were making, being prevented from doing so – even ignorant of your goal. Who else was involved? Were they fellow pilgrims, hospitable friends, or standing between you and the holy end of your pilgrimage?

Pill   Have you had to swallow a metaphorical bitter pill recently? How did it go down, in your dream? Did you spit it out? What results did it have? But the dream may be a reflection of some action or incident in your waking life, without necessarily commenting on it. This does sometimes happen.

Pillar   Yes, the Freudians would probably claim that a dream of a pillar (upright or broken, leaning or completely demolished) is concerned with sexuality; it is certainly one of the archetypal phallic symbols, and it is probably fair to suggest that whether you are male or female you should consider this attribution first. But there are other connotations. It is not by accident that sculptors and architects have shaped pillars to emphasise their likeness to *trees*, and there is the symbolism of the pillar as a support to consider: what was it supporting, was it doing so strongly or weakly and what is the parallel in your waking life, with yourself either as the supporting pillar or the fabric it is trying to hold up? In the latter case, what does it represent?

Pillow Our pillow is a friend, a comforter, placing our head upon it we seek oblivion, or at any rate peace. So could your dream pillow represent a close friend or your partner? Whether it was comfortable or uncomfortable will be important; was it making you uneasy? Keeping you awake? In that case, the allusion is obvious. Somewhere in the dream there will have been a clue to the identity of the pillow-person.

Pin Yet another possible phallic symbol; the woman who dreams that she has *pricked* her finger need look no further. This is the basis of the story of the Sleeping Beauty, sent to sleep for a hundred years by the prick she so feared when she reached puberty. Look for a symbol elsewhere in the dream for the real identity of the pin: did you borrow it from someone? Was it truly your own? There is the possiblity, on the other hand – especially if you had dropped it – that it represents something elusive for which you are seeking; only you will know what.

Pipe A pipe is one of the great symbols in our time of the old-fashioned, perhaps somewhat chauvinistic male. There may be an allusion to someone you know, identified by his smoking a pipe in real life. It seems likely, however, that (if you are a woman) you need assurance, are looking for some security from the opposite sex. A man may unconsciously wish to, or feel that he should, embody the old-fashioned virtues presented by the pipe-smoking hero of fifty years ago, seen in the novels of Dornford Yates, Sapper or John Buchan. Or should you pipe down?

Pirate Setting aside the over-simple (nonetheless possible) suggestion that a woman dreaming of abduction by pirates is in some way expressing a wish for more excitement in her (sexual?) life, it will be worth remembering that pirates, if glamorous, are lawless, and that the dream may be expressing an opinion about your present behaviour. It may be mirroring your excitement at a slightly dangerous enterprise, or – if the dream ended badly – issuing a warning.

Plane See **Flying**.

Planet Something distant, inevitable, serene, unachievable? Could there be a reference to some ambition which you hold dear but which seems unattainable? And in that case was the dream encouraging you to go for it – to climb on board your metaphorical rocket and head for the *stars*? It is possible. Remember that the planets have their traditional attributes: there may be a hint of some kind there, even if you are not aware, consciously, of the allusions: the *Sun*, a masculine planet, is associated with power, with the colour gold, with youthful vigour; the *Moon* (feminine) is associated with instinct, with silver, and has stood both for extreme youth and extreme age; *Mercury* (of ambivalent sexuality) is associated with communication, with the colour yellow, and with bisexuality; *Venus* (feminine) is associated with harmony, the colours green and blue, with feminity, love and desire; *Mars* (masculine) is associated with energy, the colour red, with masculinity and passion; *Jupiter* (masculine) is associated with expansion, the colours blue, violet or orange, with age and intellect; *Saturn* (masculine) is associated with limitation, the colour black, with reason, rationality, analytical thought. The three 'modern' planets only have those qualities fairly recently allowed them by astrologers – *Uranus* is associated with change, uncertainty, a sense of awe; *Neptune* is associated with cloudiness , *Pluto* with elimination and sudden change.

Plants Look for some waking association between any particular plant of which you dream and yourself. In general, plants have always symbolised life itself – they have the force of life, 'the force that through the green fuse drives the flower', but without the capacity for thought; so it is possible that the allusion may be to your own enjoyment of the simplest process of living; a suggestion that you should stop theorising and get on with life. But this is the most general of suggestions, and you should look for particular symbols to direct you to a more particular meaning. Uprooted weeds, for instance, may stand for some fault you are eager to eradicate (or which, at any event, should be eradicated); vegetables for those practical virtues which you need if you are to live life satisfactorily; decorative flowers for the arts, or your affections and their objects. There are numerous possibilities. In ancient myth, plants often sprang from blood shed by the gods – a suggestion that they may represent the outward manifestations of your most secret wishes.

Plaster   If you were plastering a wall, remember that this activity conceals faults or fills in gaps; there may be an allusion to something in your waking life you are eager to disguise or patch up. The same sort of symbol could lie at the back of a dream in which you are putting a plaster over a wound: helping it to heal, protecting it from further injury, maybe, but also hiding it. Is there a waking parallel? Did you get plastered the night before?

Platform   See **Stage**; but remember that we associate a platform with a personal speech rather than a stage performance, so the allusion is very likely to be to some more personal statement, perhaps one you are making to yourself, rather than to your attitude to the public in general. If you were on a *railway* platform, are you about to set off on some kind of journey?

Plough/Ploughing   Though there is a possible sexual connotation (the plough as masculine, the earth as feminine), there is also an association with fertility, of preparing the earth to bear fruit. So there could be an allusion to conception, possibly predictive. Or are you ploughing on with some heavy task, living a rather boring and predictable life, ploughing the same furrow?

Plumage   Plumage is, or has been, both decorative and symbolic of *royalty*, kingship, power. There could be an allusion to pride (in your image, maybe) or to a folk memory of the feathered headdresses of Indian and other chiefs. Feathers are also associated with flight, so there may be a suggestion that you should use a particular attribute to help you to soar, either in terms of your personality or of your work. Or had someone ruffled your plumage, upset you in some way?

Pocket   We speak of a person 'having someone in their pocket' if they are dominating them, or using them in some way. Could your dream bear that allusion? There may be a financial reference (was there a hole in your pocket?).

Poison   A dream involving poison is unlikely to be pleasant in its allusions. Were you the poisoner or the poisoned? Are you (or is someone else) in some way spreading poison – by gossip, intentionally or unintentionally? Have you a wish to get someone out of your way? Or do you fear someone is trying to usurp your position?

The dream seems likely to involve some kind of warning. If you were the victim, have you some personal traits of which you should rid yourself?

Pole   A pole is likely to be a phallic symbol, and how you were using it, its purpose, whether it was strong, weak, damaged, decorative or admired, is likely to be important.

The Pole, North or South, is in a sense more interesting; distant and extremely inaccessible, people have expended great efforts to reach it, so it may represent an ambition, an aim in your life, the attainment of which you may be beginning to despair. Was the dream urging you on (i.e., were you plodding purposefully forward) or warning you?

Police   A dream about authority. A warning (were you being arrested?) or a justification (were you arresting someone else – i.e., bringing them to book?). Much will depend on your waking attitude to the police, and your past experience of them. See **Trial**.

Politician   Your view of politics and politicians will be important, but the interpretation of this dream may well depend on other symbols – *platform*, perhaps, or *crowd*? An actual dream of yourself or someone else as a politican is (sadly for democracy) likely to be a pejorative one, since the word has become in our time associated on the whole with equivocation, deceit, uselessness.

Polygamy   Wish-fulfilment? If a man's dream was of living with and enjoying several wives, it may have been an enjoyable sexual rumination; a woman dreaming of being one of several wives may unconsciously be reflecting on the faithfulness or otherwise of a partner. But there are other possibilities: the women in the dream may stand for something else – for proliferating ideas, maybe; or do you feel that you should be more single-minded?

Pool/The 'Pools'   See **Water**, first of all; then consider what sort of a pool was in your dream, and try to relate to it. Diving into a pool might be a reference to the exploration of your emotions, or a desire to dive deeper into them; swimming with someone else may suggest you want a greater emotional intimacy with them. The *landscape* around the pool may be suggestive of its context.

A dream of winning 'the Pools' was probably wish-fulfilment

though a dream of finding the right combination of teams should not altogether be ignored!

Postcard   See **Letter**; but remember that a postcard is more open – that you don't mind who knows its contents, and may even *want* someone other than the recipient to know them. Is there something significant there? Is there a secret you would like known, but which you don't actually want to reveal, too obviously, yourself? The dream may be suggesting an oblique solution. If the postcard was of a specific place or person it will be important to work out the reason for that allusion.

Postman   The bringer of news – and of personal news rather than the kind brought by a newspaper or newscaster. See **Letter**, **Postcard**, **Parcel**, if any apply; if you are waiting for the postman or dream that something has happened to detain him, consider whether that may refer to news which you had hoped to hear. Who was the postman/woman in your dream? You?

Pot   Like all containers, this symbol is likely to be female in origin; since you looked it up under this name (rather than **Vase**) it seems likely that it is a very personal symbol – one tends to make pots oneself; when one buys them, or if they are decorative, one usually alludes to them under some other name. So consider whether there is an allusion to a friend or partner; someone whom, in a sense, you have 'made' – by helping them to shape their personality (as a teacher?). If you are a man, have you 'made' them sexually? Was the pot broken, were you mending it, was it merely decorative, a receptacle for something valuable or just pretty? Likely to be a complex dream to analyse: ask (see p. 45–6) for more clues.

Poverty   A dream of poverty is likely to allude to some kind of deprivation – poverty of spirit, or to loss. It is an abstract concept, so look to other symbols in the dream: how was the poverty signalled – by ragged *clothes*, or by lack of a *house*?

Prayer   You may not be aware of what you were praying for in the dream; but the suggestion must be that in waking life there is something you deeply desire, but which seems out of reach – you are not doing anything practical in order to attain it, but relying on prayer (though of course if you are devout, praying most certainly *is* doing something!). It might be well to look for a more practical approach to the problem, and the dream may, in other ways, be suggesting this. What was the atmosphere; were you convinced your prayer would be answered?

Preacher   The interpretation of the dream will depend on what the preacher was saying, or at least, his attitude to the congregation. Were you the preacher, even if in the dream s/he appeared to be someone else? If so, then do you have some kind of message you need to deliver to society at large, or less obviously to a particular person (was s/he in the congregation)? It is most likely, because of the context, to be a moral message; so the criticism may be of others' morals, or of your own; could your unconscious be rebuking you for some aspect of your present behaviour?

Pregnancy   Though this could be either a wishful dream, or a predictive one, remember that we sometimes speak of being pregnant with an idea; so is there something to which you are about to give birth? – a plan, an idea, an artwork of some kind? Or is the suggestion that you should in some way be more productive? This is not impossible even if you are a man – the pregnant woman in your dream may represent the more feminine, creative part of your own personality. Consider whether something about her might tie in with your conception of yourself.

Present   What sort of present? And were you glad to receive it, or disappointed when you opened it? We can only speak here of an abstract present. If it was a particular thing, you must focus on that and on its associations, remembering however that a present is in general something we pay for only in thanks, or by our response to the person who gives it. So the dream may be a hint about your relationship with someone (the giver), and again its meaning may hinge on whatever was given. A mystery present which you do not undo may represent a facet of the personality of your friend with which you have so far not come properly to terms. If you gave yourself a present in the dream, this may be a hint that you deserve a break, or a reward for some unrecognised action. Is this a pun on 'the present'. See **Parcel**?

Price   Thinking of *money* and its frequent alignment with emotion, the price of an object in a dream is likely to refer less to its actual cost than what it costs in emotional terms. It may be that the object represents a person (there should be a clue somewhere – a pun, possibly). Something overpriced may be attainable in waking life only at too great an emotional cost; something cheap may scarcely be worth having, and so on.

Prick   See **Pin, Needle**. If the *word* itself was particularly clear in the dream, quite apart from the action, the chances of the dream having a sexual context are emphasised. Or is your conscience pricking you? Is someone you know being a 'prick' – or are you?

Priest   A hint about your attitude to religion? That you should satisfy an innate interest or curiosity? Or a suggestion that you are ruled too much by the structure of morality within which you live – that you are too much dominated by convention (with which we often associate religion). But the interpretation of the dream will rest very largely on your attitude to religion and the priesthood in your waking life, or to a particular priest, if that is relevant.

Prince/Princess   A Prince or Princess is *royalty* in waiting, so the reference is perhaps to some position which you desire, but which at present is held by someone else. This is capable of several interpretations: you could be envying someone the place they have in someone else's heart, for instance; or someone who holds a job for which you long; or someone's house, or dog, or money – the possibilities are endless. For a man, the insistence in fairy stories of the Princess as the unattainable whose hand is eventually won must make it likely that the dream is hinting that real effort will result in success. The handsome Prince awakens the Princess, so for a woman the dream may be wish-fulfilment; though remember the toad who became a Prince when kissed – could there be a reference there? Fairy stories heard in childhood often soak into the unconscious and are strongly featured in dreams. Sometimes fathers call their daughters 'Princess'; could that be relevant?

Prison   What sort of imprisonment are you suffering in waking life? – that of an unrewarding job, of life with a small child at home, of an illness? It should not be difficult to make the connection; then look at other features of the dream. Were you planning an escape (if so, how?), resigned to your fate, being fed by a kindly hand?

Prize Not dissimilar to *present* – but even more, a reward; so this may be a self-congratulatory dream, a hint that a prize can be won, a suggestion that you should look for the rewards which are to be gained in a particular situation.

Procession Were the figures in the procession identifiable as individuals? It so, this may be a reminder of a number of incidents in your past life. However, they may all emphasise the same theme, and harp on it – if so the dream will be making a point with particular insistence. A carnival procession may hint at your capacity for enjoyment, and suggest that you indulge it more freely; a *funeral* procession will have a different meaning. Look, as always, to the atmosphere as well as the incident itself.

Professor A symbol of learning: suggesting that you should study the facts of a case, that you should rely less on instinct and more on reason? The absent-minded professor is a hackneyed symbol, but for that very reason quite likely to appear in a dream which refers to that trait in yourself.

Prosecution See **Trial**, **Prisoner**, **Judge**.

Prostitute If the dream is specifically of prostitution, then the chances are (supposing that it was not specifically a sexual dream) that it alludes to some way in which you are prostituting yourself – your talent, perhaps? Is there some way in which you are selling yourself cheaply? Much will depend on the context, as always, and there should be other clues somewhere which will help you attach a meaning to the dream. If the context is sexual, there may be a criticism of your present attitude to sex – are you selling it, in some way, rather than enjoying it as a life-enhancing gift?

Publicity If you were seeking publicity in a dream – almost irrespective of the purpose – there is probably a suggestion that you feel undervalued in some way, maybe that you should blow your own trumpet a little more. If you were conscious of someone else busily publicising themselves, on the other hand, maybe you feel in waking life that they are a little too satisfied with their own virtues; though again, you may identify with that person (dreams often work as obliquely as this, as though they hesitate to be too obviously self-critical) so consider whether you are being a little too loud in self-praise.

Pudding See **Pie** – unless there is a reference to the old, coarse allusion to being 'in the pudding club', i.e., pregnant. Or are you being accused of being a pudding – rather too plump to be wholly attractive?

Puncture There is no escaping the fact that this could be an allusion, in one way or another, to loss of virginity – your own or someone else's. But equally, it could refer to another kind of puncture: of your vanity, or of some scheme. What kind of vehicle was punctured? A *car*, a *bicycle*?

Puppet On what kind of a string? Who is controlling you – or who are you controlling? This seems likely to be a dream about manipulation, in one way or another. Consider who the puppet represented. Did it obey orders, or had it a life of its own? Did the controlling string break? All these possibilities are worth thinking about and relating to the situation which they fit in your waking life.

Purse See **Money**. The purse has had, over the years, a sexual context, referring to the vagina; so if you are a woman losing your purse, having a full purse, it may relate to this area of your life; a man dreaming of finding a purse should consider this possibility too, though it is more obscure.

Puzzle Puzzle-solving, in a dream, may well relate to puzzle-solving in waking life; are there complications which need sorting? There are the same possibilities as with a *maze*, or a *game*. The ease or difficulty with which you were coping with the problem will be important, as will the difficulty of the puzzle, and its nature.

Quarantine A similar sort of image to that of a *prison*, except that you are in it through no fault of your own. You probably feel put upon by fate, ostracised for no good reason. What can this relate to in your waking life? How sick were you, and of what sort of virus?

There could be a relationship between this and an opinion or moral attitude which in waking life sets you somehow aside from society at large, or from your particular circle. Is it worth the isolation this causes?

Quarrel Dreams do sometimes 'go by opposites', though not as literally as old-fashioned dream books suggest. But a dream of a quarrel with a loved one may be suggesting that there is not enough spice in the relationship; that too much agreement makes for a rather pallid life. But the depth or virulence of the quarrel is important. If violence was used, that is another matter. There is a possibility that you are nursing some anger and your unconscious is telling you to release it. The context of the dream should give some indication of its intention and meaning. If not, ask (see p. 45–6) for more clues.

Quarry We quarry for valuable minerals: we seek in the *earth* for something profitable. Given the association between the earth and creativity, could this refer to some new study or project? Or does it reflect a waking search for a larger income, for more security? At all events, the dream is presumably suggesting that hard work is necessary if you are to gain results.

Queen See **Royalty**.

Quicksilver See **Planet** (mercury).

Quilt People have been known to dream of cuddling under a quilt, only to wake and find that it has fallen from the bed and they are cold. But if this is not the case, think of a quilt as something protective, and intimate; strangers are rarely welcomed under most quilts. So the reference is likely to be to your private life and thoughts: do they need warming; do you feel unsure about them?

Quiver In one of Trollope's novels there is a Mr Quiverfull, who has a very large family; the allusion is an outdated one, but echoes of it may have prompted the dream. Like all containers (and this is for *arrows*!) the symbol is a female one.

Race/Racing To what waking race could your dream have been referring? – not, unless you have entered the London Marathon, necessarily a physical one; a race towards a test or examination, towards a wedding, towards promotion? In the dream were you confident of winning, or could the obstacles which were getting in your way warn you of possible weaknesses in your current plan of action? Are you feeling – or looking – rather 'racy' at present?

Rack See **Torture**; but are you racked with guilt about something?

Racket If you were playing a game and had damaged your racket, or lost it, the suggestion would seem to be that in some way either your motives or tactics have gone awry with regard to some current, waking '*game*' – which in this case could mean some manoeuvring or politicking at work, or socially. Perhaps your arguments have lost their force, or are simply faulty; or could the dream have been warning you to modify them, or be more tactful in expressing them – not to make such a racket? – or not to become involved in shady business dealings?

Radio A reference to communication, probably; was the radio broken, or too loud? And could that refer to someone's efforts to convey something to you – or the other way about? Radio voices are disembodied: there could be a reference to an inner voice to which you need to listen, or whose statements you should perhaps question.

Rags See **Poverty**.

Raid An air-raid? – though this dream will perhaps only occur to those who remember suffering in one. Such a dream is expressive of an attack of some kind, a violent, noisy and damaging one. Can you think of a waking parallel? Or do you fear one? Were you well protected, or exposed? Were you shaken, or unafraid? The circumstances may suggest the attitude you should adopt to a personal attack.

Railway See **Train**.

Rain In almost every civilisation, rain has been regarded as particularly blessed, and such imagery permeates the Bible, with its roots in hot, dry countries where rain was invariably welcome. So think along these lines, remembering that as *water* is involved there is a possibility that the reference is to your emotions. Are they being refreshed at present, or purified in some way (another common reference)? If the rain was so fierce as to be damaging, see **Storm**?

Rainbow A universal symbol of hope and promise (based, in western culture, on its appearance in the Old Testament story of the Flood, when it brought the promise of perpetual fair weather). Think along those lines, first. Is the dream giving you confidence to ignore a specific threat, backing up a optimistic attitude (or suggesting that you should adopt one)?

Ransom A ransom is paid, unwillingly, for the release of an innocent victim – so if you are paying the ransom the suggestion seems to be that you are being forced into some position or action, against your will, on someone else's behalf. If you are the victim hoping to be ransomed, are you in waking life in someone else's hands, hoping that someone, out of simple regard for you, will perform some selfless action to 'save' you in some way? This seems likely to be a complex dream to interpret, so you may care to ask (see p. 45–6) for further help.

Rape We are talking here of rape in its most violent form; if your dream was of a rather enjoyable sexual incident in which a certain amount of force was used, then there was probably an element of wish-fulfilment about the dream; there is no need to rebuke yourself about this – it will merely have been an expression of a trait in your sexual nature which is by no means necessarily dangerous. But rape as we understand it is not like that at all. So this is more likely to have been a violent and unpleasant dream. There is no escaping the fact that it may – indeed, is quite likely to – refer to some sexual problem. However, if you do not feel that this is so (and instinct is generally right where the interpretation of dreams is concerned) ask yourself how the kind of emotion that accompanies rape, or being raped, is being directed. This will not be easy, though since the emotion is so violent there may be a circumstance in waking life to which it obviously refers. However, in general, you should consider the dream in a sexual context.

It may relate to an actual waking incident – in which case you should certainly, if you are the victim, take medical advice, or at the very least consult a victim support group (these are particularly sympathetic and helpful). If the dream happens for no apparent reason, are you particularly nervous about the expression of your sexuality? The dream presents such a violent image that it is clearly sending a strong message, and again (especially if the dream recurs) you should consider asking for professional advice. A dream of being raped by a particular man will not necessarily be a warning; but you should think carefully about him and your feelings towards him. A male who dreams that he is raping someone, whether someone particular or just some anonymous person, must think very seriously about his waking reaction to the dream. It may be an expression of a violent trait in his sexual nature which he is repressing. If he has it well under control, fine; but if the dream hints at a deeply buried but extremely compulsive urge, the dreamer should think about seeking professional help. Remember, all dreams are personal messages from you to yourself: no one is forcing you to dream of being raped, or raping someone. You are in a sense *choosing* your dream, and when the images it expresses are particularly violent or unpleasant, unless you can arrive at their meaning by your own efforts, you should seriously consider consulting a psychiatrist or therapist.

Ration Not a symbol likely to occur in the dreams of younger people; but the reference is likely to be a literal one – that is, you or someone else are advised to be sparing, in one area of your life or other. If food is being rationed, the allusion is possibly to your emotional life: are you being too generous – or do you wish someone else would be?

Razor The context of the dream (as always) is important: did you cut yourself, was your razor blunt? Was it a weapon? Are you 'cutting' someone, or is that the suggestion?

Reading The book, or kind of book you were reading will be significant – supposing you to be someone for whom reading is a habit. Try to remember the title. The 'atmosphere' of the book itself might be a pointer to the dream's meaning. If you are not a great reader, the dream may be suggesting that you are missing a lot of enjoyment. But as in all dreams involving an art, the interpretation will be difficult; surrounding dreams may shed a light on its meaning.

Recipe See **Cooking**.

Recitation When we recite something, we have learned it by rote; so the suggestion is that the dream refers to something which we know well, and which we are trying to recite verbatim – to 'get right'. Might there be an allusion to some departure from the rule, some unconventional behaviour? Or are you afraid of 'going wrong' in some way? But there is the possibility that the dream refers to memory – is your memory faulty, in general or in detail? If you proudly remembered your recitation and completed it to general applause, the hint may be that you are on the right lines, pleasing yourself and others; a confidence-boosting dream. The opposite result will obviously have the opposite meaning.

Reed Are you 'a broken reed'? The ancient allusion still has force for us, and this dream might suggest that you are in some sense failing to stand up against an attack of some kind, or even to maintain your position against a wind of change. Reeds for some reason have often been associated with the passing of time, but this allusion now seems obscure and unlikely – just as we are unlikely, these days, to dream of sleeping on a reed bed.

Refrigerator One of those dream symbols which seem too easy for words: so whose affections are frozen towards you, or to whom are you being cold? Of course this is a possible interpretation – but the dream may be subtler than that. Look for clues: what was in the refrigerator? Might it have been you? Should you 'cool it' – not necessarily in the context of a relationship, but in respect of some other action? If the refrigerator was broken, or if the contents seemed to relate to you (perhaps to a particular area of life?) this seems quite likely. Look, as usual, for puns!

Refugee From what? The suggestion is likely to be that you are retreating from some situation or relationship – maybe for a perfectly good reason, but perhaps out of fear or apprehension. If there was reference to your worldly goods, then a reference to your emotions is likely. Did you have to leave them behind, to be captured by the enemy, or did you manage to rescue them? Have you managed to salvage something from the wreck, in your waking life, or have you left your heart behind?

Rehearsal   In general, we rehearse for a performance, and the reference may be of some waking situation in which pretence of some kind is involved. Sometimes we have experiences which are 'a rehearsal for life'. If the rehearsal went badly, you forgot your lines (see **Recitation**?) then the suggestion must be that you have not prepared sufficiently well. But perhaps you were confident and all went well? In that case, in a sense the dream is reassuring; but the fact that you dreamed of rehearsal rather than performance suggerts that you are still not entirely sure of your lines – or the line you are about to take – in some relevant situation in waking life. And think: was there some hint of reproach in the dream? – some suggestion that real life (i.e., honesty) is better than pretence? Remember that plays have sometimes been considered wicked because they tell lies – they are not 'real'. See **Theatre**?

Reincarnation   If you are a believer in reincarnation, the dream may reflect some concern or maybe hope for the next life: did you return as a king or as a slug? Otherwise, there might be a suggestion that you would find this ancient theory interesting, and would profit from learning and thinking about it. If the dream concentrated on the creature in whose body you had been born again, then think about its characteristics and behaviour: could they relate to some present waking attitude or action of yours?

Rejection   As with all abstract dreams – dreams in which you wake more aware of an emotion than of any particular symbol – this may have been emphasising an emotion which is troubling you in waking life; or may even be a sort of counterweight, suggesting that you are over-confident of acceptance (whether the allusion was to your emotional or practical life). Dreams often compensate for a doubt, or too much confidence, in waking life. Look at yesterday's and tomorrow's dreams of hints.

Rejuvenation   We sometimes dream that we are young again, though the dreams more often relate to actions than to a conscious-ness that we have positively been rejuvenated. Wish-fulfilment?

Quite possibly. But also maybe confirmation that we are young at heart – or a reminder that we are, essentially, the same people we were when we were fifteen.

Relatives   Think, on waking from a dream of relatives, of the people concerned, their relationship to you, their faults and virtues, and in particular what you think of and feel about them. If the dream does not relate directly to them, i.e., if it is not a reflection of some characteristic which you have recently noticed (illness, maybe, or simply ageing), try to relate it to yourself and your own personality. The dream may have suggested you become more, or less, like them. This can be true of dreams about any other human being; but blood relationship underlines the possibility. The context, as always, is vital – does something need doing, or undoing?

Rent   Paying rent gives us the right to live in a particular place; so the allusion may be to the cost of being who and what we are – in terms, perhaps, of the psychological or other sacrifices we may have to make, and how we feel about them. Refusing to pay rent suggests that we find it increasingly difficult, or even impossible, to continue to subjugate an inner longing to what seems an outer necessity (we *want* to be an artist, *have* to be a stockbroker). Such a dream would clearly be a danger signal. Or was the rent (and the pressure) being increased? Someone paying us rent may owe us more than we realise, in waking life; or are we being a mean landlord, and extorting too much from them? Worried about a rent bill not yet paid? Again, things may be getting on top of you.

Rescue   From what? The suggestion is that you need rescuing in some way, but look for other symbols in the dream. If you are rescued from the *sea*, then the allusion may be your emotional life; but other people involved (the rescuer, or the rescued if you are doing the rescuing) will clearly be important.

Restaurant   See **Cooking**? If you were serving, then there is a hint that you are in some way contributing to the emotional satisfaction of others (who were the customers?), especially if you were serving food you provided yourself. In a restaurant with other people? Are you seeking contact, looking for psychological back-up? A difficult dream to interpret, for there are likely to be a number of possible allusions. Perhaps your memory focuses on one particular aspect, one particular symbol? Because *food* is involved, the connection is quite likely to be with your emotions.

Revolution   Are you in some way concerned, in waking life, with changing your present state in some way? If you were leading a revolution, or taking an active part in one, this seems a possibility: and there is the suggestion of violent, sudden change, though motivated by yourself. The dream may be suggesting this or warning against it, depending on the circumstances. If you were a victim of a revolution – being made a *refugee* or even being executed – the dream may be reflecting your concern about changes being forced upon you in waking life. Consider your dream reaction: frightened, protesting, antagonistic, steadfastly opposed?

Rice   Rice is thrown at weddings to encourage the fruitfulness of the married couple, so there is a strong connection with the conception and birth of children. This could be a wish-fulfiling dream, a hint or even a prophesy! Rice has also, in some societies, been a symbol of spiritual food; dreaming of eating a rice pudding may, even in our time, carry a deeper significance than we think!

Riches   A dream in which we are particularly conscious of being rich may allude to a waking preoccupation with money, but is more likely to refer to intellectual or spiritual riches, so carefully consider other symbols in the dream and what you were doing with the riches. Hoarding them (laying up knowledge for the future?), spending them (using knowledge to further your position?), envious of them (envying someone else's knowledge or perhaps intellectual power?). See **Gold**? **Silver**?

Riding   This dream must be interpreted *apropos* your own feelings about riding, presumably horse-riding; if not, think about the *animal* concerned, and in any event, see **Horse**. Does the dream relate to progress: were you jumping obstacles? Successfully or unsuccessfully? Were you worried or sanguine about them? But perhaps you were hunting? If so, what (who)? Bareback riding has an undoubted sexual connotation; that is a possibility, if slight. On horseback, one has a command of the landscape lacking when one is on foot. Was the landscape significant? This may well be one of those dreams which is difficult to interpret without support from other dreams.

Ring A ring carries much of the symbolism of the *mandala*, and this is true either of circular buildings, stone circles, or finger-rings. If the latter, there is almost sure to be a reference to the most important aspect of the ring in modern times – its appearance as a visible symbol of a human relationship, strongly hinting at marriage. Wish-fulfilment is a possibility; finding a ring may reflect your hopes about a new relationship, or the desire for one. The loss of a ring may reflect concern about the way a relationship is developing, or not developing; or about a long-term relationship which seems to be deteriorating. In ancient times, rings often indicated sovereignty (kings and queens, such as they are in modern times, are still usually invested with a ring at their coronation, and the Pope wears Peter's ring as a symbol of authority). For the Chinese, and the early Christians, a ring symbolises eternity. (Was your ring an 'eternity ring'?) About other rings there is something magical – think of the so-called 'fairy rings' found in the grass, of the ring around the Moon which is something special, of the ring of fire which surrounds Siva in Hindu legend, about the rings in Wagner's operas and the ancient Norse sagas, or Tolkien's modern one. So there may be a suggestion that your feet are too much on the ground, and that you should think more about the mysteries of existence.

Riot What kind of riot? Against what? The suggestion must be that the dream reflects something in waking life against which you are tending to rebel. But a riot suggests a lack of discipline; so this may be a strong hint that you need to plan more, need to set your thoughts in order – it is your thoughts that may be rioting; the dream may merely be pointing to some confusion in your mind. Are you living a somewhat riotous life at present?

Ritual What kind of ritual? A religious one? This is most likely, and the dream seems to be suggesting that some waking action or thought needs formalising. But as with all abstractions, look first for other symbols, then at surrounding dreams, and finally ask (see p. 45–6) for assistance.

River See, first of all, **Water**; and remember that this usually signifies a comment on your emotional life. The dream may well relate to the flow of your emotions – so was the river in flood, or was the water very low; was it placidly flowing or in spate? Is there a suggestion that your emotions need releasing, or that on the contrary they are flowing out of control? All sorts of symbolism is possible within such a dream; the breaking or construction of a dam, for instance; the meeting of river and *sea*; perhaps you were trying to swim upstream (with what success?) or drifting happily with the current. More generally, a river often symbolises life itself; so if your waking emotional state seems not to be a focus, apply the dream to your life in general. A river estuary has been seen as the point at which life meets the infinite, and will have much the same significance as a *gate* or *doorway*, though relating more to your relationship with the infinite than with personal development.

Road Because of our conception of time, we often think of life as a road stretching from life to death, and this may well be the symbolism to which your dream alludes; it is more likely to refer to your material life and prospects than the rather similar image of a **River** (see above). So were you travelling along it? – hopefully? – reluctantly? What were the obstacles, and did you overcome them? Were you putting your best foot forward? Was there a bend around which you could not see? Was the road uphill and difficult, or downhill and easy? This is a dream in which your feelings will be important. There may be other symbols within it which will refer you to one particular incident or problem in your waking life, though the dream may be a more general comment on the stage of life through which you are passing.

Robe Since you have chosen to look up *robe* rather than, say, *cloak* or coat, the garment in your dreams seems likely to have had a special significance, probably related to our idea of a robe as a ceremonial garment – one worn by a particular person, perhaps a *king* or a *priest*. And it in turn may have something to do with your image (a robe is put on over other garments, in order to present a particular picture to an onlooker – usually one of dignity or state). Were you wearing the robe proudly, or was it torn and disreputable? A comment on how you are at present seen by others, or believe you are seen? If you were discarding it, do you wish to be rid of or lay down responsibility? Was your robe a bath-robe? If so, had you donned it after a bath, and cleansed your system of something or someone? Or were you merely hiding your nakedness – concealing some all-too-true fact about yourself?

Robber See **Theft**.

Robot Robots obey us, but do so automatically; they are clever, but they imitate man rather than counterfeiting his abilities. Are you in some way behaving as a robot in your waking life, accepting arguments or instructions blindly, when you should question them? Or are you treating someone else like a robot, exacting unquestioning obedience from them?

Rocket For male dreamers, very possibly an allusion to orgasm; this may have a physical explanation, or may refer to a sexual difficulty if, for instance, the rocket fails to ignite, soar and 'go off'. It could on the other hand be a symbol of ambition; but you can apply the same test.

Rod See **Cane**.

Roof See **House**; a specific allusion to the roof may be puzzling; a roof damaged by gales might suggest some concern about a prospective shelter – worry about your home, your job? But look for other symbols in surrounding dreams; if necessary ask (see p. 45–6) for more identifiable symbols. Dreaming that your roof is leaking, you might care to check it; your unconscious may have spotted a weakness that your conscious self has missed.

Rooms See **House**. Discovering new and unfamiliar rooms in a familiar house is a frequent and encouraging symbol prompting you to broaden your horizons – or may reflect your beginning to explore new avenues of interest. A locked room can be the symbol of some mystery you are trying to penetrate.

Rope A rope can bind you, or someone else, and so may represent some constriction: were you cutting it, struggling to escape, binding someone else? How might this relate to some restriction in your waking life, or your desire to restrict someone else in some way? However, you can use a rope to escape – up a rope ladder, or down a knotted rope. In India, that is the case – the Indian Rope Trick symbolises man's escape from earth to the mystery and grandeur of heaven. Is there a parallel there? Or were you spinning a rope, and therefore preparing either to bind someone or make an escape? Remember that a bound figure could be you, even if you seem to be looking on. Is someone giving you more rope, even enough to hang yourself?

Royalty   In England, almost everyone has at some time dreamed about the Queen or some other member of the Royal family. This preoccupation with royalty is difficult to explain, though there is a reference to the King or Queen as archetypal Father or Mother of the State, so perhaps it has something to do with the way in which everyone associates the country with its ruling family – in which case the allusion is to your feelings about where you live. On the other hand such dreams are quite often comic, in which case there may be a hint of a wish to 'take down' those in authority over you. Obviously, if you are royal (and see **King**) everything will depend on what is happening to you: are you being crowned (and therefore revered – unless someone is 'crowning' you in a less regal manner!) or dethroned, or abdicating? The reference in any case is likely to be to responsibility and/or social position.

Rubbish   What, or who, is 'a load of rubbish'? What the rubbish actually *is* is perhaps less important than the fact that this is the word to which you have turned; the allusion is a pejorative one, so look to your waking life for the reference – then remember your dream and your attitude to the rubbish, whether you were clearing it up, sweeping it under the carpet, or whatever. The hint given by your dream will probably be a fairly obvious one.

Ruin   The allusion may well be a literal one: what is ruined? Your home? Someone associated with your job, or with a personal relationship? Or a building associated with a personal emotion or characteristic? A ruined church might represent the desuetude of your religious sense; a ruined railway station or airport the destruction of your travel plans, and so on.

Running   The desire to be first? In what race? For promotion, for the attentions of a particular person, for a job? Once you have decided (and see **Racing**), remember how you felt in the dream. Did you trip? Were there other contestants or were you running alone, and therefore competing only against yourself?

Rust   See **Iron**.

Sack The most obvious explanation is the punning one – 'getting the sack'. Could the dream have reflected your uncertainty about your future, or feelings about an employee? If something was trapped inside a sack, then there might be the suggestion that you are hiding something, or that someone is about to divulge some mystery. But in that case, why a sack rather than some other container? Look to the first suggestions first.

Sacrifice The solution of a dream about a sacrifice must lie in the reason for the sacrifice: human and animal sacrifice was designed to placate the gods – do you feel there is someone with whom you must ingratiate yourself? Or have you been chosen as the lamb who must be slaughtered to satisfy someone else? Look for other symbols in the dream, though it could simply be the result of your feeling put-upon.

Safe Were you locking something in a safe, or safe-breaking? In either case, the object which was being safeguarded should give you a clue to the meaning of the dream. It may represent a secret, an aspect of your character which you want to keep from public view. As with all symbols of security, it could represent virginity, and a man dreaming of opening or breaking into a safe should keep this in mind. See **Lock**, **Key**.

Sail A symbol of hope? Were you on a desert island and watching for the possibility of rescue? If so, have you in some way been isolated recently? What or who is likely to come to your rescue? The dream may be making a suggestion. If you were sailing in a storm and the sail broke loose, or was bowling you along at a great rate, the allusion may be to your emotional life (on which the elements often comment). Was there a suggestion of losing control? Or of making the best possible use of some element of your personality?

Saint A difficult subject to interpret for a typically agnostic modern man or woman. The suggestion must be that the dream refers to some part of your personality which seems to you to be 'good', to be the better part of you; so whether you were listening to the saint, reverent towards him, or scornful and derisive, will be important – as will other people's reactions. The crucifixion or tormenting of a saint strongly suggests that you are under psychological pressure. The symbol seems likely to be rather similar to a dream of the *Madonna*, if a little less forceful.

Sale What was being 'sold off'? Was it a reject sale, or a sale of damaged goods? The idea seems to be one of devaluation. There could be a reference either to this or to finding a bargain, getting something 'on the cheap'. Since money is involved, the reference might be to your emotional life: are you 'selling yourself too cheaply'? Or not valuing someone, or their devotion, sufficiently highly?

Salt Salt is enormously important to our physical well-being, and man has always recognised the fact; so a large number of super-stitions have attached themselves to the mineral, and it has become symbolic of other necessary elements of our spiritual life – of life itself, of immortality, wisdom, fidelity. It has been used to dismiss a visitation by the Devil, and to spill it has always been a symbol of misfortune, a waste of life in some way. So to dream of hoarding salt is a suggestion that you are much concerned to hang on to your life as it is, to maintain the status quo; to dream of spilling salt may well indicate that in some way you are wasting yourself, physically, spiritually or morally. A dream of using it to ward off evil could refer to some contest between good and ill which is on your mind at present.

Sanctuary Taking refuge from someone or something? What does that someone or something represent? Look for clues in the other symbols of the dream. Similarly, *where* were you taking sanctuary? In a *cave* or a *church*, or someone else's *house*? The dream's purpose is to draw attention to the fact that you need help, protection, and that it must be particularly reassuring – not merely a bolt-hole, but some specially safe hiding-place. You could want to take refuge 'in' someone else. Maybe you want to retreat back into the womb, the ultimate safe place. Again, look for clues elsewhere.

Sand We still often associate sand with time, despite the fact that sand-clocks have long since vanished, and even egg-timers are now electronic! The idea of the sands of time running out is still very much a part of our folk memory and must be the first image that occurs to us when thinking about a dream of sand, even if there seems no obvious allusion. Dreaming of lying comfortably on a sandy beach may have this kind of connotation, if you were specially conscious of the comfort of the sand, giving you a pleasant resting-place: you have enough time. Walking on sand is difficult and can even trip you up; much more dangerous is quicksand – the association may still be with time, but the allusion to the difficulty of making progress (though in that case, why did your unconscious choose sand as the symbol, rather than, say *mud*?).

Saucepan   So what's *cooking*? Remember that containers often represent the feminine, so *cherchez la femme*. Was everything coming along nicely, or were you over-hasty, turning the heat up too much?

Savage   See **Tribe**; a specific savage may represent some savage element in your own personality which you may not feel you have sufficiently under control. Look for other clues: what was the savage wearing, was any part of his/her body particularly prominent, or was it the behaviour which was out of place?

Saw   There is always the pun, of course: who was it that you saw? More literally, a saw is both an instrument of destruction and of creation, so what was being sawn is important: were you (or the person wielding the saw) cutting down a *tree* or preparing *wood* with which to build something? A saw has teeth: have you visited, or should you visit, the dentist?

Scales   A symbol still much associated with justice, for scales have for thousands of years represented the way in which we balance one thing against another – good against evil, truth against equivocation. So what was being weighed, and what does it stand for in your life? The reference could be to some current problem which you are trying to sort out – 'weigh up' – in your own mind, or to someone in whom your confidence has perhaps been shaken; or there may be a physical question to be decided, with two options to choose between.

Sceptre   Difficult to avoid the suggestion that this could be nothing but a phallic symbol, and an extremely confident one at that.

Proudly bearing your sceptre, who were you trying to impress? Being presented with one, who was trying to build your confidence? Whose *king* were you? It is possible that the dream could have merely been about your conception of your own superiority, your confidence in your own power. But your unconscious, choosing this particular symbol, which has always stood for physical strength, surely had something else on its mind?

School A dream that we are back at school is not all that uncommon, generally seems to indicate that we are not as sure of our place in the world as we may think – that we don't know as much about life as we believe. The dream may be your unconscious's compensatory attempt to shake your confidence a little, to point out that you don't know everything; maybe that you should be a little cautious. There may be an allusion to some new learning task that you have undertaken, or are about to undertake. There may be an implied rebuke, if you have to wear a dunce's cap or stand in the corner! If you were the *teacher*, of course, that's another matter. But must you school yourself to do something?

Schoolmaster/Schoolmistress See **Teacher**.

Scorpion Something dangerous and frightening: the question, as always, is why your unconscious should have chosen this particular symbol. Perhaps the poisonous tail is a clue. Is someone spreading poisonous gossip about someone? Are you the gossip? One hopes not – but the dream may be pointing out the damage you can do. No civilisation has suggested that scorpions represent good; so you must look to the idea of evil, suffering or pain for a solution. Could there be a Zodiacal reference to Scorpio?

Screen A screen hides things, but also protects you from draughts. What purposes did it serve in your dream? If you or someone else were hiding behind a screen, what do you need to conceal in waking life, or what do you suspect someone else is keeping from you? Did you throw down the screen, or were you discovered behind it? Are you screening someone? If the screen was merely protective, is there a suggestion that you should take a little more care of yourself in some way?

Screw The possibility of a pun should not be ignored, even if you do not normally use that kind of language. For a man, a dream of driving in a screw, or a *nail*, may not be without sexual significance. But you can screw someone in the financial sense too. Or you, or someone else, can be 'all screwed up'. Who and why? Look for other clues in the dream.

Sea   Almost always a reference to our emotions, for early man believed that everything originated in *water* – in a wild and undisciplined, mysterious and illimitable ocean. As the source of all life, the sea contains everything, is the basic material from which everything we know grew, though the allusion is more often to our spiritual and emotional lives than to material things. Being such a general symbol, it is extremely difficult to interpret; but it is fair to suggest that any dream in which the sea is central, whether calm and placid or unruly and undisciplined, is likely to have its basis in our emotional life. Hopefully there will be other symbols in the dream which will help you to 'place' it more accurately; if not it may be a case of studying those dreams which precede and follow it, or asking (see p. 45–6) for elucidation.

Seasons   Each season carries its own expectations: Spring, of hope, rebirth; Summer, of fulfilment, of fruition; Autumn, of fading hopes, melancholy and harvest; Winter, of cold, the death or at least temporary disappearance of living things. A dream in which you are specially conscious of a season may reflect any of these emotions – but it is worth noting that the Chinese believe that the seasons represent the natural order of things, that they are inevitable and immortal; there is a possibility that your dream was an attempt to put something in proportion.

Secret   What was the secret? Were you about to blab it out? Is there a reference to some secret in your waking life, and could the dream have been prompting you either to keep or reveal it? It may have confirmed or warned, depending on the context.

Secretary   The dream will probably be personal, and may involve your attitude to service and in particular to a person you serve, or who thinks you should serve him/her; or to someone you wish to see in a subservient capacity. But it will depend much on your view of what a secretary should be and do.

Seed   A sexual dream is a possibility, especially for a man. But the planting of seed and its germination need not necessarily refer to human pregnancy – it could represent an idea which you wish to plant in someone's mind – or which needs to grow quietly until you have the means to develop it properly, or the time comes to harvest it. Hindu temples preserve seed as a representation of life itself, and this is a strong symbol which can appear even if we are not conscious of its basis.

Seesaw   On the face of it, a reference to indecision, so the first thing to consider is whether, in waking life, we are vaccillating, unable to make up our minds about some person, idea or action. What was your relationship to the seesaw? Were you balancing it successfully? Or was someone on the other end much heavier than you and keeping you 'in the air'? If so, who was it? Or were you the one who was anchoring your end of the seesaw solidly to the earth – the person on the other end disappointed and protesting? Were you let down with a bump, or did you 'let someone down'?

Selling   What were you selling, and what did it stand for? The action of selling suggests that you wanted to get rid of something, if possible for profit. But see **Market**, **Sale**.

Serpent   See **Snake**.

Servant   A dream of being a servant may be putting us in our place: perhaps we have been over-confident lately – paying too little attention to someone whose authority deserves respect. On the other hand, the dream may reflect an attitude of resentment in waking life; or the wish, if someone else was the servant, to put someone in their place. All depends on the people involved, and on the relationship with them (in the dream). The very term 'servant' has, these days, a pejorative connotation which it did not necessarily have years ago; pride in service is now out of fashion – yet the dream may be suggesting (if you were not uncomfortable or ashamed) that you should think about the service you are giving to your employer. There may be an allusion to the well-known Biblical phrase about the 'good and faithful servant'. A compliment from you to yourself, for work well done?

Sewing   A creative act, also one which may indicate care for the future ('a stitch in time saves nine'). What kind of garment were you making or mending, and to whom did it belong? That will almost certainly be significant. Were you being neat and careful, or careless? Were you confident that your work would last? The dream may be a suggestion that you should be more careful about any waking task which requires the kind of attention sewing usually demands. Or could there be an allusion to sowing – wild oats, perhaps?

Sex   There are allusions to sex and sexuality in many dream symbols, and we have referred to this in the first section of this book (see p. 25). The purely sexual dream, leading to orgasm and/or emission, is common chiefly with adolescents (unless an adult is more or less severely sexually deprived). Allusions to sex in dreams are another matter. Just how common these are is still a matter of opinion, with the Freudians continuing to insist, though with decreasing coherence, that almost every dream symbol is sexual in nature. However, it is certainly true that our sexual needs or cravings are often expressed in dream symbolism. This can sometimes be very uncomfortable, especially if (as is frequently the case) we have thoroughly suppressed the instincts to which the dream refers. What our dreams ask is that we should freely admit that human sexuality is extremely diverse – much more diverse than puritans allow – and recognise the fact. There is no such thing as an unnatural sexual act, if by that we mean one unknown elsewhere in nature: incest and rape, for instance, are common in species other than man. This does not mean that we should, or need, express openly those inclinations to which our dreams refer. (It may, however allow us to be much more tolerant of those whose sexual proclivities are less conventional than our own.) Recognising a sexual element or symbol in a dream, we should ask ourselves whether there is a suggestion that some repression or other is giving rise to the kind of tension which may prove troublesome. If not – relax and enjoy!

Shadow   This could be a literal reference to our psychological shadow (see p. 37): ask yourself what the shadow represents. Some societies believe that the shadow represents the soul, and that the disappearance of one's shadow is fatal; self-criticism would be the obvious explanation of such a dream. But are you in someone else's shadow, or are you casting a long shadow over someone else's life or character?

Shells   There is a connection with *water*, probably the *sea*, so refer to those if apposite. Shells themselves have sometimes had a sexual connection, representing the female genitals; there is that possibility too. The conch shell has, from time to time, been important to various peoples: sometimes as the counterpart of a *trumpet* : was one being sounded, in your dream? There has been a Christian connection, too, shells playing a part in the ceremony of baptism (the *water* connection, again). A shell is one of the emblems of Venus; could there be a reference there?

Shepherd   The allusion to the Good Shepherd is irresistible to anyone brought up in the Christian tradition. But that is not a specifically Christian image – the Egyptians, the Greeks, the Buddhists all had their Good Shepherd, and of course Krishna was connected with shepherds. Was your shepherd herding *sheep* or *goats*? Were you one of the flock, or the shepherd himself? Might any sheep and goats have represented people you know? Have you been trying to categorise your friends or colleagues recently, dividing the sheep from the goats? In that case the dream could have been your vision of your place in society – or against society: maybe you were doing your best to escape from the herd? Your feelings about the dream, as always, will be important: did you resent being herded with others into the restriction of a pen, or feel pleased to be part of the herd?

Shield   The idea of protection is the paramount one: against whom were you shielding yourself? Or who was successfully protecting themselves from your thrusts? A shield was, in mythology, sometimes equated with virginity. What was the shield like? Of what metal? Was it large, and therefore highly protective, or did you feel it was inadequate? Are you shielding someone, in waking life? Was the dream encouraging or discouraging you?

Ship   Always spoken of as feminine, ships venture out on the *sea*, which as we have seen almost invariably represents our emotions. Are you storm-tossed, emotionally? If so, was the dream reassuring? Did you reach harbour or was there a shipwreck? There may be a reference to a particular woman (perhaps your mother: there is a certain resemblance between the protective ship and the womb). Writers have sometimes drawn the analogy of the Ship of Life, crossing uncertain waters; probably another allusion to your emotional life. The atmosphere in the dream – of calm or storm, assurance or nervousness – will certainly be important. If you are familiar with the I-Ching, a boat represents crossing the water – going ahead with plans, while remaining aware of any dangers involved. Also travelling.

Shipwreck See **Ship**, above. Remember, this is not likely to be a predictive dream; more likely a warning of psychological rocks ahead, or of a practical difficulty of some kind. So examine the course of any project to which you think the dream may refer – and prepare a lifejacket, just in case!

Shirt Occasionally men dream of being out in the street clad only in their shirt (a variation on the *nudity* dream). The dream may simply be taking you down a peg or two: have you been over-confident or a little too superior lately? Was the shirt uncomfortable? Have you a 'hair shirt' of some sort to wear, at present, in waking life? Are you contemplating or have you taken a financial risk lately: likely to lose your shirt?

Shoe In ancient times the shoe was a symbol of freedom, for only slaves went barefoot. These days, however, the allusion may just be physical (are your shoes too tight?) – unless you are too big for your boots in some way! Foot fetishism apart, women's shoes strongly attract some men (and can certainly be taken as sexual symbols). Taking off shoes, however, can be a sign of reverence. Was someone else wearing the shoe in question? Could you want to *shoo* them away? Did the shoe fit, as in *Cinderella*?

Shooting See **Gun**. Who were you shooting at, and why? Or were you giving a demonstration of skill? If so, to what could that allude in your waking life? Yes, if you are a man, a woman could certainly be involved, in which case the dream is not so much a hint, more a statement of intent!

Shop There is a similarity between a dream of a shop and of a building full of *rooms*: the allusion may well be to your mind, full of new ideas (or of old ones that need clearing out, rearranging or cataloguing). The kind of shop in question may give you a hint about the area of your waking life to which the dream is alluding. But have you choices to make? Are you spoiled for choice? Remember underground slang: has someone shopped you? Or are you about to shop them?

Shrinking Shrinking, like Alice after drinking her potion, suggests some diminution of self-esteem or a hint that you are not quite as large in other people's estimation as in your own. Even if the shrinking figure did not seem to be you, that may be the dream's intent (but see other symbols within it). Some object which is shrinking may well carry different allusions; what could the object symbolise? (It may still be some aspect of your character or personality.)

Sickness To dream that you are sick does not necessarily mean that you are ill, though it may be some kind of suggestion that all is not completely well. If you are actually feeling tired or exhausted and not yourself, then the dream may be trying to overrule your refusal to see a doctor. Take the hint.

Siege The suggestion is of an attack on yourself – on something you probably hold dear. For a woman, it may be, in the old-fashioned phrase, an attack on your virtue; and you may even see it that way, though men these days do not on the whole 'lay siege', or have to! Was the enemy gathered around a castle or a town? What was its name? – there may be a clue there.

Signal Traffic signal? Railway signal? Whichever, the important thing is whether it was at red or green, stop or go – and whether you felt inclined to obey it, or planned to overshoot it. If the latter, and a crash ensued – or even a near miss – then the warning is very obvious. Such a symbol should not need a great deal of interpretation: it must surely refer to some decision or action which is much on your mind at the moment.

Signature Your signature is in a very real sense your self; even if we sign a brief note to someone, we are making an affirmation just as real as if we were witnessing a document in front of a solicitor. So whether you signed confidently and with a flourish, or hesitantly, is important. And what were you signing? The reference is no doubt to a decision of some kind.

Silver   Through its association with the Moon, silver has always been regarded as peculiarly feminine (gold, on the other hand, is considered masculine), and has been related to chastity. There may be an allusion here, or one to money. The other symbols in the dream will be important in deciding just what it means: refer to other entries.

Singing   If you are a singer, wish-fulfilment – or a warning, if you are in danger of straining your throat. Otherwise, a celebration, or just an indication of general happiness?

Skating   Skating is a marvellously free form of movement, provided you are adept at it; to most of us, watching the champions, it seems to require little effort, and the most elaborate acrobatics are performed with ease. If you were the skater, and doing well, this may be a reassurance in the area where it is most needed. On the other hand, if we venture on the *ice* we feel insecure on its slippery surface; and there may be a warning that we need to keep our balance in some area of our waking life. It may be worth remembering that ice – thin or otherwise – is strongly related to *water* – so there may be a reference to your emotional life. Or should you be 'getting your skates on'?

Skeleton   Do you need to reduce some complex situation or argument to its bare bones? This seems the most obvious suggestion, though as usual the context will tell you more. Otherwise, the dream may have something to do with your attitude to *death*; this would certainly be the classical interpretation, especially if the figure is carrying a scythe or wearing a hood – such a dream (though the image will be familiar to anyone interested in the Tarot) is less likely now than a generation ago. In any event, such a dream should be thought-provoking rather than frightening. Was the skeleton hidden in your cupboard? So what is the scandal someone is hoping to conceal?

Skin   Our skin is an important part of the self we present to people: the dream may therefore be about our image. If it was spotty and disfigured, the allusion is obvious; if fine, smooth, and clear, then presumably you have little to worry about. A snake sloughing its skin may be an allusion to the necessity for change (but see

Snake!). If you are concerned or worried about your skin, the dream may be wish-fulfilment.

Skull See **Skeleton**; the skull has always been specifically a *momento mori* – so see **Death**, remembering that it is by no means a negative symbol. Remember too that in some societies the skull has been a reference to the inheritance of knowledge from ancestors.

Sky See **Weather**.

Skyscraper A phallic symbol? New York would probably be glad to assent, and the shape of the oldest skyscrapers seems to derive from the sexual fantasies of architects! So a man dreaming of the demolition of a skyscraper, or of it collapsing, may well have something to think about. Ascending a skyscraper suggests something else. Of course if you live in a skyscraper, or would like to live in one, the dream may mean something else altogether – yet the urge itself, some psychologists would suggest, may not be unconnected with sexuality.

Slaughter On the face of it, this might be expected to be a highly unpleasant dream, and is likely to have been very forceful. But (see **Death**) it may be a preparation for rebuilding: maybe some characteristic of your personality, and trait, some attitude really needs to be killed, and your unconscious is tired of the resistance you are putting up. What was being slaughtered is the strongest hint of the meaning of the dream.

Slavery No one longs to be a slave, to anyone or any thing, and your dream is more likely to allege slavery to an idea or an attitude than anything else. Were you complacent about your slavery, or longing to escape from your shackles? Keeping someone else as a slave – even if it was not anyone you recognised – may carry the same interpretation; but if the slave was someone close to you, there is a suggestion that you are in some way looking upon them as your possession. Think again. Slavery *en masse* is more likely to refer to a social attitude, your view of your own 'class' or situation in life.

Slimming Unless you have a problem with your weight, this is more than likely a reference to some idea which needs rationalisation, 'slimming down'. Were you successful or unsuccessful?

Slums A dream that you are living in a slum seems likely to be a reference to dissatisfaction with the present circumstances in which you are living – not necessarily with your physical surroundings, but perhaps with your job, or with your attitude to it and to life in general. Do you feel that there are better things towards which you should aspire? Your attitude in your dream is important – whether you were escaping from the slums, or trapped in them. Physical places, in dreams, are often allusions to states of mind, and this may be the case here. You may be capable of better things, of lifting your mind from mundane matters to something more worthwhile.

Smoke Ascending smoke has been seen, in the past, as both a signal and a symbol of escape from earth to heaven. These days, the former is probably most likely. Was the smoke white or black, and could that be a hint of the dream's intention? Was the smoke a smoke-screen: and if so, what was it hiding, and are you at the moment putting up some sort of concealing barrier between your real feelings and your actions, or in some way hiding from the outside world?

Smoking It used to be the case that a young person, dreaming s/he was smoking, was looking forward to adulthood. Since smoking became a disreputable act this presumably no longer happens; and the symbolism must now be rather obscure – unless of course you are trying to give up smoking and it is a wish-fulfilment dream. A dream of smoking in a non-smoking zone, or of upsetting someone by smoking, may refer to some other act of which you are not specially proud or which may cause trouble – or it may suggest that you are being particularly objectionable and bloody-minded! Remember 'there's no smoke without fire'; are you failing to recognise some emotional state suffered by someone else?

Snail The form of the snail's shell is not unlike a simple *labyrinth*, so it has sometimes been taken as the symbol of something hidden and mysterious. But we associate snails with slowness, so it may be a hint that you should speed up some process, perhaps a thought-process – or slow down in some way!

Snake One of those dream symbols at which everyone winks, knowingly: ah, yes, a fear of snakes equals a fear of the penis. Well, it is true that some psychologists would claim that the snake is the archetypal phallic symbol and it is fair to consider the possibility first, examining your attitude to the dream snake and what it meant to you, then relating your emotions to your sexuality. The snake however has a long and extremely convoluted history of symbolic meaning in many civilisations, sometimes related to sex and sometimes not. The Christian story of the snake as presiding over the tree bearing the fruit of knowledge is clearly sexual in origin, given the frequently manic early Christian assumption that sex equalled evil. Often found in the secret places of the earth, the snake came to represent underground, occult, often magical forces, but also considerable energy, and was usually considered to be not only wise but extremely devious. More subtle analogies are too many even to list; they vary from civilisation to civilisation. Many of them are now obscure. If you have recurring dreams about snakes, or a snake, you could – unless you wish to seek professional help – look the subject up in a good dictionary of myth and legend. One general thing to note is that when the snake is represented as being attacked, by an eagle for instance (it is often seen wriggling in an eagle's talons, in early art), it invariably represents the principle of evil being subjugated to the power of good. This is worth remembering.

Snow   Untrampled snow has always been a sign of purity, virginity, or at worst, frigidity; so if you were plodding through it in large boots, or trying to prevent others from doing so, the allusion is obvious. There may be a connection with a particular person or place – note the other symbols in the dream. There is, as with *ice*, a connection with *water*, so the emotions may be involved: are you being particular cold, at present, emotionally? Was the snow melting? Were you hoping for a thaw?

Soldiers   Soldiers represent the male principle at its roughest; no doubt unjustly, in a civilian context they suggest rape and pillage – so a dream in which they are involved is hardly likely to be either pleasant or comforting, unless the promise of sexual ravishment is rather attractive to you. If a particular soldier was recognisable the meaning will be less general, and especially if he is not actually in the army, there may be an element of wish-fulfilment or of fear – the context will decide the question.

Soup   Are you in it? Or 'in a stew'? Or in hot water? Were you adding salt or spice? – perhaps you should add a little vigour and positivity to your arguments. Confused by the number of ingredients? – then how should you cope with them? See **Food**, **Cooking**.

Sowing The immediate reaction must be that this is a reference to impregnation; so the dream may refer (if you are a woman) to a desire to become pregnant – and remember that this is one area in which prophetic dreams are not unknown. If you were not sowing the seed, who was? Of course, the dream may have been more abstract than that. If you are a man have you a conscious wish to father children? Or it may have been an apprehensive dream: were wild oats involved? It is likely that some symbol in the dream will point to the woman involved. This dream could also refer to sowing new seed for the future – new ideas, a new career, new beginnings in some shape or form. See **Seed**, **Sewing**.

Space A dream of space, unless you long to become a spaceman or woman, seems most likely to be associated with the space within – with the exploration and expansion of your own mind. Were you setting out for a particular destination? Was the lift-off and flight trouble-free? Was anyone else involved?

Spear Freud suggested that all weapons were phallic symbols, and this certainly rings true of the spear in particular (not only because of its shape, but the way it is carried and thrown). So the first attempt at interpretation should certainly move in that direction. At whom was the spear thrown; were you afraid of it or throwing it with exultation? Early societies saw it as a fertility symbol, too; could there be a connection there? The Christian association of the spear with Christ's passion is less likely to play a part in modern dreams.

Spectacles The necessity to examine something more closely? Shortsightedness on your part – or someone else's – about some project or person? Or, if you had lost your spectacles, the inability to see what is in front of your face? The suggestion that you physically need spectacles, or new ones? Are you making a spectacle of yourself?

Speed The circumstances of the dream should explain it; and your emotion – whether the speed was exhilarating or frightening, whether you were afraid of a crash or convinced of your safety. How were you travelling – by *car*, and if so whose car? See **Flying**. Were you speed-*skating*?

Spelling   This is likely to be a rather obscure dream, but a dream of not being able to spell suggests the inability to work something out, get something right. On the other hand, since illiteracy is generally regarded as shameful, there may be an allusion to some aspect of your waking life which you would rather no one knew about. The word which you could not spell may represent a clue to the dream's intention. Do you need to spell something out in detail?

Spending   See **Money**. If you were spending freely, the allusion may well be to the freedom with which your emotions are being expressed; or the opposite may be true. Remember that 'spending' is a euphemism for male ejaculation.

Sphere   A sphere is the symbol of perfection; also of the world itself; when carried (as a king carries an orb) it is a symbol of command. It is also a *mandala*. A very general symbol, then; you may have to look for more clues, or ask (see p. 45–6) for elucidation. If more than one sphere was involved, the temptation would be to ask to what idea or person you simply wish to say 'Balls!'

Sphinx   The Sphinx is a figure of mystery, possessed of great knowledge; it is difficult to believe that any dream which involves it is not in some way involved with a lack of understanding. Look for other symbols in the dream for the basic subject.

Spices   If you were adding spices to food, then the suggestion seems to be that some area of your life lacks spice. What sort of food were you cooking? Where was the cooking taking place?

Spider   What is your attitude to spiders? Most people are obscurely afraid of them, though in the Western world they are chiefly harmless. Was the spider spinning a *web*? – in which case are you planning to trap or entangle someone, or are you the trapped victim? In ancient myth the great spider spun the threads of destiny, and the web itself can sometimes be a general symbol for life and its complexities, in which we are seeking a pattern.

Spinning   See **Spider**, if relevant. There is an equivalent symbol in the action of spinning threads on a wheel: many myths have the vision of an ancient woman spinning the *web* of fate. So the preoccupation may be with the shape of the future. How did the spinning go? Was there a complex pattern; were there any faults? What *colour* was the cloth? Were you consciously planning to make a particular garment? Does the dream reflect your hopes or fears?

Spine   As with any dream of a particular part of the body, there may be a reference to some weakness or actual pain. If not, then are you being spineless about something, failing to face up to it? Do you need to put some spine into an idea, see that it has strength and backbone?

Spiral   A very ancient symbol which seems originally to have represented expansion, but had many other meanings in various societies, sometimes representing the air, sometimes the revolutions of the planets, a whirlwind, a maze. The appearance of the pattern alone might seem to suggest a state of confusion, presumably about some particular problem. It is also a basic pattern of growth. Otherwise, look for the symbols which surround it, or ask (see p. 45–6) for further references.

Spire   A church spire, soaring towards the heavens, was originally a symbol of aspiration towards the heavenly state, a finger pointing towards God. The same meaning could inform a modern dream, particularly if you are of a religious nature. On the other hand, like any upright and pointed object, there could be a phallic interpretation. The context of the dream should make this clear. The appearance of the spire, whether it was plain or highly decorated, its state of repair, the kind of building to which it was attached, whether you are ascending or descending it, building, repairing or demolishing it – all this is relevant.

Spitting   These days, usually a symbol of distaste or contempt. So were you spitting at someone? And if not, at what – and what does that something represent? Occasionally we still spit for luck. Could that be the allusion?

Spoon   We use a spoon to eat with; so the dream may relate to our means of obtaining sustenance – perhaps intellectual or spiritual.

This is particularly likely if you were conscious of the spoon itself rather than the *food* it was bearing to your mouth. The spoon could represent a teacher, a course of lessons, one's own appetite for learning. A valuable *silver* spoon clearly adds importance to the subject; a *wooden* spoon might indicate a more practical and down-to-earth attitude. What you were actually doing with the spoon – eating, or stirring things up – will be equally important. Locking a spoon away might indicate a refusal to be interested in something, a conscious decision to set aside the means of learning, to refuse to help yourself.

Sponge An unlikely subject for a dream? But no subject is really unlikely. A sponge soaks up water; people are sometimes said to soak up knowledge or learning like a sponge. Are you in the middle of a learning project at the moment? Or is someone using you as a sponge, to mop up their own mess?

Sport To dream of being involved in a sport may reflect an interest in or need for physical exercise – or could involve wish-fulfilment, if you are an ambitious sportsman or woman. Objects involved in a sport may be significant; they should be found listed elsewhere in this directory. Do not think only of your physical self: the allusion may be to another area of your life, suggesting the need to move about, to be more athletic, in your thinking processes for instance.

Spy A dream of being a spy, or discovering one, seems to suggest some insecurity about your own image and the way it is presented. Are you in some way 'under cover'; is someone closer to finding the real you than is comfortable? There may be a much more literal allusion to some current waking action of yours; other clues in the dream should make this quite clear – in which case your success or failure, or any other feeling in the dream should obviously be applied to it.

Square A square seems from earliest times to have represented the earth (the *circle* representing the heavens – see **Mandala**). There is also the traditional equation, which seems to have begun with Confucius, of the square with honesty, being 'on the square', as Freemasons put it. The square represents order rather than chaos, a basically solid, secure and dependable state of things. To this has more recently been added the suggestion that to be square is to be out of fashion, out of date, not in tune with the times. Any of these allusions may apply in your dream, depending on its context.

Squash   A quick-moving game of squash could refer to the speedy development of a waking situation whose complexities may relate to the rules of the game. So the suggestion may be that you should be even more vigilant and quick, or that you should relax. But there is surely also a reference to your competitiveness. Were you winning the game? Losing? Falling over a little too often? And see **Sport**.

Stabbing   See **Knife**.

Stable   The old myth about the labour of Hercules, condemned to clean out the Augean stables, may still find an echo; it is a never-ending job. Could it relate to some laborious and not altogether agreeable task which you must perform in waking life? It may be a reflection of the tedium you are experiencing – or a punning reference to the stability of some project or situation. In Christian mythology we remember Christ's birth in a stable; so there may be an allusion to (ill-deserved?) poverty.

Staff   A staff in the sense of a walking-stick is likely, in the case of a dreaming male, to be phallic in its implication – so if you are hitting or attacking someone with it, think on. Using it on a walk, in a perfectly normal manner, may simply be an expression of contentment. A dream involving a human staff of work-people will be more difficult to interpret, unless there was a particular theme: ask (see p. 45–6) for help.

Stage   There are too many references to the stage as a representation of life, for us not to grasp at that idea first. Unless this is a characteristic 'worry' dream – i.e., you know you have an important part in a play but cannot reach the stage – think first about the part you were playing and the piece being performed, and try to relate them to present circumstances. Are you pretending to be something you are not? Were you forgetting your lines, which suggests lack of confidence? Or was this happening to someone else, which might suggest that it is you who are confident; someone doesn't known their part, is letting you down. Did you know the play well, and so is the developing situation foreseeable and going according to plan? But remember all the time the suggestion of pretence: the stage reflects, but is not, real life. Or is there a pun – a new stage in your life?

Stain   On your character or reputation? That is the most obvious suggestion. What was stained? What *colour* was the stain? Was it easily removed? Were you particularly ashamed of it, or sorry that it happened?

Stair   It has been suggested that a dream of climbing stairs generally has a sexual context, and one can quite see why. So think about this first – was the climb difficult or easy, careful or careless, did it unduly exhaust you, was someone waiting at the top or could you not reach the top? But there may be the context of ambition: in which case much the same questions apply. Remember that a *house* can often represent your life, so you may be reaching out and up towards some new ambition or experience. Jacob's ladder, in the Old Testament with its climbing angels, symbolised the aspiration to mount from earth to heaven, from the material to the spiritual. Have you such aspirations? How successfully were you climbing?

Stamp   The allusion may be to money: you have to buy a stamp. And was the message worth the price of the stamp? Stamping a letter shows a decision to send it, so rather like fixing a seal it is a conclusive act. Should you make a final decision – now? But perhaps the stamp refused to be properly fixed or was peeling off. In which case, a little caution might not be a bad thing.

Star   The way to the stars has always been difficult if not impossible – yet man has always aspired to reach them; and the first possibility is that the dream refers to some ambition (perhaps corporeal, perhaps spiritual or intellectual) which, though it seems beyond reach, is nevertheless dear to you. If the stars were burning brightly and serenely, a comforting and encouraging dream; obscured by clouds or growing fainter? – the suggestion is less reassuring. Stars were gods, in ancient days, so there may be a quasi-religious reference. The Hindus regard a star as a symbol of constancy, and the reference has leaked into western mythology too. The dream may be encouraging you to be faithful – whether to a person or an idea.

Starvation   It is possible that you should have had a snack before going to bed. But dreams working as they do, the allusion is more probably to your need for less substantial food. Perhaps your mind is given insufficient food in some way you can recognise – a particular problem may be solved only after you have fed more information into your cranial computer, or you may not have enough to think about. Dreams of this sort sometimes occur when we have just finished a complicated task and the mind has not yet got used to the lack of a knotty problem – or sometimes when we have just retired, and have ceased to cope with daily problems at work. So there may be a suggestion that you should start a new project of some kind, or take some existing one further. Could you be emotionally starved?

Station   The suggestion is of a terminus, and therefore of some target, some place you want to reach, some objective you want to attain. Was the *train* making for or drawing into the station, or was there a delay? Were you waiting at the station, surrounded by your *luggage*? This would have a different connotation – the suggestion that you are about to set out on a *journey*; what were the announcements on the tannoy saying? The dream could be reassuring, or offer a warning of some kind.

Statue   Of whom? Of yourself? In which case, was it a tribute? – or was someone trying to pull it down or deface it? The recent demolition of statues of Lenin and Marx, in the Eastern communist countries, is fresh in our minds, so there may be a comment on some attitude or theory of yours which is unacceptable to others – or to your better self. In a similar way, your dream attitude to a statue of someone else, a friend or loved one, could certainly be admiring – or critical. Could you be putting someone on a pedestal? And if so, is that pedestal as firm as you may think?

Steam   Were you letting off steam, and could this be a hint – or an indication – or a warning? But steam still represents power, so perhaps you need to get up steam in relation to some project or other. We are also somewhat afraid of steam: there could be a warning here. Are you in hot water?

Steps   See **Stairs**, or **Footprints**?

Stew See **Soup**.

Stick See **Staff**, **Twigs**?

Stigmata This is a more prevalent dream symbol than might be supposed in an age when Christianity is in decline; the marks of the nails which pierced Christ's hands are said to have appeared, miraculously, on the hands of modern saints. Such a dream is likely to relate to religion, but also to your view of yourself. A saint? Really? Or are you metaphorically being crucified by someone – emotionally hurt?

Sting What were you stung by? A *bee*? A *wasp*? Remember that a bee dies after using its sting. It is a slight, but irritating and painful injury; so do you simply need 'waking up' in some way? Or could you be the wasp, wanting to wake someone else to a more lively appreciation of a situation or of a problem of yours? The part of the body on which you were stung may be relevant.

Stitch See **Sewing**? A dropped stitch could be a reminder: have you forgotten to do something? Again, neat or careless stitching could be an allusion to a job on which you are engaged at the moment.

Stomach Unless prompted by an uncomfortable or painful stomach, the punning allusion seems relevant: is there a waking job for which you simply have no stomach?

Stone The strength of stone is still its main characteristic; and stones as such have been used as part of religious buildings from the most ancient times – they often marked sacred sites, and stonehenges are to be found all over the world. So the reference may be to some extremely deep-rooted characteristic – perhaps a prejudice. Was the stone new, proud and upright or ancient, worn and tumbledown? Stones carved in phallic shapes are to be found all over the world, too, in ancient sites, and this is an allusion that cannot be dismissed out of hand. A broken stone can symbolise the end of something; or *death* – thinking of tombstones. The symbolism is extremely complex, and if surrounding dreams offer no clue, ask (see p. 45–6) for help. See also, **Jewel**?

Stool A stool is a means of support – but less substantial and supportive than a *chair*; a three-legged stool is sometimes fairly unbalanced, so there may be an allusion to some support-structure in your waking life which is less solid than you may think. A stool can be the means of reaching for something: are you using someone, in that sense, to gain advantage? Or are you merely constipated?

Storm   The obvious allusion would be to some kind of storm in your waking life. So consider your dream emotion: fear, confidence, hope, despair?

Stowaway   A stowaway wants to get somewhere without paying for it; and the other allusion is to secrecy. So are you trying in some way to get a free ride in waking life? Are you sneaking your way into someone's emotions, or taking advantage of them? (Do not forget that if you are stowing away on a *ship*, there is an oblique reference to *water*, which generally represents your emotions.) The ship may be a reference to your home, or the firm for which you work; are you in some way taking a free ride there?

Stranger   See **Man**.

Strangulation   This sounds like a nightmare. If it was not suggested by some constriction around the neck, then it is certainly a reflection of subconcious fear; and if you cannot relate it to any aspect of your waking life, and certainly if it recurs and is really frightening, you should seek professional help.

Straw   Was this a straw in the wind? – a suggestion that you have overlooked some clue, in waking life, which might bring about the solution of a problem; or were you casting a straw on the wind, and in that case should you find some way of testing public opinion about some planned course of action? Straw (unless it is thatch, which is another matter) suggests insubstantiality – but can also be comfortable; were you lying on a straw *bed*?

Stream   The allusion is to *water*, so the emotions may well be involved. Was the stream running freely, or blocked? Was it *muddy*, or crystal clear? Were you drinking from the stream, bathing in it? Was it cold and frigid, or warm and welcoming? All questions to apply to the area of your emotional life to which you feel the symbol may apply (and remember that an instinctive feeling that a dream applies to one particular area of your life is very often reliable).

Street The life of a busy street could certainly represent your present life, or life as a whole – crowded with incident or remarkably quiet. Were you rushing along it, or merely observing it? Was something or someone holding up the traffic, and if so were you impatient to remove the obstacle, or patiently waiting for it to go of its own accord? This could all relate to present problems or merely allude to how positively enjoyable life is at the moment. Other people or objects which particularly came to your attention should be treated as important, however, and may be a clue to a more individual meaning of the dream.

Strike A strike stops work – but stops it for a reason; so is there either a suggestion that you should put an end to a particular situation, or that someone else is about to do so? In which case, did you want to resolve the strike – was it a source of frustration – or did you feel that on the whole it was justified? Has an idea struck you?

String How long is a piece of string? Was there a reference to some situation which you can't see the end of, or which needs untangling? Was the string holding something together, just preventing it coming apart, or actually breaking? Are you stringing someone along – or they, you?

Struggle Who or what were you struggling with? The reference must surely be to some contest in your waking life – it could be with a person, a situation or an emotion; other symbols in the dream should provide a clue.

Stumble A dream that you are stumbling, or have stumbled and fallen, seems a warning which you should apply to an area of your waking life suggested, perhaps, by other symbols in the dream.

Stunt There may be an allusion to *juggling*, or perhaps you were an *acrobat*. But the very word is on the whole pejorative, so see **Trick**, **Trickster**.

Submarine *Water* is involved, the *sea*, so above all the dreams seems likely to refer to your emotions – and to your desire to examine them to their depths. If there is a particular waking problem that is emotionally taxing or disturbing, you should devote more time to analysing it rather than simply passively experiencing it, or suffering under it. Were you conscious of the submarine safely sinking to great depths? Or was there the suggestion of danger? – in which case are you being over-analytic? A submarine under strain, or under attack, suggests that you are under psychological pressure, and should seek means of escape.

Succubus   See **Incubus**.

Sucking   An action associated with infancy, but also strongly erotic; dreaming of sucking your thumb may be a suggestion that you return to the simplicity of babyhood, in some context or other; or the dream could have sexual connotations. Search it for more clues. Are you being a 'sucker'? Or feeling insecure?

Sugar   So who do you regard as sweet? – or too sweet? – or not sweet enough? What were you doing with the sugar? Does your life need sweetening – or are you think of giving someone a 'sweetener'? Were you taking a sugar-coated pill?

Suicide   The end of a project, or the suggestion that you should end one? Do not take this as any reference to your ending your own life, or anyone else's intention of doing so. See **Death**.

Suit   A suit of clothes hides our nakedness, but also has has much to do with our image; there may be either a suggestion or a criticism, in the latter case – or a reference to 'disguise' of some kind in the former. What have you to hide? Are you in a job, performing some task, in a partnership, which doesn't suit you?

Summer   See **Seasons**.

Sun   Pages could be taken up in exploring the various myths and legends connected with the Sun; but above all, civilisation has associated it with great power and energy, and seen it as the source of all life. A dream of an eclipse, then, may well allude to waning powers – or perhaps to a lack of energy spent on a particular project. Being sunburned may suggest that you have been too dangerously near the centre of things, and should in some way keep your distance. The Sun also represents the father, just as the Moon represents the mother; the former masculine, the latter feminine. That may be worth remembering. The Sun represents light (knowledge) as opposed to darkness (ignorance): so, a strong hint pointing you towards an increase of knowledge in one particular area? If someone else was brightly illuminated by the sun, this would seem a strong mark of your regard or admiration.

Surgery   If not motivated by simple apprehension about a coming operation, focus your mind on the part of the body on which surgery was being performed, and if there is any suspicion of anything wrong, consult your doctor. Amputation of a limb may allude to some factor which needs 'cutting out' of your life – do you know a Mr Legge? Is someone putting the finger on you? Have you been putting your foot in it? Are you paying 'an arm and a leg' for something? Consider the puns – but perhaps you should ask (see p. 45–6) for more clues.

Swamp   Since *water* is an element, this may be an allusion to a not altogether straightforward emotional situation, in which you may be bogged down. Was it difficult to escape? Were you actually drowning? Or was rescue in sight – and if so, what form did it take? Any sign of another person involved would obviously be significant.

Swimming   First of all, as always when *water* is involved, remember that the dream is very likely to concern your emotional life. Whether you were swimming or *drowning* is obviously important. Perhaps you were making good progress – even winning some kind of race? Perhaps you were being swept along by the current, totally out of control, or being pulled down by the water or the weight of your clothes. The manner, weakness or strength of your swimming probably mirrors your attitude to your emotional life. Are you coping? You may need help – this is very likely if you were drowning. You could be out of control if you were being swept along, but doing very well if your efforts were getting you where you wanted to be. Were you out of your depth – and is this illustrative of your present feeling? Your dream swim could be just a pun – that life is going swimmingly for you – this would be most likely if you were enjoying a lovely swim in warm, placid water.

Swinging   A swing seems to represent vaccillation – one minute up, the next, down. But then there is the modern sense of the word – being slap up-to-date; and the sexual connotation, too. So have you been procrastinating about some decision you have to make? If so, how you got off the swing in your dream will be very significant. A sudden fall or jump – or a gentle stopping of the swing? If you were 'swinging' – having a good time, uncaring of the eventual consequences – then your dream may be suggesting that you let up and try to enjoy life a bit more – or giving you a timely warning that you are taking certain risks. Or was there, do you think, an element of wish-fulfilment in your dream?

Sword   This may have been a phallic symbol, especially for a male dreamer. The sword is an aggressive weapon, held within a sheath; here, symbolically, are the masculine and feminine principles aptly portrayed. But it is important too, especially if you were being destructive of life, to ask yourself whether you are feeling particularly aggressive towards someone – whether you wish them harm in some way. Or, even more importantly, you may be cross with yourself, or for some reason not like yourself very much at the moment. These are important issues; consider them carefully, asking your dreams (see p. 45–6) for more help, and if confused getting professional advice.

Table   A table is important to us: we eat from one, often work at one. It can be a symbol of authority: we often think of our father sitting at the head of the table. There is an association with the *altar*. If it is really a central symbol (i.e., not just something being used for ordinary purposes) think of it as bearing something (there may be a pun there: what can't you bear?). See **Food**?

Tail   A pun seems really very likely: have you been telling tales, or tale-bearing? Or is there an association with *monkeys*? Are you at the tail-end of something?

Tape   These days the chief association is probably with recording tape: was someone recording you (i.e., taking notice of what you say)? Or were you editing a tape (taking notice only of what you *want* to hear)? Has someone got you taped? Were you caught up in red tape?

Target   What was aimed at the target? – see under the relevant symbol, **Gun**, **Arrow**, or whatever. But the target itself will certainly be important: what or who did it represent? Look for every possible association.

Tarot   The Tarot pack is in itself the most fascinating set of symbols, and the more you know about it the more complex the symbolism of your dream is likely to be (but the readier you will be to interpret it). Look for what specific cards represent – or, more likely, *who* they represent. See **Cards**.

Tart   The pun is obvious – it may even be quite difficult to conceive of anyone dreaming of a tart except in a punning fashion. So who is the tart? What were you doing to it/her? Was your dream expressing your real feelings about her? Was the tart unexpectedly delicious, or in the end too sweet – or expensive? Did it crumble as you picked it up?

Tattoo   A tattoo is famously or notoriously difficult to eradicate, so your dream may concern something which you feel you should or must remember, or some thought which you desperately want to retain. The words or picture tattooed are obviously important – but so is the part of the body being tattooed. Were you trying to remove the tattoo? Then ask the same questions – but why should you be so eager to forget?

Taxi   See **Vehicle**, **Car**? But you hire a taxi; you pay for it; you cannot be certain of the goodwill of the driver. Was he taking you in a direction in which you did not want to go? If so, look for the parallel in waking life. Who was the driver? Did he overcharge? – is something you seek likely to prove more expensive than you think?

Tea   For many or most English people, *the* social drink – and so likely to refer (if you were taking tea with someone) to your social life. Remember the atmosphere: happy or uneasy? Who was there, or who failed to arrive? Consider your waking relationship with them. Are you neglectful – or are they? Are you simply not being sufficiently considerate, in a social context? See **Thirst**?

Teacher If the teacher was unknown to you, the reference is probably to your – perhaps unconscious – need for knowledge. What kind of knowledge? What was the dream teacher teaching? If you knew the teacher, what are your recollections of him or her? Happy or unhappy? What is the association? Is your dream suggesting that a present waking preoccupation will make you happy or unhappy? If you were teaching, whether the class was attentive or inattentive may comment on your present relationship with those who depend on you.

Team Most of us are involved in teamwork of some kind: so what is your present team, and how does the dream comment on it? Were you a happy, efficient member, or out on a limb? How did the rest react to you? How was the team doing, and what part were you playing? The comment may well be a social one, rather than entirely personal. If you were captain, was this wish-fulfilment?

Teeth First, consider the practical considerations – did you wake with toothache, or gnashing your teeth, or with a loose tooth? Have you an appointment with your dentist? Remember, dreams can sometimes warn you of physical weaknesses before your waking body recognises them, so this may be a hint that you should make that appointment. But teeth have always suggested attack, presumably a hangover from the age when they were a major weapon; so who or what do you want to get your teeth into? If you dreamed of dentures, is there something false in your current waking attitude to someone or something? Teeth endure even longer than bones, and so can be a symbol of endurance.

Telephone Above all, a telephone, before conveying a message, attracts our attention: so perhaps your dream is telling you that someone badly needs to make contact in some way – not necessarily verbally, perhaps emotionally. You yourself could be the telephone, desperately ringing to attract the attention of someone else. Did you 'get through'? Was the line clear, or was there interference? Were you ringing Enquiries? Think over all these suggestions, always with the word 'message' in mind.

Telescope What, in your waking life, do you need to see more clearly? Someone? Some situation? Because a telescope (as opposed to binoculars) is usually used to look into space, there may be an intellectual or spiritual connection: perhaps you are worried about your own place in the wider scheme of things. Consider what you were observing in your dream. Men might remember that a telescope (which, after all, one erects, or draws out so that it becomes longer) could be a phallic symbol; at what – or who – were you pointing it?

Television If your dream was about something you saw on television, then forget the set itself: it was simply the means of jogging your unconscious. If you dreamed of something involving the television itself it is another matter. The screen is in one way a barrier between you and reality, as well as a conveyer of entertainment and ideas. So maybe it is suggesting that there is, or needs to be, a distance between you and the symbol you saw on the screen. Consider this with regard to the symbol itself. If the TV had gone wrong, or was destroyed, or you attacked it, you must think what it means to you – what you chiefly associate it with. Maybe you need to get more involved in current affairs, need to take life less – or more – lightly.

Tenant A tenant does not own the place where s/he lives, and is to some extent unsure of it. So are you rather unsure of your personality, of your place in society or at work? Were you unable to pay the rent? Or was it too high? Try to make the connection between the circumstances of the dream and the circumstances of your life. See **Landlord**?

Tennis Any *game* of which you dream is likely in some way to comment on your waking life; so whether the game went well or ill, whether you were cheating, will be significant. The fact that scoring in tennis includes the term 'love' may be meaningful.

Tent A temporary accommodation, referring to something in waking life which seems secure or even permanent, but may not be (was the tent secure, keeping the rain out or letting it in?). There may be an association with freedom, especially if you are an inveterate camper. Is there some situation from which you want to escape? Look, for enlightenment, at other symbols in the dream. Are you *intent* on some form of action?

Terminus Have you reached the end of something? – your tether, perhaps? Remember a terminus can be the start of a journey as well as the end of it. Did you know where you were going or where you'd come from? Could you find your ticket, or had you lost it (a reference to your motivation)? The presence or absence of other people may help you to place the dream and work out its specific reference. See **Railway**?

Thaw See **Water**: it seems very possible that the *ice* in your dream referred to some emotional blockage, some refusal to 'let yourself go' in some way – but your emotions have won; the ice is about to break. There seem to be no circumstances in which this could be a warning or negative dream: when ice thaws, even if a flood occurs, it is still a release and a relief.

Theatre Whether you were on-stage or merely a member of the audience will be crucial – if you were performing, so will the audience's response. This may be a wish-fulfilment dream, or a warning that the centre of things is sometimes not a comfortable place to be. If you forgot your words there may be a reminder of uncertainty; if you remembered them, of glibness. Great applause will be reassuring. As a member of the audience, did you admire the actors? What they were performing should suggest the symbolism involved, for it will doubtless refer to some area of your life. Was your dream encouraging you to take centre-stage and show off a bit?

Theft If you were the thief, what you stole may well represent something you feel you have achieved by some rather underhand method; you may fear discovery – were there any policemen about? If something was stolen from you, this could be a reference to something which you have lost against your will – a job, someone's affection? At all events, someone will be the loser in the waking situation to which the dream refers.

Thermometer A reference to temperature is usually to emotional temperature, so look for other symbols in the dream which may indicate what you have got yourself in a state about. Remember that dreams can be a warning: if you feel a little out of sorts, by all means take your temperature – though if in the middle of the dream you wake in a sweat because you are too hot, forget it!

Thirst If you dream that you are thirsty, you very often wake to find it true. However, if this is not the case think of the phrase 'to thirst after knowledge', and look for other symbols in the dream as an indication of the area to which you should give extra study.

Thread   In ancient myth, thread indicated the continuity of life, the thread of knowledge, the umbilical cord, and it is by no means impossible that your dream may have something to do with creativity: were you sewing, or knitting? This can often mean that some area of your waking life needs expansion, further consideration, 'working on'. If the thread broke, or was knotted or tangled, the inference is obvious, and all you must do is consider on which area of your waking life the dream was commenting. Other symbols should offer a clue.

Threshold   Rooms or houses, in dreams, often stand for new experiences or areas of life; and the threshold is the beginning of something new. The ancients saw it as a boundary between the 'real' and the magical' world (a boundary which today seems very vague to many people). Was the *door* closed? Were you prevented from entering? Or were you welcomed? Ws the *room/house* familiar or unfamiliar – i.e., should you spend more time on a special area of life, or open out a new and rewarding landscape?

Throne   The seat of majesty, authority, knowledge, wisdom, power. Were you securely seated upon it? Lucky you. But if you were tottering, or the seat was insecure, or you were merely struggling to reach it, perhaps you are less of a complete person than you think. Someone else on the throne probably symbolises power over you in some way, maybe emotional. Again, what was your attitude? Were you trying to dethrone them, or seat them more firmly? But don't just think of power – think of knowledge and wisdom, and your search or need for it. See **Royalty**?

Thunder   For primitive man, thunder was the Voice of God, or of a particular god, and the thunderbolt was his means of punishing man. That idea is far too deeply rooted for us to be able to ignore it, even in a modern interpretation of a dream. If you wake in the middle of a storm, it is reasonable to assume that thunder may have broken into your dream from the outside world; but if not, then it will certainly be worth considering whether your conscience is rebuking you for some action or attitude, or whether you are unconsciously aware that someone else, in a position of moral if not real authority, disapproves of you. (Thunder was/is invariably a symbol of disapproval; though applause can be 'thunderous', this never seems to be the case in dreams – even for actors?) Voices can sound like thunder – a particular voice? Or the voice of public opinion? Thunder sometimes announces a *storm* and *rain*, and if either are associated with the dream – or even if they were not obviously a part of it – you should look at the suggested interpretations of those symbols.

Ticket A ticket to ride? A ticket of admission? Maybe a sign of approval ('That's the ticket!'). There are various possibilities. Think of what sort of ticket it was, and where it allowed you to go – what kind of entertainment it promised; and relate that to your waking life: what associations are there with the place to which you were hoping to travel, or the show you were paying to see? Consider the price: if the ticket was expensive, and you were grumbling about it, have you in some way paid too much for some action, some position at work or in society – are you having to pay too heavily for a particular friendship or companion? If you were pleased with the ticket, was the dream simply confirming that some kind of expenditure, perhaps emotional, was worthwhile?

Tide The association is with *water*, the *sea*, so check these symbols. We speak of a tide of emotion or opinion, and those are possible associations – in waking life, are your feelings for someone or something growing, or at a peak? Is the tide turning – *a* tide, at least? Or are you searching for some support to 'tide you over' in a crisis? Are you even in some way 'tied up' in a project or a relationship?

Tie Freud spoke of a tie as a sexual symbol – sometimes of impotence (it hangs limply and is tied in a knot!). Of course this may be so – it is more likely to be the case than with many other articles of clothing; so men dreaming about a tie should certainly consider it (women too, for that matter; it could relate to a partner's sexuality, or your attitude towards it – were you, for instance, helping to tie the knot, or unknotting it?). Like most articles of dress, the symbol is likely to be a highly personal one; its *colour* may be significant. But remember other possibilities, too: are you hoping to 'tie the knot' by formalising a partnership? Are you 'all tied up' in some way – or inviting someone to 'get knotted'?

Tomato   The tomato was supposed to have been the 'love-apple' which Eve offered Adam in the Garden of Eden (with what trouble-some consequences we all know!). There may possibly be a reference here – and even if you were unconscious of the reference, the tomato certainly has a suggestion of the erotic about it; so whether you were taking an enjoyable bite at it, presenting it to someone else or selling it, this symbolism will be worth considera-tion. Your liking for or dislike of tomatoes will be relevant – as with any dreams of *food*; and as with all such dreams, the reference is likely to be to your emotional life. The tomato takes on rather a different significance if you were throwing it at someone, or some-one was pelting you!

Tomb   A dream of a tomb is not necessarily anything to do with physical *death*; it is not always – or even often – unpleasant: the tomb can be a beautiful one, in delightful countryside, wreathed with wild flowers, and very often refers to the burial of an aspect of oneself, of an outworked attitude or idea, with the inherent sug-gestion that you have 'risen again' and are a new person, the old you sloughed off like a snake's skin. It is also the case that the tomb has strong associations with the womb, so the reference to being 'born again' is really quite strong. Consider whether this might be the case; whether you have in some way rejected your old self and become a new person.

Tombstone   See **Tomb**, above. In Dickens' *Christmas Carol* Scrooge dreamed that he was shown his tombstone, associated with his stingy and selfish life; and to dream of your own tombstone may be a reference to your feelings about your life as a whole, and in particular, to other people's view of you (they, not you, erect your tombstone!). So your emotions in your dream very probably refer to your inner convictions about your life, and are quite likely to be self-critical. Look at other clues as to the particular area of your life that is being criticised (unless you are such an unpleasant person, and so wasting your entire life, that its every aspect is being criticised!). If the tomb was beautifully cared for, clean and white and noble, then your unconscious may well be paying you a splen-did compliment!

Torch   The idea is of shedding light, whether the torch is a modern one or a flaming brand. It may be that the former suggests some practical problem, the solution to which you are groping towards in waking life, while the latter may refer to some more intellectual or spiritual problem; but that is by no means necessarily the case. A flaming torch has often represented life – as light does; and its sudden extinguishing had been taken to represent **Death** – but see our definition of that! The connection with light and darkness – i.e., intellectual illumination or the darkness of ignorance – is also worth consideration; people often said of a leader that 'his torch burned bright'; were you lighting the way for someone other than yourself? Last but not least, there could be a phallic reference.

Torture   Could there be a connection with some kind of coercion in waking life? Who was doing the torture? Or who was being tortured? is someone emotionally torturing you? Don't be afraid of confronting the possibility that there may be a connection with some deep-seated sado-masochistic feelings; and don't let this worry you unless it becomes an overmastering emotion. It is more likely that the dream has something to do with punishment – either of yourself, for something of which your unconscious disapproves, or of someone else who you would like to see get their comeuppance.

Tower   Yes, of course Freudians would claim that all towers are phallic symbols; and it is worth considering the possibility. The analogies are obvious – a falling tower and impotence, a rising tower and confidence in growing sexual powers, and so on (see **Chimney**). But long before Freud, a tower was taken to symbolise watchfulness, and sometimes protection – sometimes a princess was imprisoned at the top of one. In that case there was also a sexual significance, for the rescuing knight had to mount the tower to deliver her (or she may have let her hair down for him to climb – and *hair* is another powerful sexual symbol). So there seems no getting away from the fact that the dream's meaning may lie somewhere in that area. Remember, too, the ivory tower (out of touch with reality), a tower of strength. Or are you towering over someone – or someone over you?

Toy   First of all, think about the significance of the toy itself: was it one of which you were uncommonly fond, as a child? What associations does it have – happy, or sad? And with what present waking preoccupation might it have a connection? A mechanical toy may suggest that your life is too ruled by convention. (Look for a possible pun – perhaps on a name.) There may, yet again, be a sexual connection: even today the word has those connotations – you can toy with someone's affections, and not too long ago 'toying' was a synonym for lovemaking.

Traffic   The traffic of a busy town could symbolise life itself, and your progress or lack of it could refer to your progress in everyday life, or at work. Look for other symbols to suggest which particular area of your life is under examination. A traffic jam could reflect the fact that in some way your life has come to a dead stop; dreaming of speeding, even uncontrollably, might be a suggestion that you are allowing something – an idea, a person – to run away with you. As we point out, a *car* or a road vehicle of any kind seems very often to be a phallic symbol for a male dreamer; in that context, good steering, speeding or an accident which drives you off the road, all have very obvious significance.

Train   See **Traffic** (above), or **Car** – for again, for male dreamers, there is very possibly a sexual significance – the classic copulatory symbol is of a train plunging into a tunnel. (It may be necessary to point out here that these are not merely our interpretations; they have been accepted now by generations of psychologists.) Nevertheless, the meaning could be completely different, so consider the context – was your journey forced, or necessary, or merely for pleasure? Who else was involved? What was the landscape like? (We knew a retired engine-driver who had a recurring dream of riding in a carriage simply enjoying the landscape – as, in his retirement, he was merely enjoying watching the world pass by.) If the rails seemed important, see **Tram**, below.

Tram   Like a *train*, a tram travels on rails; so the reference may well be to some aspect of life which is very much under control, the tracks having either been laid by yourself, or by someone else, or by society in general. Was your tram leaping the tracks? – or moving contentedly, smoothly, along them? Did they lead to the terminus you wanted to reach?

Tramp   We think of tramps, in general, as being rather disreputable – but free: so the dream may be wish-fulfilment. Maybe you want to, or should, throw caution to the winds and simply let yourself roam about at will – defy convention, in thought, or behaviour, or some other way. But a vision of yourself as a tramp might reflect concern about other people's view of you or your behaviour. Someone you know, appearing as a tramp, might be attracting a certain amount of scorn in waking life.

Transvestism   Not necessarily a comment on sexuality, yours or anyone else's, but merely a suggestion that you should give the other side of your nature more expression: if a man, that you should cultivate sensitivity; if a woman that you may need to be a little more assertive. Clothes reflect the personality of the person (sex) that wears them; so a dream of wearing someone else's clothes – or the clothes of another sex – suggests that you are seeking, or need, some of his/her/its qualities. 'Dressing up', sometimes in the clothes of the opposite sex, has long been a part of carnivals and celebrations; could the dream have been a suggestion that you need to loosen up and have fun? Almost certainly it was not any kind of comment on your gender, or uncertainty about it – unless the dream is a matter of wish-fulfilment; and don't be distressed about that!

Trap   Were you laying it for someone else or about to fall into one, trapped? The nature of the trap may give a clue to the meaning of the dream; but what you felt about it is much more important. It seems most likely that the dream is a warning, so think about your waking life and the possibility that something unexpected may be in store which may bring about a fall of some kind.

Treasure   Something valuable, sometimes placed on show, sometimes hidden. A symbol of what you treasure most? Maybe a person, but more likely some personal attribute? The nature of the treasure should offer a clue. Were you hoarding it, burying your talents, hiding your light under a bushel (how deeply was it buried)? Should you be spending it, using it, making a positive display? If you found treasure, was it a happy experience, or did it lead to quarrels and violence (as so often it does)? Was it protected – by bars, or walls, or hidden traps, or by guards or a mythical monster? What do you so deeply desire in waking life, but perhaps fear to seek or approach because of what seem over-difficult problems? The ancient adventurers were usually helped by the supernatural – could your waking search need spiritual assistance?

Tree   In ancient times the tree was almost always a symbol of life
– whether real, or spiritual; and in a sense that is at one with the
Freudian suggestion that it has a phallic significance, even if the
mythological tree was usually feminine. Fed by *water* (emotion) it
grew towards the *sky* (the spiritual), and out of the dead *earth*
(nothingness). The *apple* of the knowledge of good and evil was
picked from a tree, which grew in Paradise – so the growing tree can
also be a symbol of immortality. The idea is not confined to
Christian mythology – the Chinese and Japanese, the Hindus and
the Sumerians, all had heavens in which sacred trees bore fine fruit,
though usually fruit made of precious stones. The Australian abori-
gines believed that a great tree supported the heavens themselves,
and in many societies the action of climbing a tree symbolised
progress towards heaven. The tree, then, is an extremely complex
symbol, and you may well need to ask for additional help from your
dreams before you can work out the symbolism. You could start
with your own position *vis-à-vis* the tree: whether you were taking
your ease beneath it or eating its fruit, climbing it or falling out of it,
cutting it down or nurturing it? Try to relate your action (or
inaction) and emotion to your current waking attitude to your life
itself.

Trespass   The idea of trespass, of being where you should not be,
may relate to feelings of guilt about some action of your waking life.
Try to remember the landscape and your feelings about it, which
should provide a clue to the area of life to which the dream referred.

Trial   If you were on trial, consider whether an attitude or action of
yours would be likely to upset someone, or perhaps public opinion.
The identity of *judge* or *jury* will obviously be important. If you were
either, then the idea that you are in some way sitting in judgment
on someone else must be a possibility.

Triangle   The idea of the triangle has been of considerable significance in history (see also the number *three*), often in religion representing man, woman and an invisible godhead (in Christianity
Father, Son and Holy Spirit); in human relationships it can represent father, mother and child, or two partners and a threatening
third person. A triangle with the point upwards conventionally
represents the masculine (and fire), one with the point downwards,
the feminine (and water). In our own time, the idea that first comes

216

to mind is the 'eternal triangle' which signifies some kind of emotional turmoil; so consider whether the dream may be telling you something that your conscious mind does not want to recognise. If the reference is to some recognised fact, what happened to the triangle, or the circumstances in which it appeared, will be significant. But remember that it is an age-old symbol of truth and confidence; it may be a reassuring symbol.

Tribe We are all members of a tribe, of one kind or another, and that feeling is remarkably strong: so to dream that one belongs to a primitive, uncivilised tribe may be a reference to the kind of behaviour of which your friends and contemporaries may disappove (this may not mean that you are behaving badly – just unconventionally). But it depends what the tribe was doing, and whether in your waking state you remember it with pleasure, displeasure, shame. Attacked by a tribe, you could look for a waking fear that you have stepped outside the bounds of conventional social behaviour and fear disapproval.

Trick/Trickster The whole point of trickery, or conjuring, is to gain the confidence of someone, and convince them that what is false, is true; so whether you or someone else were the conjurer, the point of the dream seems fairly obvious. Whether the trickery was successful or not is also clearly important. Relating the dream to your waking life should not be difficult – nor should deciding whether it was a warning or confirmation of your own success (whether warranted or not must be your decision!). The Trickster in some guise or other appears in the mythology of most countries, and is generally taken to represent the physical aspect of life – less dependable than the spiritual, and more likely to press us into foolish actions.

Triumph Yours, or someone else's? A complimentary dream, surely, unless the triumph was in some way flawed or spoiled.

Truck See **Car**; remember that a vehicle of any kind, if a man dreams that he is driving it, may be a phallic symbol. What was the truck's cargo? Was there a co-driver? But there is also the pun: with whom will you 'have no truck'?

Trumpet Almost always regarded as an accompaniment to triumph: 'The trumpet shall sound.' Were you 'blowing your own trumpet'? – a sign that you should make sure your abilities are recognised and applauded? Or was someone else blowing their trumpet, and making an unpleasant noise? If you play, or would like to play the trumpet, there is the possibility of wish-fulfilment.

Tunnel Like all holes in the ground, a symbol of femininity; certainly this interpretation is not to be ignored, especially by male dreamers. Could there be a reference to a desire to climb back into the womb? – a longing for security? See **Cave**; but a tunnel is specifically man-made, so the reference is more likely to be extremely personal, and you should look elsewhere in the dream for clues. Your emotions will also be extremely important: did you feel confident and happy, or nervous, fearful, claustrophobic or uncertain? There could be a reference to a personal relationship; more rarely, to some work on which you are engaged (was the tunnel actually leading somewhere, or did you think it was a dead end?).

Twigs Twigs have often been used in divination, and while you may not consciously be aware of this, there is the possibility that the allusion in your dream was to the future, or its uncertainty. Were the twigs neatly piled, or scattered at random? Was the reference to some uncertainty in your present waking life? Were you picking up the twigs, setting them in order? Have you just 'twigged' something?

Twins A dream of twins, if you are pregnant, may be wish-fulfilment or a genuinely prophetic dream; this has been known. But more generally the idea of twins has been a reference to duality – world myth and literature is full of stories of two brothers, often one good, the other evil – Cain and Abel, Castor and Pollux, Baldar and Loki; the conflict between them is usually, but not always, resolved by the 'good' triumphing. So a dream of twins may represent the two sides of your (or more rarely, someone else's) personality; consider their actions and your feeling towards them. Dreaming that someone you know has become twins, or has a twin, it will be worth considering whether the dream was trying to show you a side of them whose existence you have not previously suspected. Also remember that Gemini is the sign of the twins.

Umbrella As a form of protection, a dream umbrella may refer to your need to protect yourself from some kind of an attack – more probably verbal or ideological than physical. Did the umbrella leak? If so, is there a hole in your argument? Was it blown away, or turned inside out? Are you aware of the idea that it is unlucky to open an umbrella indoors?

Umpire An umpire giving some decision for or against you may represent your own conscience, or some superior figure. So whether you accepted the decision, or hotly contested it, will be significant.

Underclothes Normally hidden, these may represent some facet of your personality not normally on view – so if they were torn or dirty, you may be doing a little self-criticism. If someone else exposes their underclothes, the reference may similarly be to something about them which you suspect but have never seen.

Underground See **Cave, Void**.

Understudy 'Standing by' to appear for someone else, take someone's part, will have a different significance for a dreaming actor than anyone else. In general the suggestion seems to be that you envy the person concerned, as understudies often do; or you may consciously or unconsciously wish them ill so that you can do their job, hopefully better than they. Did you succeed or fail? Have you studied insufficiently (under-studied) for some test or explanation?

Undertaker See **Death**: the undertaker is most likely to be involved in some way in a new project you are planning, or into which you have been pitched. If he has come to take away a coffin, or a body, you must consider what that represents: what trait of your character would you wish to see removed or buried? What current task will you be glad to see the last of? There is also the pun: what are you undertaking or about to undertake?

Uniform   As the word suggests, a uniform is meant to impose uniformity, to encourage conformity, to persuade one that one is in some way the same as everyone else, expected to behave in the same way (it is the chief reason for clothing members of the armed forces in this way). So there seems likely to be an emphasis on this aspect of your life. Were you proud of your uniform (glad to conform), or did you hate it (long in some way to be different)?

Urine   Children often dream of urination as they wet the bed; but assuming that no incontinence is involved, or that you don't wake up painfully aware that you need to urinate, the dream – given our quite irrational association of urine and faeces with dirt – may concern some personal trait or attribute of which you wish to be rid. A sexual connotation is possible but not very likely.

Urn   See **Vase**; but an urn, as such, is associated with ashes and therefore *death*. What was being carefully preserved in the urn? Are you clinging too ferociously to some aspect of the past? The figure in the Zodiac sign, Aquarius, pours liquid from an urn: could there be an association there? Or is this a statement about your earning capacity?

Vamp   See **Woman**.

Vase   In many world mythologies, a vase symbolised Woman (perhaps in the abstract); a full vase suggested knowledge; someone pouring from one, the dissemination of knowledge; a man pouring from a vase symbolised an offering to the gods, and remember the water-pourer who is the symbol of the astrological Zodiac sign Aquarius. Don't forget to consider whether you may be the vase into which someone is putting something. What is it? And what does it represent? The contents of the vase will in any case be important (its shape may be, too). If you are putting something into it, it may represent someone who you wish to affect (by putting something into their mind). But see, too, **Urn**.

Vault   There are obvious similarities with *cave* or *tomb*; but if you think of the place you visited in your dream as a vault, then there may be an association with *death*. Certainly the dream may be even more mysterious than usual, having an association with secrets. Are you trying to hide something (possibly some new idea or break away from your usual activities)?

Vaulting   Very likely a suggestion that you are (if the vault was successful) surmounting some problem, or at least psyching yourself up to do so. The dream also suggests 'vaulting ambition'. Look for other clues. For men, there is a possibility that the pole is a phallic symbol and that your ambition is the conquest of someone: were they standing by, or suggested by some other symbol in the dream? If the pole breaks, there is an obvious warning here – or a reference to some conscious or unconscious doubt.

Vegetables   Consider every association with the vegetable you saw, handled, ate: not least, its shape. Apart from a general reference to life, life-giving properties, nourishment, the symbolism of the dream is likely to be personal, perhaps based on someone you associate with the particular vegetable (seen eating it, peeling it, *cooking* it). What was being done to the vegetable may well be important – if you were chopping the end off a carrot or extracting the pips from a tomato, the meaning of your dream is likely to be very different. Or was the dream suggesting that you are vegetating at present?

Vehicles   See **Car**, **Train**, **Ship**.

Veil   A veil is often associated with the idea of secrecy, particularly on a personal level; in early Christianity, the hiding of sexuality, and thus a symbol of chastity or modesty; in Islam what is hidden is traditional knowledge – lifting the veil is to reveal the nature of divinity. We in the West may associate the veil with widowhood or with weddings, or with becoming a nun. Which, will presumably have been clear in your dream. But there will still be the suggestion of concealment: are you trying to conceal pain, or happiness, from yourself or anyone else. If someone else was veiled, might there be a suggestion of deceit?

Ventriloquism   There is surely a reference to deception of some kind, to things being not what they seem? Were you 'throwing your voice', or was someone else? And to what purpose? What the voice was saying, and who it imitated, is also important. Who was the ventriloquist's dummy?

Vibration   Not something most likely to occur in a dream; mentioned here because many people who have had out-of-body experiences while apparently asleep have claimed that these began with a sense that their bodies and spirits were 'vibrating' in a peculiar manner.

Victim   Someone who is victimised is the subject of undue pressure of some kind; look for parallels between the victimisation in your dream and any situations or events in your waking life, then try to match up other symbols which may have occurred in your dream.

Victory   There may be many symbols in a dream which seem to suggest that you have been in some way victorious: see **Wreath**, or **Crown**. Over what have you triumphed? Some disability or shortcoming, someone? Or were you defeated? But remember, the ostensible subject may not be the real one in your waking life.

Villain   As with everything else in dreams, a villain may not be what s/he seems. If you saw yourself as a villain, there may be a reference to behaviour of which you are rightly (if perhaps secretly) ashamed.If someone else is the villain, carefully examine any situation involving them in waking life – remembering that your dream may be a warning. But perhaps the villain represents an action rather than a person: was he smoking, for instance, or taking some other 'villainous' drug?

Vine   The vine has been for almost every civilisation a symbol of life, generosity, fruitfulness in every sense, and thus sometimes of sexual passion – though in early Christianity it was seen as the Tree of Life, with its many branches. Were you gathering grapes (i.e., getting the best out of life?) or were the grapes withered on the vine, maybe a sign that you are neglecting some area of your life, spiritual or corporeal? Were the grapes being stolen (someone else plundering your intelligence or taking advantage of you)? Are you a clinging vine?

Vinegar With its bitter taste, vinegar has usually symbolised something unpleasant, unpalatable (if also sometimes good for one – in Christian myth it stands for Christ's Passion, at the very height of sacrifice and self-immolation). But while considering it from this point of view, remember that we use it to spice up salads and some other *foods*: so is some area of your life lacking in interest (spice)? The general context of the dream should offer a clue to its meaning. If you were drinking vinegar, presumably you need to take an unpleasant lesson to heart; if you were adding it to food, some area of your life needs a little excitement.

Vineyard See **Vine**. If a whole vineyard produces plentiful fruit, or is being plundered, the compliment or warning is obviously on a larger, more comprehensive scale.

Violence Violence, in a dream, must be seen in context; it need not be frightening or unduly worrying – it may simply be a kind of safety valve, the release of emotion or sexual tension. Look for other symbols in the dream, and examine them.

Violin The meaning will be connected with your attitude to music: if you are a keen amateur or professional, then this may be a wish-fulfilment dream. If you or someone else is playing excruciatingly badly, there may be a suggestion that your life in general, or some area of it, is badly out of tune; if you are tuning the violin, the implication is obvious. In general, the violin seems to suggest beauty and emotion – so look at the symbol from this point of view: there will be all sorts of possibilities. Putting a violin away in its case may symbolise your determination to put practicality above emotion, for instance. Does the saying 'There's many a good tune played on an old fiddle' strike a chord? Or are you fiddling something or someone?

Virgin An allusion to virginity in a dream is more often than not an allusion to innocence, rather than anything sexual (though clearly there could in some cases be an element of wish-fulfilment). There may be a feeling of 'untouchability' which again could refer to almost anything – a cherished scheme which you don't want others to interfere with, for instance. In some myths the virgin or *virginity* was taken as something to be scorned, even something evil – life-denying. Are you being overprotective, in any sense, in your waking life? – of a person, an idea, a possession? Remember the virgin as the symbol of the astrological sign of Virgo; does the context of your dream suggest a person of that Sun-sign? A specific reference to the Virgin Mother or the Virgin Birth is another matter; it is possibly religious, or at least in some sense a spiritual suggestion, but remember that in some world myths the Virgin Mother was not technically a virgin, just unmarried.

Virility   A man dreaming that he has abundant virility, or that his virility is failing, is no doubt preoccupied with the technical attributes of his masculinity. The important thing is whether his waking sex-life is in trouble. If so, the dream is properly suggesting counselling – or maybe a little restraint!

Voice   A disembodied voice, in a dream, would in ancient days no doubt have been believed to be the Voice of God (or of a god). Today, it is more likely to be the voice of your conscience, your inner self – in fact, the voice of your dreams themselves; but if you are directly addressed in this way, though it is possible that the message is an important one, dreams usually send their messages obliquely and it may be that this message is simply nonsense. As with all dreams, it may be judged by its vividness; if it remains with you, if you can't forget it, then work on it. If it seems, on reflection, meaningless – don't worry about it. Subsequent dreams will reveal all, if there is anything to reveal!

Void   To dream of being in a void, stranded in blackness, is extremely unpleasant. It may possibly be a simple physiological phenomenon; but on the other hand it may be an important reference to your being in some way 'lost', in waking life. Since the meaning must necessarily be obscure if there is no other symbol to refer to, ask your dream for elucidation (see p 45–6) – without fearing that coming dreams will be as unpleasant as this one.

Vomit   Presuming that the dream is not simply the result of your feeling physically nauseous, a dream that you are vomiting refers to something in your life which you want to get rid of – or which your subconscious insists that you should! Look for other clues. If someone else is vomiting, are they someone who in waking life may disapprove of you, your attitude, your actions? Or do you feel they need to shed some of their personal characteristics?

Voyeur   Sexuality will almost certainly be involved – that is what Peeping Toms are usually concerned with – and the context be one of overt voyeurism. So this will almost certainly be a comment on this area of your life. If someone was watching you, are you over-satisfied with your sexual performance (maybe you have the right!) – or if you were watching, what was your reaction? Were you envious? So should you look to your laurels? Of course, this may just have been an entertaining sexual fantasy – though very few dreams are for entertainment only.

Wages   A dream that your wages are being cut, or increased, could refer to your present work and your satisfaction or dissatisfaction with it, or be an anxiety dream. But it could relate to other areas of your life, so carefully check any symbols in the dream, remembering the association between *money* and emotion. Do you remember the Biblical text about the 'wages of sin'?

Wagon   Some kind of burden is suggested, which is either being satisfactorily carried, or is too heavy, or an insecure load. This could refer to work, or to responsibilities. What was on the wagon – you? – and what could this refer to in your present life?

Waiter   Were you being waited on, or serving someone else? A reference to your work, or your ideas of service. If carrying a tray through a crowd, or balancing it under difficulties, maybe a comment on a rather sensitive task before you? But maybe you are asking this of someone else?

Walk   A walk through an unfamiliar landscape suggests exploration, the opening out of new horizons; especially if it is leisurely and unhurried, this is a pleasantly encouraging symbol. A walk through familiar countryside may suggest nostalgia, even living in the past.

Wall   Sheltering walls – every city once had its wall; many houses are still guarded by one – suggest protection in general: perhaps your attitude to your partner or family. Was there a breach in the wall? Were you attempting to climb it, or strengthen it? Apply this to your present circumstances. Are you searching for something which you are unable to achieve because of some obstacle? Do you want to keep the world out? Are you taking an unrealistic view of life? The demolition of a wall can be a telling image of freedom – e.g. the Berlin Wall.

Wallet   A very private container for secrets. If you lost it, or it was stolen, this may indicate concern about having 'lost your way' in a psychological or spiritual sense. But a wallet contains money and credit, which is often unconsciously associated with love – have you lost someone's affection or esteem, or are you afraid it may be stolen from you? Are you jealous?

Wand   Dreaming of a stick or baton is one thing; dreaming of what you recognise as a wand is something else, and must infer that it had magical properties. So this is a dream of power – power which you wish to wield or which someone else is wielding over you? A white wand usually signifies white magic, and therefore good: in that case, an encouraging dream. Otherwise, a suggestion that you are using power in the wrong way, or suspect someone else of doing so. In the Tarot pack, wands represent the fire element – energy, growth and enterprise.

War   There are obviously many contexts in which you could dream of war, but in general the suggestion is of the disintegration of order, things falling apart. The context should suggest which area of your life is in focus. An eventual victory should indicate success after the battle; defeat may suggest that your dream is warning you to prepare for failure. The face of the enemy will be important: if you never see it, consider whether this is not an internal battle you are fighting with yourself. That is quite frequently the case. Is there some area of your life, some attitude, which is confusing you at present? Think about the landscape of the battle – there may be a valuable clue there.

Washing   The washing of hands has always been a symbol of trying to cleanse ourselves of evil: perhaps you bitterly regret some recent action (the context of the dream may offer a clue).

Wasp   A wasp does not carry the same positive symbolism as a *bee* – it is non-productive, and moreover it can sting more than once and harm only its victim. You are far more likely to be stung by a wasp than by a bee – even in a dream – and the reference seems almost certainly to be on the edge of unpleasantness: is someone having a go at you? Or trying to wake you up in a fairly radical way (perhaps having failed to do so by gentler means)? Are you ready to administer that kind of shock to someone else? Or is someone buzzing round you, and you, sensing danger, want them to stop? Did you successfully swot the wasp?

Water   One of the most important of all symbols, which finds a place in every known civilisation. It has always been considered – long before modern science confirmed the fact – that water is the source of all life, and therefore of everything we know, so it signifies life itself, our purpose, our destiny. For the same reason it has always signified the mother and been associated with birth. Water cleanses and regenerates (see **Washing**), and in Christian baptism is a sign of renewal and rebirth. If you dream of diving into water, this could be symbolic of a search for meaning in life, if not for *the* meaning of life. It also suggests the exploration of your own unconscious, for which water is also a powerful symbol. A dream of dividing the waters, as Moses did, is similarly a dream of exploration and enquiry – probably successful. Dreaming of walking on water would suggest that you are confident you have solved the problem of your own identity to your own satisfaction: you are in charge of your own destiny. See **Swimming**. Crossing the water, by whatever means, suggests some movement in understanding – a progress from one set of beliefs to another.

Waves   Obviously see **Water**; but also consider whether you are 'making waves' i.e., trying to make anyone's life difficult at present. Or are you surviving someone else's obstruction of your aims?

Weapons   Freud would suggest that almost every weapon is a phallic symbol, and this is often true – but the nature of the weapon is clearly significant: if you are threatening or being threatened by a *gun*, a *spear*, a *knife*, you might certainly consider any possible sexual significance; a *sword* or a *stone* may have other meanings – may be symbols of power, either real or desired. A dream that you are playing with a weapon may be a sign that you have put aside violence as a merely childish way of resolving problems.

Weather   Weather, in a dream, will be a significant chiefly in setting the mood, unless a specific symbol, such as *thunder* or *lightning* are prominent. Beautifully clear, sunny weather will give a dream a different 'flavour' from dull, drizzly, overcast weather. Take this into consideration. Remember the pun: 'whether'.

Weaving   A symbol of creativity, from time immemorial: goddesses of time and fate were often depicted sitting at the loom, and the idea of fate and destiny is very strongly associated with this activity. The creation of something from a mere tangled mass of wool or yarn is significant, and the warp and weft (the vertical and horizontal strands) symbolise the combination of opposites – male and female, body and spirit, good and evil, night and day – what you will. To dream of weaving a perfect piece of cloth is obviously encouraging; faulty work must suggest flaws in some current activity or argument. What were you weaving? There should be some clue in your dream which will show you where the symbol is to be applied.

Web   It is the idea of deceit that first comes to mind, perhaps because of Scott's famous lines, 'Oh, what a tangled web we weave, When first we practise to deceive . . .' But the ancient allusion was to the web of time, where all life was laid out in a strict, fated pattern – life at the outside of the circle, death (the spider) at the centre. A journey across the net is a dangerous journey through life. If you were a fly caught in the web, apply the dream to some possible trap awaiting you in waking life. If you are spinning a web, are you trying to catch, or deceive, someone?

Wedding   Wish-fulfilment, perhaps – whether you were bride or groom, or even someone trying to stop the marriage. But could bride and groom themselves be symbols, representing two ideas you want to amalgamate? Try looking at the symbol as one of joining together, not necessarily involving human beings at all.

Weeds   Sometimes beautiful, but in general undesirable, sometimes positively choking the cultivated flowers of the garden. A strong growth of weeds may represent aspects of your personality which you recognise (at least unconsciously) as being undesirable, and which are standing in the way of progress, whether spiritual or real. If you were trying to uproot them, an encouraging symbol; if they entirely took over the garden, a warning. Could they represent other people? If so, look for a pun in their names. Are you being 'a weed' – failing out of nervousness to take necessary action?

Weeping It is not uncommon to suffer deep depression in the course of a dream, often for no very clear reason. This may be the result of some very simple recent incident; it should not be taken as a warning or a prophetic dream – though if it is clearly associated with some person or activity which you recognise, then it will be worth considering on that basis. If someone else is weeping, the image could reflect your concern for the person in waking life – or perhaps some action of yours which is giving them pain. Is the weeping nostalgia for a way of life you have forsaken, or been forced to forsake? Again, the context is vital.

Weighing The Christian, Islamic, Egyptian and Hindu idea that after death the good we have done is weighed against the evil, is still very pervasive, and the *scales* very much associated with the abstract idea of justice. So scales may relate to some action of yours, some decision you must make, or your estimate of some person or situation. What was being 'weighed in the balance'? And was it found wanting?

Well Truth was traditionally supposed to be found at the bottom of a well. There were many sacred wells, not only in Greek mythology but in Christian reality – and there were also 'lucky wells'. Earlier the association was with femininity, and later with the psyche (see **Water**). Were you jumping in (looking for truth), falling in (being shown the truth despite yourself) or even being thrown in (forced to take notice)? What was in the well, or what did you hope to find there?

Whale An association with *water* suggests that the whale, the largest mammal, represents power over the unconscious; but remember the story of Jonah, which for Christians symbolised the descent into the grave, from which he was eventually released. A mere dream of a whale swimming may suggest a wish to establish and reinforce your ideas of your own place in the universe. A dream of being swallowed may indicate a desire to explore the unconscious. Are you a conservationist?

Wheel   See **Mandala**. In many civilisations the wheel represented the known universe, with the *sun* at its centre and the spokes representing its rays. All the known ancient Sun-gods had the wheel as their emblem; and its associations since then have always been with the force of life itself, the unmoving centre and the changing exterior, the truth surrounded by moving fashion, and so on. The wheel has also become 'the wheel of fate', representing *karma*, the round of existence, to the Buddhist 'the wheel of the World and of Law', to the Egyptian the potter's wheel on which Man was made, to the Greeks the Wheel of Life, to the Hindus the representation of perfection; also the circle of the *Zodiac*. Solely in Christian myth has the wheel on the whole been insignificant (the emblem only of St Catherine). This is one of the most difficult dream symbols to interpret, for although we may resist the suggestion, most of us will consciously or unconsciously have been affected by the traditional associations of the symbol. So a damaged wheel (even a punctured tyre) can very possibly be a powerful symbol of destiny gone awry – though on the other hand it may well be merely a symbol of delay. The entry under **Mandala** may be a help; but this is very possibly a case in which you may have to appeal to your dreams (see p. 45–6) for further help. Do not hesitate to do so, because this may be a more important dream than you realise.

Whip   In ancient civilisations a whip was the mark of authority, but in Roman mythology it also denoted virility and fertility: Roman brides were whipped for that reason – so were fruit trees. This symbolism may not be entirely dead, and certainly sexual symbolism might be involved (not necessarily in a sadistic sense). It is worth remembering the Christian significance – not only of Christ whipping the money-changers from the Temple, but 'whipping the Old Adam' (i.e., sin) out of man. Who was wielding the whip and who was being whipped is significant. Should you whip up your enthusiasm for something?

Whirlpool   See **Water**; but the whirlpool has often been a mysterious image, with magical connections; there may be a reference to 'getting to the centre of things' – or being drawn unwillingly into some argument or emotional entanglement.

Whirlwind   Not dissimilar to *whirlpool*, but traditionally associated with great energy, and with witchcraft (witches and warlocks 'rode the whirlwind') – so this may be a rather darker symbol than the other.

Wig   In Egyptian civilisation the wig was an important symbol of authority, and in European civilisation that tradition continues, in some countries, in the courts of justice. The allusion should not be overlooked. But see **Hair** and **Beard**: in males there can often be a sexual significance, or a connection with personal image and power. There is also sometimes something ludicrous about a wig – the very name now has comic associations not connected with the word 'hairpiece' or 'toupée'. So if the word itself comes clearly to your mind, it is possible your dreams may be trying to puncture personal pomposity or ambition.

Wind   As insubstantial and mysterious as life itself, the wind has been associated with the spirit and its power over us – often more vital and persistent than the body itself. Was this a destructive wind, one carrying seeds, one which was blowing you away or refreshing you? If carried by the wind, see **Flying**, but was someone or something other than yourself motivating the flight? Is the phrase 'the wind of change' significant? Or are you (on the most ludicrous level) suffering from flatulence?

Window   Protecting you from the elements, a window is also an artificial barrier; so are you putting an obstacle – or some distance – between yourself and someone else, or something else? What were you looking at through the window? Or was someone looking at you? If the latter, were they trying to get to you, or attract your attention? If you were looking at a landscape, was it some sort of Promised Land? Did you throw open the window – and if so, is this an invitation to open yourself to someone, or to new ideas?

Wine   From ancient times wine has represented a life-giving force, in some cases truth or wisdom, but importantly in the Christian tradition, the blood of sacrifice. In almost every known religion, wine and blood are symbolically one and the same. With whom were you sharing wine? Someone you admire and wish to emulate, and whose wisdom you want to share? Was the atmosphere friendly? If you spilt wine, could this be a warning against disregarding or going against advice? (Look, again, for the person concerned.)

Wings   In the Christian religion wings symbolise divinity (angels and saints wear them); Buddhism represents wisdom in the same way, and other western religions entertained similar traditions. So if you dreamed that you grew wings the suggestion is of enhanced knowledge, wisdom or spirituality. If you had wings which were torn off, a rebuke is implied; other people seen with wings suggest your admiration of them. See, if apposite, **Flying**.

Witch   To dream of witches may seem a simple nightmare, and in childhood it may be. Adults, however, will consciously or unconsciously be aware of witchcraft as evil as well as frightening, and to dream of someone as a witch may suggest mistrust. If you, a woman, were a witch, perhaps your dreams have recognised unworthy plotting on your part. If you were riding a broomstick, the sexual connotations seems unmistakable; or maybe you wish to fly, spiritually – to travel or explore new dimensions.

Woman   A man's sexual dream of a woman need be nothing more than wish-fulfilment. Other dreams in which an unknown woman is the central figure should be approached via other symbols within them. There will be a different significance for male and female readers. Remember, all men hold dear, in their subconscious, the idea of the archetypal woman – Woman the ideal, the *anima*, the figure with whom all other women are compared. Could this have been she? Or did she represent the female side of your masculine nature?

Womb   It is rare for one to dream one is back in the womb, though dreams of birth are not uncommon – if sometimes disguised (as descending a waterfall, passing through a watery tunnel, and so on). Some psychologists suggest that we all carry an unconscious memory of the process of our own birth. A dream of being back in the womb is fairly obviously one in which we are crying out for security, for someone else to look after us and protect us from the world. The desire to return to the womb is that of someone afraid, for some reason, to face the real world.

Wood   The fact that Christ was a carpenter is significant, for wood has always been regarded as one of the basic elements of life on earth, and the carpenter's tools as shaping the order of things. If you were carving wood, then what you were making is clearly important, but so was your motive – were you making something for someone else (i.e., paying tribute) or for yourself (i.e., perhaps shaping your future life, or trying to impose order on your present life)? If the wood was a **Forest**, see under that symbol; being lost in a wood or forest suggests confusion: whether you eventually found the way out, or woke while still completely lost, is important – but in any event it seems likely that the dream refers to some confusion in your waking life, or suggests that the situation is confused even if you think that the way forward is clear. Look at the context – where were you going? Who was with you? See, perhaps, **Tree**?

Wool   If you were *knitting*, there are obvious similarities to *weaving*; if merely winding wool, then perhaps you are problem-solving in real life, and the way the wool was wound will suggest the present state of play. What you were knitting, and for whom, will be important – and what happened to the garment. Was it a pullover – and if so, are you about to deceive someone (pull the wool over their eyes)? Or are you being woolly, or employing woolly arguments?

Worms   The association between worms and death cannot be ignored; if they were devouring someone, this unpleasant dream may be an indication of your attitude to them, which is likely to be, consciously or unconsciously, antagonistic. The dream may be a comment on your fear of *death*. But remember the good done by worms in the garden: this could be a dream of regeneration – especially in view of some worms' talent, when chopped in half, to go happily on their way as two worms.

Wound   The symbolic wound of Christ comes to mind, but such a dream symbol would probably only be likely to occur to someone with a keen preoccupation with theology (though see **Stigmata**). Wounds to any part of the body must be considered carefully: it is possible that there may be a reference to some injury not as yet recognised in the waking state. If someone else is wounded in your dream, question your attitude to them – if the injury is to their eyes, are you afraid of what they may see in you? If to their hands, are you in physical fear of them; if to their feet, do you want to impede their progress?

Wreath   In past ages there were triumphal wreaths as well as mourning wreaths, and today the Christmas wreath, though associated with Christ's victory in *death*, is on the whole a happy symbol – as is the bridal wreath. If you were being crowned with a wreath, you are clearly very pleased at the moment to be you! But did the wreath wither or fall from your head? Wreaths at a funeral need not symbolise, much less predict, death; they may mark or celebrate a new start.

Yoke   Relatively few people have ever seen a yoke, yet the allusion has power in the unconscious, where it symbolises discipline, enforced slavery or, at best, control. So were you yoked, or controlling someone else by its use? And were you happy, either way? A comment, it seems, on your need for discipline or to impose it on someone else. What about the pun, though: see **Egg**?

Youth   To dream of being young is often an affirmation that one feels young, that one's ideas are fresh and youthful, and an affirmation of physical well-being. Occasionally, one dreams of one's parents or elderly relatives being young; this can be a splendidly affirmative and comforting dream, especially if they are dead.

Zodiac, the   The signs of the Zodiac are themselves associated with certain symbols. If you dream of these symbols, there may be an allusion – since most people have at some time read about them, and probably unconsciously remember them – to people of that Sun-sign or to the characteristic of the sign. The signs are Aries (the *ram*), Taurus (the *bull*), Gemini (the *twins*), Cancer (the *crab*), Leo (the *lion*), Virgo (a *virgin*), Libra (the *scales*), Scorpio (the *scorpion*), Sagittarius (the *centaur*), Capricorn (the *goat*), Aquarius (a man pouring *water*), and Pisces (two *fish*).

Zoo A zoo is a place of captivity, if now often moderately pleasant. It seems possible you may wish to see someone removed from your life, though unharmed. What animal were you looking at? And who, in your waking life, may they represent? Would you be quite glad if they went away? If you yourself were in a cage, might this be a comment on your present feelings? Do *you* want to 'get out'?

Suggested Further Reading

There is a very great number of serious books about the nature and interpretation of dreams, and we can only suggest here a few which will take you further along the road to understanding them. Do not be too nervous about going straight to the works of Freud and Jung to discover their theories at first hand: fortunately they both wrote extremely clearly and well, and have been well translated. Freud's theory is explained at length in *The Interpretation of Dreams*, which is included in the collected edition of his writing published by the Hogarth Press. Jung's writing on dreams is scattered through his collected work, which is published by Routledge, and has an excellent index which will lead you to relevant passages. Perhaps the best of his books for the general reader is his fascinating autobiography, *Memories, Dreams, Reflections*, also published by Routledge. *Man and his Symbols* (Aldus Books) is a collection of essays edited by Jung, and is a good general introduction to the theory of symbolism in dreams. The best single book explaining Jung's theories is *On Jung*, by Anthony Stevens (Routledge). A second book by Dr Stevens, *Archetype: a natural history of the self* (Routledge) is extremely useful in explaining the theory of the archetype.

J. C. Cooper's *An Illustrated Encyclopaedia of Traditional Symbols* (Thames & Hudson) and Tom Chetwynd's *A Dictionary of Symbols* (Paladin) will be of a great help in fleshing out many of the symbols whose meaning is so complex that our own summaries have had to be brief. *The New Larousse Encyclopaedia of Mythology* (Hamlyn) will also be useful; our own *The Immortals* is a more popular approach to the same subject.

As to other general books on dreams interpretation, those by Ann Faraday – notably *Dream Power* (Hodder & Stoughton) and *The Dream Game* (Temple Smith) – are always thought-provoking. Our own

Dreaming (Mitchell Beazley) is useful to those who want to know more about the mechanics and physiology of sleep and dreaming.

D. and J. P.

About the Authors

Julia and Derek Parker are well-known authors and writers. For several years Julia was president of the Faculty of Astrological Studies. She studied counseling techniques and is trained in the Jungian approach to dream analysis. They are also the authors of *Life Signs* (Piatkus).